THE TRANSACTIONS OF

THE SOCIETY OF ALUMNI OF

BELLEVUE HOSPITAL

FOR 1897-'98

NEW YORK
D. APPLETON AND COMPANY
1898

1944

CONTENTS.

SOCIETY OF

ALUMNI OF BELLEVUE HOSPITAL.

Meeting of October 6, 1897.

The President, Dr. ROBERT J. CARLISLE, in the Chair.

Address of the President.—Gentlemen of the Society: Should any one doubt the development and growth in strength and importance of this society, let him compare her youthful days with these, when she inaugurates her president; and, were he to stand where I do now, he would be deeply impressed with the responsibility placed upon him. He would feel also, as I do, that to be president of the Society of Alumni of Bellevue Hospital is a high honor, and one of which he may be justly proud.

I am proud, therefore, gentlemen, of that honor that you have conferred upon me, and when I say that during my term of office I will strive to be as active, diligent, and efficient in advancing the interests of the society as my immediate predecessor has been, and to be as worthy of a place in the long honor-roll of those who have preceded me, I think you can ask no further declaration or assurance from me.

My experience as chief steward had almost produced on my mind a wrong idea of the character of this organization. Although I knew, in a general way, of its twofold purpose in life, I had nearly become convinced that it was a society of gastronomers banded together for the furtherance of the art of gastronomy. There is no doubt that the bump of alimentiveness, as the phrenologist says, in this body is a large one (and why should it not be in a society of alumni?), but it is located, methinks, in the abdominal and not in the

1

cerebral region; and I had arrived at the conclusion that amicability and love of kind had their centres likewise in the abdomen, but higher up, say in the scrobiculus cordis; so that as the first centre became larger the last two became deeper. Be that as it may, I now approve of the custom in vogue, of placing the vice-president in charge of the social department, as a wise one. To have a perfect idea of a whole, one must have a vivid conception of all the parts. It is a fact that you can get at a man by way of his alimentary canal better and easier than in any other way—and when one has put potential energy in, he has a right to expect kinetic energy out. As in the normal man, so also in an association of normal men: when the body is well nourished, each and every part is well nourished with it. I commend these few suggestions to my successor in that office.

This being the beginning of a new year with us, it would be proper in an address of this kind to review the field of scientific research, to sum up the established facts, and to point out in what manner our energies should be put forth to further the advance of medicine and surgery. I wish I were capable of doing it. The new developments in all departments of medicine are bewildering in numbers. It is hard to keep pace with them—in anatomy, physiology, and chemistry. To refer to but a few: in anatomy, for instance, the recent investigations in the histology of the neurone made possible by the newer microscopical technique, and their possible bearing upon the physiology of the nervous system; the revelations in the anatomy and physiology of the blood, both in normal and in pathological states; in physiology and in chemistry, the work done and being done in regard to the functions of the ductless glands, suggested by the discovery of the therapeutic value of thyreoid extract—you know of them all and it is not my intention to rehearse them. But I would like to mention a subject of great interest in which much work is being done that gives promise of much good result, and that is, the subject of intoxication in disease. The work of Pasteur in proving that bacteria were the cause of putrefaction, suggesting the possibility that poisons produced by bacterial growth were the causes of many of the symptoms of diseases known to be of bacterial origin, led on to the recent work in physiological chemistry and pathology looking to the discovery of a toxic principle or principles, either bacterial or metabolic in origin, which acted as the causes of many diseased states. The bearing of this on the ætiology of gout and of the so-called lithæmic condition, on some of the diseases of the skin, in epilepsy, tetany, etc., is but suggested.

In connection with epilepsy I beg to quote from the sixth edition of the work on *Practice of Medicine* of the late Austin Flint, as showing the wonderfully thoughtful and close observer and advanced physician that man was. Under the head of epilepsy, page 825 (this was written in 1886), he says: " In a large proportion of cases of epilepsy no sources of centric or of excentric irritation are apparent. That under these circumstances the epileptic paroxysms are due to the action of an internal and at present unknown toxical agent seems to me the most rational hypothesis. Epilepsy, according to this hypothesis, is a toxæmia analogous to uræmia, the toxical agent being produced at variable intervals, the quantity and the continuance of its production not being sufficient to endanger life; and in this respect the contrast with uræmia being striking. If this pathological view be correct, knowledge of the nature and source of the toxical agent, which may, perhaps, be acquired, will, as we may hope, render this disease controllable." It is in this class of diseases, it seems to me, that much good work will be accomplished in the not far-distant future.

I wish to take this opportunity to refer to the reports of work done here—our published *Transactions.* . Our reports being the evidence of our work and its character, every effort should be made to keep them abreast of the times. The papers read, whether they report original investigation or not, should show that the author is fully cognizant of the progress made in the particular department of science under discussion; and, if for any reason the report is incomplete, it ought not to be because the writer did not know better; and in the discussion no one should attempt to discuss a question who is not informed on the subject; he should come prepared, and in discussing be exact and stick to the point.

I thank you again, gentlemen, for this honor and your kindness to me in the past, and bespeak your aid in upholding this society as the peer of any.

Osteosarcoma of Jaw; No Recurrence in Ten Months after Excision.—Dr. J. W. S. GOULEY presented a patient whom he had shown to the society during the past winter. The case was that of the young man from whom he had removed the superior maxilla of the right

side for an osteosarcoma—a very dense osteosarcoma
in which there had been some giant cells and spindle
cells, but in which the osseous element had largely
predominated. · He said that the tumor had not apparently recurred in the ten months that had elapsed since
the operation. It was evident that the man's speech
had decidedly improved, and he had now learned to
eat without removing the dental appliance. No food
whatever passed through the nose. That no recurrence
had taken place was probably due to the fact that the
tumor had been undergoing a progressive rather than a
retrogressive change. It was well known that sarcomata
which tended to become converted into fibrous tissue
were less malignant than the other varieties. In another
case of this kind he would prefer to sacrifice less tissue;
it would have been better, he thought, if he had preserved more mucous membrane and periosteum. The
starting point in this case had not been the periosteum,
but the bone itself.

Dr. A. B. JOHNSON said that the result in this case
was most excellent, yet it had occurred to him that
the dental plate could be so fixed in the mouth as to
allow of the patient chewing upon it. He was reminded
of the case of a child whom he had presented to the society about two years after the removal of a sarcoma of
the lower jaw. There had been no recurrence then,
and he had heard quite recently from the child, and the
. report had been that there was still no return of the
disease.

Pyosalpinx.—Dr. FREDERICK HOLME WIGGIN presented the uterus, tubes, and ovaries that had been removed by the abdominal route on September 20th for
pyosalpinx from an Armenian—A. S., aged about thirty-five years—a patient at the City Hospital. No previous history could be obtained, as she was unable to
speak English. Vaginal examination had shown fixation
of the uterus and enlargement of both tubes. After
the removal of the uterus, the round ligaments had
been fastened to the vaginal wall to prevent its descent,
and the wounds in the latter closed. The peritonæum
had also been brought together and closed. After the
insertion of the sutures in the abdominal wall, the abdominal cavity had been filled with saline solution, and
this had been allowed to remain in the cavity. The patient had made a good recovery, with the exception of
a few superficial points of infection around the sutures.
The uterine and tubal infection was probably due to
gonorrhœa.

Pyosalpinx and Appendicitis.—Dr. WIGGIN also presented a tube and ovary removed by operation on October 3, 1897, from a woman, thirty-seven years of age, a patient of Dr. Rodger's, of Woodbury, Conn. The woman had been married fifteen years. Her first menstruation had occurred in her fourteenth year, and for about eight years had been irregular, tending to recur about every five or six weeks, but without pain. She had been married at the age of twenty-two, and eleven months afterward had been delivered of a child. There was a history of some infection having occurred at this time. Two other children had been born later. Three years ago she had had a miscarriage, followed by an illness of several weeks. Since that time menstruation had been regular. She had complained of a great deal of pain on the right side, and had given a history of recurring appendicitis. The examination had revealed a spot of localized tenderness over "McBurney's point." The vaginal examination had shown the uterus to be enlarged, but in fairly good position, and the right tube to be considerably enlarged. A week after this examination the uterus had been curetted, the perinæum repaired, and then an incision made over the right rectus muscle, which had been split. On introducing the hand into the pelvic cavity it had been found that the appendix was adherent to the tube and ovary. Between the time of the operation and the first examination there had been a free discharge from the uterus, and the tube had shrunk somewhat. The appendix was about seven inches long, and somewhat inflamed and thickened. It had been evident that the cause of the peculiar tenderness over "McBurney's point" was an area of localized peritonitis on the cæcum, limited to one side of the base of the appendix vermiformis, and measuring about an inch in diameter. The tube had been very much inflamed and the ovary enlarged, so both had been removed. The stump of the appendix was turned into the cæcum and a running suture passed around it, according to the method of Dawbarn. So far convalescence had been satisfactory.

In answer to a question, Dr. Wiggin said that he had done an abdominal and not a vaginal hysterectomy because his experience had led him, in a case of fixation with probable septic complications, to prefer the abdominal route. It could be done more quickly and the exact condition could be better determined. He now confined the vaginal operation to cases in which the uterus was more or less movable, and where there was reason to believe there were no long-standing adhesions.

- - ---

Meeting of November 3, 1897.

The President, Dr. ROBERT J. CARLISLE, in the Chair.

Case showing the Result of Resection of the Rectum for Anal Fistulæ.—Dr. FREDERICK HOLME WIGGIN presented such a case. The patient, J. N., thirty-eight years of age, had been admitted to the gynæcological ward of the City Hospital on December 20, 1896. Fourteen years previously she had had syphilis, and a year later abscesses had formed in both buttocks. Two operations had been performed on her, but both had been unsuccessful. When he had first seen her the condition had already existed eight years. At that time she had been in a pitiable condition, the buttocks being so indurated and inflamed that she could not sit down with comfort, and there had been sinuses which had opened in either buttock and in the left labium majus, discharging gas and fæcal matter. He had injected hydrozone into each of the external openings of these sinuses, having first placed a small Sims's speculum in the rectum, and had been able to locate the internal openings, which were from one to three inches from the sphincter, by the escape of gas. Laying open the sinuses would have been too extensive an operation, and hence it had been decided to resect the diseased portions of the bowel and bring down the healthy part of the gut and attach it to the skin, and so shut off the fæcal matter from the sinuses. In doing this operation he had first divided the perinæum and secondly the tissues lying between the posterior margin of the anus and the coccyx, and with the aid of heavy silk sutures, the ends being left long and placed on either side, the parts had been retracted and the diseased bowel had been dissected out and about three inches of it had been amputated, and finally he had attached the margin of the healthy gut to the skin and closed the perineal wound, leaving the wound posterior to the gut open with gauze in it. The latter gradually healed by granulation. A few weeks later he had freely incised the sinuses in the buttocks, and had found large cavities separated by bands. These bands had been broken down so as to convert these cavities into one large cavity, which was curetted. The whole wound had then been swabbed out with pure carbolic acid and carefully dressed so as to secure healing from the bottom. The sphincter had been divided above and below, and there had been in consequence a good deal of prolapse of the mucous lining of the bowel. To overcome this, he had endeavored to produce a moderate stricture of the bowel by repeated applications of the Paquelin cautery. The woman had been discharged from the hospital last August, and at the present time there was good control of the bowel.

Dr. ROBERT T. MORRIS said that so far the result seemed to be very excellent, and if it was as good after three years the case would be quite a remarkable one. The danger was from slow cicatricial contraction, and he would like to know what operation Dr. Wiggin proposed to do to remedy this should it occur. He also asked if he had had any experience with the method of twisting the rectum upon itself one or one-and-a-half times and suturing it to the skin for the purpose of giving control of the bowel movements. It was theoretically a good operation, but in two cases in which he had tried it the sutures had not held the bowel in the twisted position.

Dr. PARKER SYMS said that an anus from which the sphincter muscle had been lost was never able to control diarrhœal or fluid evacuations, although it might be entirely competent to control solid fæcal matter. He would expect it to be very difficult to get proper union in the operation alluded to by the last speaker, owing to the interference with the circulation of the parts caused by the twisting of the bowel.

Dr. WIGGIN said that he had had no experience with this twisting method. The reason he had followed the line of procedure that he had described was that at the end of the operation, as a result of rather free hæmorrhage, the patient had been in such a bad condition that he had felt justified in taking some risks about the control of the bowel. If the tissues continued to contract until trouble arose from that source he would be inclined to free the bowel again, and perhaps pass it through an opening in the gluteal muscles on one side. He expected to be able to keep this patient under observation for a long time, and therefore hoped that he could make a later report on the case.

Paper.

A CASE OF PEMPHIGUS NEONATORUM ASSOCIATED WITH A GENERAL INFECTION BY THE STAPHYLOCOCCUS PYOGENES.

By L. EMMETT HOLT, M. D.

On December 19, 1896, there was admitted to the Babies' Hospital an infant nine days old with many bullæ over its shoulders and the lower part of its body. No history of syphilis was obtained in the parents or in two other children. The infant was brought from a home of great destitution and squalor, and had evidently been greatly neglected from the time of its birth. The mother was unable to nurse the child, and its food had been principally fennel tea, with occasionally a little milk and water added. At the time of admission it was said that the baby had had no food for twenty-four hours.

The child was certainly a vigorous one, for, in spite of this neglect, it was still plump and well nourished, weighing seven pounds twelve ounces, showing no evidence of its previous starvation. The body was exceedingly dirty, and looked as if there had been no bath given for a week. The bullæ were chiefly about the shoulders, buttocks, and thighs. They were from a quarter of an inch to an inch in diameter; none were present over the chest or back, none upon the feet or hands, and only two upon the face. Some of them had evidently just appeared. These were flaccid, and had slightly turbid contents; others had ruptured, showing a deep red base formed by the cutis vera, and still others showed superficial ulceration and were discharging pus. There was a moderately severe purulent ophthalmia, with an abundant discharge of pus. The navel was normal; examination of chest and abdomen negative; pulse good; temperature, 98.2° F.

An examination of the pus from the eye showed an abundance of pus organisms, but no gonococci. The contents of one of the bullæ on the neck and another from the thigh both showed pure cultures of the *Staphylococcus pyogenes aureus.*

On the following day the general symptoms became worse; the morning temperature was 99.6° F.; the evening, 102.5° F. There was quite marked general prostration and many new bullæ appeared, especially over the lower part of the abdomen and the thighs, some of these being two inches in diameter.

Upon the third day the child grew worse very rapidly and lay in a dull, semistupid condition, refusing food, and, in spite of free stimulation, lost steadily. New bullæ appeared in regions previously unaffected, especially over the forearms, legs, and feet. These came out with great rapidity, and often attained in twelve hours the size of an inch and a half in diameter. The epidermis would soon rupture, leaving an appearance much like that seen in a burn of the second degree. This appearance on the hands and feet is well shown in the illustrations. The temperature from this time ranged from 100.6° to 101.8° F., and death occurred from exhaustion on December 22d at 5 A. M., about sixty hours after admission.

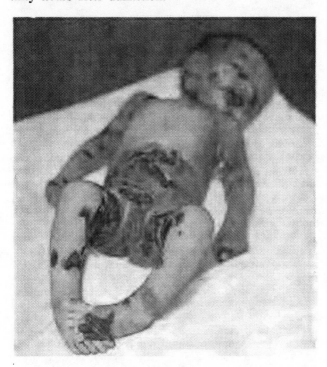

The illustrations are made from photographs taken after death.

Autopsy and bacteriological examination by Dr. Wollstein and Dr. Cordes thirty-one hours after death.

The body was well nourished and showed an extensive cutaneous eruption. Brain moderately congested.

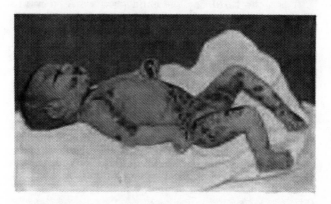

Larynx congested, and covered with a thin, grayish film, which peeled off easily, showing the reddened mucous membrane beneath. No membrane in the nasopharynx. Lungs: Large areas of atelectasis in both lower lobes, with emphysema anteriorly and many punctate hæmorrhages on the surface of both lower lobes, with much general congestion. Thymus: Many punctate hæmorrhages. Liver and spleen swollen and congested, otherwise normal. Kidneys intensely congested, Malpighian pyramids appearing almost hæmorrhagic. Suprarenals much congested, and showed small hæmorrhages. Mucous membrane of œsophagus and stomach intensely congested. Peyer's patches and the solitary follicles of the colon swollen and intensely congested, but mucous membrane generally normal.

Cultures from the lungs showed a *Staphylococcus pyogenes aureus* and the *Bacterium lactis aerogenes.*

The spleen and left kidney showed *Streptococcus longus;* the liver, *Streptococcus longus* and *Staphylococcus pyogenes aureus.* The bullæ upon the skin showed pure cultures of *Staphylococcus pyogenes aureus.*

Cultures of the *Staphylococcus pyogenes aureus* were injected into a mouse, which was found dead at the end of twenty-four hours. The same organism was recovered from the heart's blood and at the site of injection.

Regarding the use of few medical terms does more confusion exist than with respect to pemphigus. Ordinarily it is used to designate almost any cutaneous lesion characterized by bullous eruption. The acute form of the disease seen in very young infants certainly has little or nothing in common with the chronic form seen in older children and in adults.

Hereditary syphilis is responsible for a certain proportion of cases of pemphigus seen in newly born children, and many writers have been disposed to regard all these cases as syphilitic. The facts, however, do not warrant such a conclusion. In the case here reported there was no evidence whatever of syphilis, either clinical or pathological; but the symptoms during life, post-mortem findings, and the cultures all indicate a process of an acute general infection, of which the bullous eruption was only one of the manifestations. This bears out the findings of Strelitz and others, and shows that there are certainly cases of so-called pemphigus which are simply varieties of sepsis in the newly born. It is my opinion that many cases formerly regarded as syphilitic will be found to belong to this category.

Dr. ALEXANDER LAMBERT asked if there had been on the heart valves any evidence of endocarditis.

Dr. HOLT replied in the negative, and stated that there had been no lesion of the heart.

Dr. GEORGE THOMAS JACKSON said that pemphigus neonatorum was very rare in this country. This use of the name, moreover, was wrong; it was not, in his opinion, pemphigus at all. The first cases of this kind that he had observed had been many years ago at the Nursery and Child's Hospital. Three children had been affected, and all had had beautiful pemphigus blebs, but they had really been suffering from impetigo contagiosa. In foreign literature there was much said about contagious pemphigus. In true pemphigus pus cocci were not found, unless the blebs had become purulent. Another case of supposed pemphigus he had seen some years ago in Bellevue Hospital. This had also appeared to be one of impetigo contagiosa, and he had accordingly expressed the opinion that it would subside quickly under the use of salicylic acid ointment. This prediction had been verified. In view of these facts, he would protest against the use of the term " pemphigus." True pemphigus was a chronic

disease, running a course with relapses—a disease of
the nerves rather than a pus infection.

Dr. EDWARD B. BRONSON said that he had seen
the case reported by Dr. Holt, and it had not seemed
to be an example of real pemphigus neonatorum. The
child had certainly not been syphilitic, and the disease
had run a very different course from that of typical,
essential pemphigus. It was well known that under a
great many conditions what might be regarded as a
pemphigoid process might occur in the skin. Anything which caused marked vital depression seemed to
predispose to the formation of the blebs—*i. e.*, a separation of the cuticle and an effusion of serum underneath. When this effect occurred without any definite
assignable cause as an essential or idiopathic form of
disease it was called pemphigus. Undoubtedly there
was some general (probably internal) cause for the
lowered vitality in the skin, but inasmuch as the cause
could not be identified we called it an " essential " skin
disease. But just the same process might be the effect
of injury to the skin, as in the blisters from traumatism,
from excess of heat or cold, or from acrid irritants.
It might likewise result from injurious influences proceeding from within. That form observed in infants
suffering from hereditary syphilis, know as pemphigus
neonatorum syphiliticus, did not usually occur without
some other lesion of the skin, such as a syphilitic
erythema or a papular eruption. The pemphigus was
simply an exaggeration of the usual effect, and was
due to the fact that the skin reacted much more power-
fully in children than in adults, blistering being produced where ordinarily there would be only an erythema or a papulous eruption perhaps. Sometimes in
local infections one would find a similar process taking
place. For example, in impetigo contagiosa there was
ordinarily only a very superficial pustule having a thin
wall. But in some cases in which this infection of the
skin had lasted a considerable time it seemed to cause
such a lowering of the vitality as to produce a condition very closely corresponding to what was found in
true pemphigus. Again, there was a condition described as pemphigus hystericus, in which a single bleb
might be formed as a result of a peculiar nervous influence. In some cases when blistering had been produced by hot applications in patients suffering from col-
lapse, apoplexy, shock, or some other state of great
nervous depression, the effect could not be accounted
for by the degree of heat that had been applied. In

one instance he had seen blisters produced in a case of hemiplegia on the paralyzed side only, notwithstanding that the hot-water bottles had been applied to both limbs alike. The blistering was a pemphigoid effect, due to the lowered vital tone. The production of lesions corresponding to those of true pemphigus was often, therefore, really a symptom which might be common to quite a number of pathological conditions.

Dr. HOLT said it was true that a great number of diverse conditions had been grouped under this term " pemphigus," but his object was simply to report a case under the name by which it was usually described. His case was clearly a septic one.

Paper.

ABSCESS OF THE LIVER OF UNUSUAL ORIGIN.

By ALEXANDER LAMBERT, M. D.

R. L., aged fifty-six years; cook; was admitted on July 29, 1897, and died on August 22, 1897. Family history negative. She had had a fever thirty years ago which lasted two weeks. Previous history otherwise negative. She had been a regular drinker of whisky.

Three weeks before admission she became overheated while ironing clothes, and nausea and vomiting, with a chill accompanied by fever and sweating, followed. There was pain in the abdomen, also any other symptom asked for. She had chills and fever every day, the bowels were irregular, and the appetite was poor.

A physical examination showed that the patient was poorly nourished and very anæmic. The lower edges of the ribs were compressed inward. The tongue was dry and red, and the pulse was small and frequent. The patient was stupid and apathetic.

The breathing was high-pitched and harsh over the entire surface of both lungs. There was dullness on percussion at the base of the right lung behind. The heart was not enlarged, there were no murmurs, and its action was rapid. The firm, sharp edge of the liver could be felt an inch and a half below the free border of the ribs. There was no tenderness on pressure. It seemed to be slightly enlarged. The spleen was apparently normal.

The bowels were constipated. The urine was of a clear amber color, with a slight mucoid precipitate, and

acid. The specific gravity was 1.013; albumin, four
per cent.; there was no sugar. Microscopical examination revealed pus cells and a few epithelial cells, but no
casts. A week after admission the specific gravity was
1.016, and albumin eight per cent.

The patient took her nourishment well and slept
most of the time. She never complained of pain and
remained in a sleepy, apathetic condition. The temperature on admission was 102.4° F., the pulse 110, and
the respiration 22. The temperature ranged from 100°
to 102° F. for five days, and the pulse from 90 to 106.
The temperature then came down slowly to 99°, following the administration of ten grains of quinine three
times a day. It rose again, however, to 102°, and varied
for two days between 98° and 102°. Then for ten days
it ranged between 98° and 100°, rose to 103°, and for
four days remained high, with one remission to 100°,
then dropped to 97°, and until her death five days later
varied between 97° and 102°, being usually highest at
night, but never with any sudden rise or fall or chill.
The pulse varied between 88 and 116; usually, however, it ranged from 90 to 100. Small fly blisters were
applied to the epigastrium in order to obtain serum for
Widal's test, but no blister could be raised on the dry,
harsh, thick skin. The blood was tested and gave an absolutely negative reaction. The blood was very thin
and watery. The patient gradually became weaker and
more sleepy and apathetic, and died twenty-three days
after admission. The diagnosis was chronic nephritis
and cirrhosis of the liver, with unknown cause of the
fever and death.

At the autopsy the following conditions were found:
The body was emaciated, and the general muscular
volume was small. There were extensive post-mortem
discolorations over the abdomen, and post-mortem cyanosis over the entire posterior surface of· the body.
There were areas of vesication present over the epigastric region. The face, arms, and upper portion of the
thorax presented large patches of yellowish pigmenta-
tion. Both pupils were contracted to a pin point.

The panniculus adiposus was small in amount and
highly colored. The muscles of the thorax and abdomen were very small in volume, but were firm and of
a fairly good color. The pericardial exposure meas-

ured four by three centimetres. The pleural cavities were free. There were no pleuro-pericardial adhesions present.

The heart was small, and it was surrounded by a small amount of light-colored adipose tissue. The epicardium was negative. The heart chambers were not contracted. The muscle was soft and light-brown in color. The aortic and mitral segments were slightly thickened, and other portions of the endocardium presented a few diffuse thickened areas. The arch of the aorta appeared to be slightly dilated, and the intima presented a few atheromatous areas. The coronary arteries showed endarteritis of a moderate degree. The heart weighed eight ounces.

The peribronchial lymph nodes were not enlarged. The mucous membrane of the trachea and bronchi was congested. The bronchi contained an abundant purulent secretion, and in places they presented spindle-shaped dilatations of small extent. The lungs were emphysematous, and the posterior portions showed extreme congestion, probably hypostatic. The apices on both sides presented several cicatrices, evidently healed tubercles. Three isolated calcareous nodules were present in the left lower lobe, also probably tuberculous in origin.

The inferior surface of the right lobe of the liver was densely adherent to the subjacent tissues, and on separating these adhesions a large amount of a greenish-yellow pus gushed from the lower surface of the liver. On removal, the right lobe of the liver was found to be completely riddled with communicating cavities of a large size. These pus accumulations were limited by dense walls of fibrous connective tissue, the inner surfaces of which were covered by masses of granulations and pus clots. These granulations did not appear to be tuberculous in character. The lower wall of the abscess cavity was formed by the dense peritoneal adhesions already mentioned, which glued the upper border of the stomach to the inferior surface of the liver. On close examination of the wall of the abscess cavity a

pin incased in calcareous matter was dislodged from the
wall of the main cavity. The pin was of the ordinary
variety and measured twenty-seven millimetres in
length. Both the head and the stem of the pin were
incased in calcareous matter, so that it measured nearly
three millimetres in diameter. The liver, as a whole,
was not enlarged. The capsule was thickened and
scarred. The left lobe was not involved in the suppurative process. It was of a light mahogany in color, and
showed congestion with considerable increase of the circumvascular connective tissue. The weight of the liver
after the pus cavities had been flushed out was two
pounds and ten ounces. The pus was examined microscopically and showed bacilli and micrococci, but no cultures were made.

The gall bladder was small and it contained a small
amount of a light-yellow mucoidlike secretion. The
spleen was not enlarged. The capsule was rough and
thickened. It was firm in consistence and of a dark
mahogany color. It weighed four ounces. The lesser
curvature was involved in the plane of adhesions mentioned before. The stomach was small, and the mucous
membrane was generally atrophied. At a spot situated ten centimetres from the œsophageal entrance
and two centimetres anterior to the mesenteric attachment of the lesser curvature the mucous membrane was found to present an old circular cicatrix
measuring fifteen millimetres in diameter. This area
was surrounded by a ring of indurated tissue, but no evidences of recent inflammation were present. The base
of the cicatrix was found to be very thin, and, although
it was completely healed over, it was very evident that at
one time perforation of all the coats of the stomach wall
had been present. The process was undoubtedly an old
one, probably of months' or years' standing. This ulceration was situated directly beneath the centre of that
portion of the liver containing the abscess cavity. No
peritoneal adhesions, aside from those already mentioned,
were present. The intestinal coils were flaccid. Both
large and small intestines showed quite extensive post-

mortem changes; no lesions were evident. The pancreas was small, and its tissue was firm and a dark pink in color. The adrenals were very small, and their tissue appeared to be largely fatty.

The kidneys were slightly enlarged. The capsules were thickened and generally adherent. The cortex was fairly thick and regular. The markings were distinct. They were firm in consistence. The cortical portions were light purple in color and the pyramids were considerably darker. There was a marked increase of the perivascular connective tissue. The right renal artery was plugged near the hilus of the kidney by a yellowish embolic mass. The capillaries and the small vessels of both kidneys were injected. The bladder was small and contained a small amount of turbid urine.

The uterine annexa were held by a few fibrous bands. The ovaries were atrophic, but the right ovary presented a cyst three centimetres in diameter, which contained a clear serous fluid. The tubes were normal. The uterus was small and its mucous membrane was atrophic. The fundus contained two small fibroid masses.

The skullcap was thin and asymmetrical in form, the arching being fuller on the left side. The depressions for the Pacchionian bodies and for the middle meningeal arteries were deep. The dura mater was somewhat thickened. The pia mater was very opalescent over the parietal lobes. The brain was asymmetrical. The right hemisphere was considerably smaller than the left, and the convolutions on this side were smaller and less perfectly marked. The vessels of the base showed considerably thickened walls. The cortical layer of gray matter was thin and irregularly distributed. The ependymata were normal. The tissue was firm and solid in consistence. The right lobe of the cerebellum was considerably larger than the left.

The spinal cord was not examined. The autopsy was performed by Dr. Harmon Brooks, pathologist to the Fourth Division of Bellevue Hospital.

2

Paper.

A CASE OF PRIMARY SARCOMA OF THE HEART.

By ALEXANDER LAMBERT, M. D.

J. C., aged thirty-nine years. Irish. His father died of phthisis. He had measles and whooping-cough when young. He has had pain in the joints, but no other rheumatic symptoms. He had an attack of grippe three years ago. He is a moderate drinker, and smokes and chews. He drinks considerable coffee. He has had gonorrhœa, but denies syphilis. Ten years ago he was kicked in the chest by a horse, and suffered from a broken sternum and several broken ribs in the pericardial region. During the past two years his voice has changed from deep bass to one that is husky and high-pitched.

The present illness began five days before admission. The patient had been shoveling snow in the streets for two days, and when he came home at night he had a chill, followed by dyspnœa and pain in the chest. He was forced to go to bed. He had a cough of a distressing character, with muco-purulent expectoration. His appetite was poor and he vomited a little; since then the symptoms have persisted. He complained of pains across the chest, beneath the shoulder blades, in the small of the back, and at the lower end of the sternum. On admission his temperature was 100.8° F., the pulse 90, and respiration 36.

The patient was well nourished, the jugular veins were prominent, the face was slightly flushed, and the pupils were dilated. The chest bulged slightly on the right side in front. There was exaggerated breathing at the right apex in front, with prolonged and high-pitched expiration and broncho-vesicular voice. Behind, on the right side, there was dullness of the entire lung, with diminished vocal fremitus; from the spine of the scapulæ to the base the voice was of a nasal quality and diminished. The breathing was very much diminished. Just below the angle of the left scapula there was a small area where the breathing was exaggerated, with prolonged and slightly high-pitched expiration and broncho-vesicular voice and crepitant râles.

The heart apex in the fourth intercostal space was an inch and a half internal to the mamillary line. The sounds were weak, but no murmurs were present. The second pulmonic sound was not exaggerated. The action was somewhat irregular. The pulse was small and compressible. The liver extended an inch and a half too far downward and was tender on pressure. The spleen was large and there was tenderness over its area.

The patient's pneumonia developed in areas in both lungs, and cleared up in a week, except a patch on the right side behind, at the level of the eighth rib, which persisted. Ten days after admission a pericarditis friction rub was heard, but no fluid could be demonstrated in the sac. At the same time a pleurisy developed in both pleural cavities, with effusion in both cavities. The fluid drawn from the right pleural cavity was bloody, while that from the left was clear serum. The patient perspired profusely. There was marked cyanosis of the face and neck, extending to the clavicles, while the patient was lying down; when he sat up the face became white, though the lips remained blue, and there was then a distinct though slight cyanosis of the body as far down as Poupart's ligaments, the legs remaining white. For nineteen days longer the pneumonic patch persisted. The profuse sweating and cyanosis remained, also the dry pericarditis. During this time, when the left chest became filled with effusion and the heart was pushed over to the right side, the right pupil became dilated. When the fluid was withdrawn the dilatation of the pupil disappeared, and the heart resumed its normal position. The effusion had to be withdrawn several times, but finally a little fluid was left in each pleural cavity, as the patient suffered less pain while the effusion separated the inflamed surfaces of the pleuræ. On the thirtieth day after admission the legs became œdematous, there was fluid in the abdominal cavity, and fluid could be demonstrated in the pericardial sac. The fluid accumulated rapidly in the pericardial sac and in the pleural cavities, and the patient died thirty-two days after admission. During his illness the temperature ranged from 99° F. to 101.8° F. with no special regularity, or with any marked irregularities. The pulse at first ran from 90 to 64; later it ran from 76 to 54. The respirations were from 20 to 40 during the first days of his illness; later from 36 to 50 a minute. The respirations were deep, though frequent.

The urinary examination on admission showed normal urine. Later there was a fair amount of albumin present, and the specific gravity was 1.035, but no sugar was present. There were no casts. The blood examination on admission showed 6,455,000 red cells, and 20,000 white cells.

The following report of the post-mortem examination is from Dr. Harmon Brooks, pathologist of the Fourth Division:

The body is that of a well-developed adult. General nutrition is good. The skin is cyanosed over the entire body, and extremely so over the face and upper portion of the thorax. Post-mortem congestion is marked over the posterior surface of the body. The subcutaneous connective tissue of the entire body is extremely œdematous, that of the face and of the pendent portions of the body being most marked. The muscles of the trunk and extremities are soft and flabby.

The abdomen is distended; it is tympanitic over the dome, but the percussion note over the sides is dull. Rigor mortis is not present. There is a small amount of panniculus adiposus. The muscles of the chest and abdominal wall are soft, anæmic, and extremely œdematous. On incising the wall the abdominal cavity was found to contain two litres of a clear, straw-colored serous fluid. The anterior border of the liver is forced downward, so that its margin projects ten centimetres below the costal border. The pleural cavities are distended on both sides by approximately four litres of clear fluid similar in character to that found in the abdomen. The superior surface of the liver is closely adherent to the diaphragm. The capsule is considerably thickened, and in areas over the superior surface is covered by recent adhesions. The liver is of a dark-clay color. The circumvascular connective tissue is considerably increased in amount. It is firm in consistence. The cut surface is granular. The weight of the liver is three pounds and a half. The external surface of the spleen is covered by recent adhesions which bind it closely to the parietal peritonæum. The capsule is thickened and contains several nodular fibroid masses. The spleen is symmetrically enlarged. The tissue is firm, but breaks easily. The Malpighian tufts are prominent. The color is dark purple.

The right kidney weighs six ounces, the left eight ounces. The capsules are thickened, and they are generally and intimately adherent. The markings are indistinct and irregular. The cortex is thin. The tissue is firm and not granular. The color is a dark purple. The circumvascular connective tissue is increased in amount. The capillaries, especially those of the cortex, are congested. The pelvis is apparently normal. The ureters are normal.

The stomach is normal in size, and it contains a small amount of partly digested food. The mucous membrane is congested and is thickened in areas; the intestines present no lesions; the mesenteric nodes are not enlarged. The pancreas is large, the tissue is firm, and it is light pink in color. In the head of the pancreas is found a circumscribed round nodule, four centimetres in diameter. It is situated on the anterior surface of the pancreas. The tissue is soft and is of a pronounced pink color. It contains many blood-vessels which are greatly congested. It is surrounded by much inflammatory tissue which is apparently of recent origin.

The peribronchial lymph nodes are slightly enlarged. They are firm, and on section presented no evidence of caseation or of metastatic neoplasm. The lungs are emphysematous. In the middle of the posterior portion of the right lower lobe is an area of pneumonic consolidation measuring eight by five centimetres.

The pericardial sac is greatly distended, measuring in its long axis twenty-two centimetres, and from side to side eighteen centimetres. The sac is somewhat peculiarly shaped, the larger end being that directed downward. No pleuro-pericardial adhesions are present. The sac is tense and smooth to the touch, but above where it joins at the root of the aorta a large, firm nodule is felt. On incising the sac about one litre of blood-stained fluid, containing many masses of fibrin, escaped. Both visceral and parietal pericardium are completely covered by a thick recent deposit of fibrin shreds. The entire internal surface of the pericardium is covered with numerous firm white nodules, in places fused into masses. The new growth is most abundant over the posterior and lateral surfaces of the pericardium. The growth has, apparently, taken place in the connective tissue below the endothelial layer, as the nodules are covered in all places apparently by the endothelial coat. On incision the nodular growths were found to be of firm consistence and almost pearly white in color. The growth is thickest about the root of the aorta, so that the aorta and vena cava are considerably pressed upon by it.

The wall of the left ventricle is almost completely involved in an apparently similar neoplasm. The growth has extended completely through the wall of the heart from the root of the aorta down to within an inch of the apex. Nodules of the growth were found in other parts of the heart wall, but the growth is apparently of longest standing in the anterior wall of the left ventricle, where very few traces of normal heart tissue remains. The growth extends to the aortic segments, the attached borders of which are involved in the growth. The trunks of both pneumogastric nerves, together with the veins at the base of the heart, are pressed upon by the growth. The growths in the heart wall are covered externally by the external endothelial coat, and internally by the endocardium. The cerebrum, cerebellum, and bulb show no gross lesions. The spinal cord was not removed below the third cervical segment.

Microscopical examinations of the nodules in the pancreas, of the growths in the pericardium, and of the heart wall give in each case the same picture—that of a typical small, round-cell sarcoma. The nodule found in the pancreas seems to be the most recent, since it is surrounded by areas of inflamed tissue, and the blood-vessels are less perfectly formed here than in the other portions of the growth. The vessels are also more numerous here. The microscope fails to reveal any points of distinction in the character or relative age of the growths found in the pericardium and in the heart wall.

The enlargement of the lymph glands seems to have been entirely inflammatory, and, though several were examined, no evidences of neoplastic invasions could be detected.

It is difficult to determine the point of the original growth from a study of the specimens. The nodule in the pancreas is very evidently the most recent, but no direct evidence is present as to whether the neoplasm was primarily in the heart or in the pericardium. The area of the heart most involved, it will be noticed, is that supplied by the left coronary artery, and the large nodule described lies directly over the origin of this artery. One should consider that this nodule occupies the space in which we usually find lymph glands belonging to the chain following the left coronary artery. But it appears extremely improbable that the growth should have originated in these nodules, for these reasons: The structure of the neoplasm is not characteristic of lymph sarcoma. If the original growths were of the lymph glands, we should expect to find other glands of the same chain involved, and a careful examination has fully excluded this possibility.

The growth is thought to be a primary one of the heart, for the following reasons: 1. The nodule in the pancreas is too small to have existed for a time sufficient for so extensive a metastatic invasion of the heart and pericardium to have taken place, and, at the same time, not to have involved, to a greater extent, the surrounding tissues; besides, the structure of this tissue shows it to be plainly a recent and active growth. 2. The heart wall has, as stated, been in places completely replaced by the neoplasm, while the largest areas of the pancreas involved are small in comparison. 3. If the growth had been primary in the pericardium, we should in all probability have found other metastatic growths distributed along those areas supplied by the same vascular trunks. Again, if the growth had been primary here, we should expect to find the endothelial coats broken through and ulcerated.

Primary sarcoma of the heart, while rare, is not of such infrequent occurrence as primary connective-tissue tumors of the pericardium, of which the writer has been unable to find a single authentic case yet reported.

The clinical diagnosis of this case was double pleurisy with effusion and pneumonic areas in the right lung at the eighth rib behind; pericarditis and a mediastinal tumor at the root of the right lung affecting the junction of the vena azygos major with the superior vena cava, the tumor being either tuberculous or sarcomatous. The enlargemer of the liver and spleen was thought to be due to cirrhosis. The diagnosis of the mediastinal tumor was based on the change in the voice, the slow pulse, and the dyspnœa, this dyspnœa being present whether there was fluid in the pleural cavities or not, and especially on the peculiar cyanosis which changed with the posture of the patient and was always limited to certain areas, depending upon the posture. These areas were those drained by the superior vena cava and the azygos.

The occurrence of primary sarcoma of the heart is so rare that the following statistics, taken from Whittaker's article in the *Twentieth Century Practice*, may be of interest: Tumors of the heart are usually secondary. In the cases collected by Berthenson neoplasms had developed in the heart cavities twenty-seven times. Of these neoplasms nine were sarcomata, seven myomata, six fibromata, two gummata, and three each carcinomata and cystic tumor. They had developed in the right auricle seven times, in the right ventricle three times, in the left auricle seven times, and in the left ventricle five times. Of the twenty cases in which the sex was mentioned, eleven had occurred in men and nine in women. Of the nine cases of sarcomata, eight had been round-celled sarcomata, and one giant-celled. Redtenbacher has reported a case of primary angeiosarcoma of the

pericardium and heart, the symptoms being those of
pericarditis and bilateral pleuritis with effusion.

Dr. A. ALEXANDER SMITH said that he had seen
this patient only once, and remembered very distinctly
the peculiar changes in his color resulting from changes
in posture. From this it had seemed easy to make a
diagnosis of pressure on the veins by a tumor. Primary sarcoma of the heart was exceedingly rare, and
there was nothing about the physical signs indicative of
such involvement of the heart. At the time he had
seen the case, he had thought the diagnosis lay between
tumor in the mediastinum and an intrapericardial
aneurysmal tumor. He believed that the condition
was so rare that the diagnosis could only be made positively on the autopsy table.

Dr. EGBERT LE FEVRE said that the clinical picture
had emphasized the impossibility of making a correct
and positive diagnosis from the signs and symptoms.
The effect on the pulse had been out of all proportion
to the growth in the heart. He had seen the patient
after the occurrence of pleural effusion in both cavities, and it had been impossible to outline the heart to
determine the extent of the dilatation. The peculiar
œdema, the cyanosis, and the breathing in the recum-
bent posture all had served to indicate merely that
there was some interference with the return circulation.
He had hazarded the opinion that there might be a
tumor pressing upon one of the large veins. As the
pulmonary symptoms and those referable to the aorta
had not warranted the diagnosis of aneurysmal tumor
there, he had been led to suspect a growth in the
mediastinum.

The speaker referred incidentally to the fact that in
the clinical history of the case Dr. Lambert had spoken
of the "curved line of Garland." This was wrong, as
Ellis had first called attention to this line, and Garland
had subsequently demonstrated it by injections into the
pleural cavity. Until recent years it had been known
as "the S-line of Ellis."

Dr. LAMBERT said that there was nothing absolutely
to point to the diagnosis of a growth in the heart. After
a careful study of the case he had expressed the opinion
that the tumor involved the vena azygos at the point at
which it emptied into the vena cava. So far as he had
been able to ascertain, this was only the tenth case of the
kind on record.

Paper.

THE OPERATIVE TREATMENT OF HÆMORRHOIDS.

By PARKER SYMS, M. D.

As the scope of this paper will be limited to a consideration of that branch of the subject indicated by
the title given, I shall have nothing to say concerning
the ætiology, pathology, or symptoms of hæmorrhoids,
nor shall I here discuss the varieties of the disease nor
attempt to specify the indications for operative procedure, but I shall pass at once to the subject properly
before us, and speak only of the operative treatment of
hæmorrhoids.

There are three well-known and approved methods
of operating upon hæmorrhoids—namely, first, by ablation and ligation, known as Allingham's operation;
second, resection of the entire hæmorrhoidal area,
known as Whitehead's method; third, ablation of the
hæmorrhoidal masses by means of the clamp and cautery.

A large experience in the treatment of this disease
has given me a favorable opportunity of testing these
various methods, of which I have taken advantage, and
I feel fairly qualified to speak of their individual advantages and disadvantages. I have tried them all,
and have carefully weighed their value, and have thereby arrived at the conclusions which are the basis of
this paper.

The objects to be attained in operatively treating
a case of hæmorrhoids are as follows:

First, to completely cure the patient of the trouble
for which you operate; secondly, to subject the patient
to the least compatible risk; thirdly, to accomplish the
desired object with the least possible delay; fourthly,
to occasion the patient the least amount of suffering:
fifthly, to produce the least possible deformity and
disability in the parts involved.

Whitehead's method involves the patient in a rather

formidable operation. It necessitates a considerable loss of blood, and this is an important matter in cases of this disease, for the patients are frequently debilitated and anæmic from the frequent hæmorrhages which are a prominent symptom of hæmorrhoids. It depends for its success upon a primary union of the wound, and therefore upon aseptic healing in a region where asepsis is most difficult to obtain. In a certain proportion of cases infection will occur, and the wound will break down by inflammation and the patient will be exposed to the danger of general septic poisoning. When these wounds are inflamed and primary union fails, the healing will be very tedious and protracted, and the circular scar which results will eventually contract, and in some instances will cause a permanent stricture at the anus. Two such cases have come under my care recently. It may be said in its favor that it is a radical procedure, and when all goes well the final healing and cure are rapidly attained, but the risks to the patient, as set forth above, are too great to be lightly considered, and I feel that it is an operation to be avoided in the vast majority of cases.

The operation known as Allingham's, which consists in excision of each hæmorrhoidal tumor with ligation of the vessels at its base, is an excellent operation in most instances, and is free from most of the risks involved in the Whitehead operation; but it is a less radical operation than the operation by the clamp and cautery, involves a greater loss of blood, takes longer to perform, and is attended by a greater amount of post-operative pain. Therefore I prefer the operation to be described.

Operation by Clamp and Cautery.—This operation can be rapidly performed. In most cases it may be completed within five minutes. It is attended by very slight loss of blood. It is radical if properly performed, curing not only the hæmorrhoids themselves, but also the tendency to rectal prolapse which is often present. In my experience the healing has always progressed satisfactorily and without inflammatory complications,

and the patients suffer less after the operation than
under the other methods. By this method the final
result is excellent, and the functional power of the anus
is never impaired.

The operation is performed as follows: First, as re-
gards the preparation of the patient. The patient
should be restricted to a simple, plain diet for two days
before the operation, from which must be excluded all
forms of alcoholic beverages. The bowels should be relieved by a purgative two days before the operation,
and by a saline on the day prior to the operation.

The lower bowel should be cleansed by an enema
about six hours before the time for the operation. No
enema should be given subsequent to that time. If
this plan is carried out the rectum will be found empty
and in proper condition for the operation. At the time
of the operation the parts about the anus should be
thoroughly washed, but no shaving will be necessary.

After the patient has been thoroughly anæsthetized
and placed in the lithotomy position, and of course the
parts properly cleansed, the sphincter muscle should be
thoroughly stretched. This must be done slowly, but
very thoroughly. To accomplish this, lubricate the two
thumbs with green soap, introduce first one and then
the other, and make steady traction forward and backward until the muscular spasm has been overcome. Further divulsion may be accomplished by crowding the
fingers of one hand together in the shape of a cone,
after they have been properly lubricated, and forcing
the hand into the anus. This stretching of the sphincter is one of the most important steps in the operation.
It must be done thoroughly, but of course it must not
be overdone, and experience alone can guide the operator to the proper exercise of judgment in this matter.

When the patient has been anæsthetized and the
sphincter divulsed, one will be able for the first time
to make a satisfactory examination of the rectum, and
the field should be thoroughly searched for ulcerations,
fistulæ, fissures, or any other abnormity. All the
prominent hæmorrhoidal masses should be grasped in

large blunt forceps, such as fenestrated sponge holders, and brought well out of the anus, producing a temporary prolapse of these masses. Should the entire circumference of the anus be involved by hæmorrhoids, it should be dealt with in three or four sections, each section containing a group of the most prominent hæmorrhoids, but leaving the ·intervening mucous membrane untouched.

Each mass should be so seized by the forceps as to raise its entire base. Now the mucous membrane should be cut through at the anal margin as far as the width of the mass to be removed. Next, the entire mass should be grasped in a special hæmorrhoid clamp, which should be constructed on the plan of the clamp devised by Dr. Smith. The clamp should be applied in the direction of the long axis of the rectum, and not transversely. Next, the mass so grasped is to be trimmed off with scissors, but sufficient of the base should be left to be dealt with by the cautery. Now, the whole cut surface is to be seared with the Paquelin cautery at a dull red heat. Next, the clamp is to be removed, and the stump carefully examined to be sure that there is no bleeding. (In rare instances it will be necessary to apply a ligature to the bleeding point.)

This completes the operation. In a majority of cases two or three masses must be thus treated. The after-treatment is very simple. The bowels should never be constipated, and if they do not move spontaneously on the second day a saline should be administered, and after that the patient should have a movement daily. The only local treatment I recommend is external bathing, and the insertion twice daily for the first week of a suppository containing five grains of iodoform.

While this operation is a simple one to perform, a great deal of care is necessary in carrying out each step, and it is only by experience that one can learn just how much or how little to do; but this is equally true of every method of operating.

If properly performed, the result is always satisfactory. Convalescence is virtually painless, and the function of the rectum and anus is not in the least impaired. During the last four years I have performed this operation considerably over one hundred times, and every patient has recovered without any complication.

Dr. S. ALEXANDER said that he agreed to most of the views expressed in the paper as to the choice of operation. His custom had been to use the Allingham operation more frequently than the operation with clamp and cautery. He had never performed the Whitehead operation, and did not approve of it. His reason for preferring the Allingham operation was its simplicity; if the anal sphincter was thoroughly dilated at the time of the operation the objections to the operation were entirely done away with. So far as his own experience had gone, he had never seen any serious hæmorrhage and had not observed any pain following this operation, and the ultimate results had been fully as good as those from the clamp and cautery if not better. It was necessary, however, to fully stretch the sphincter so as to paralyze it for about a week after the operation; in his opinion, this was one of the secrets of success with Allingham's operation. Another important point was to thoroughly cut through the mucous membrane at the base of each hæmorrhoidal tumor before tying it off. The Allingham operation was very easy to perform. If each ligature was left long, by the time the operation had been completed a number of ligatures would be hanging from the margin of the anus; when these were pulled they opened up the rectum and allowed of a very complete examination of the bowel. His objections to the clamp-and-cautery operation were that there was more danger of hæmorrhage, and complete recovery was longer delayed. Possibly the reason that he had encountered hæmorrhage frequently in performing the clamp operation was that he had made it a practice to cut close to the clamp. Another objection to the operation was that the healing of the ulcers caused by the cautery took longer than where the ligature had been used. Still another objection to the clamp-and-cautery operation was a point that had been alluded to by the reader of the paper as an advantage—*i. e.*, that by the judicious use of the clamp and cautery one was able to overcome the tendency to prolapse which occurred in a large number of bad cases of internal hæmorrhoids. But when there was not this tendency to prolapse, there seemed to be some danger of producing more or less permanent stricture of that portion of the bowel.

Dr. C. E. QUIMBY said that years ago he had done hæmorrhoidal operations, for the most part by Allingham's method. An inspection of Kelsey's hæmorrhoidal clamp led him to suggest that the action of the instrument ought to be more satisfactory if the blades were so constructed as to remain parallel to each other, instead of, as at present, the lower blade cutting clear in before the upper part had got hold of the mass at all.

Dr. SYMS said that he had never thought of making any modification of the instrument, because as now made he had found it perfectly satisfactory. In using the clamp, it was his custom to apply the blades to the tumors in an inverted position, the operation field being outside of the rectum. In this way the firmest part of the grasp of the clamp was at the base of the hæmorrhoidal tumor, or at the point where the vessels entered. The clamp did not cut the tissues; it simply compressed them firmly.

Dr. GEORGE W. CRARY said that his objection to the clamp-and-cautery operation was that in hæmorrhoids having a broad base the clamp picked up the hæmorrhoids and also a large portion of the mucous membrane, and on the removal of the clamp the edges of the mucous membrane separated and left a large ulcer, which was slow to heal. The operation answered well for pedunculated piles.

Dr. JOHN F. ERDMANN said that he strongly favored the Allingham operation. It could be done just as quickly as the clamp operation, and convalescence was as rapid as after the clamp and cautery, if not more rapid. He never kept these patients more than two or three days in bed after either operation. The pain following the use of the ligature did not seem to him any severer than after the use of the clamp and cautery. His reasons for not using the latter operation more frequently were the same as given by Dr. Crary, and also the risk of hæmorrhage. Even with unusual care in the use of the clamp and cautery, he had found spurting vessels on removing the clamp, and these had been secured with difficulty on account of their tendency to recede in the rectal field. He had recently done the Allingham operation thoroughly and quickly under cocaine and eucaine anæsthesia.

Dr. ROBERT T. MORRIS said that at the present time

we should choose between the Allingham and the clamp-and-cautery operation, and this choice would depend very much upon personal skill. He had seen some bad results from both methods. In operations for hæmorrhoids three principal things required attention—viz.: (1) The removal of the pile; (2) the control of the hæmorrhage; and (3) the prevention of infection. This last element was the factor which caused the most trouble. Unless one was very skillful in leaving a very small slough, the danger of infection from the slough was not unimportant—he had seen infection occur in this way—though in the hands of a careful and watchful surgeon the danger was comparatively small. Personally, he preferred the Allingham operation at present. It cured the patient with very little danger of infection or hæmorrhage. One very important point had not been discussed by the authors in connection with the Whitehead operation. In that operation the linea pectinata was removed, and with it a special sensory apparatus of the anus. Stroud, in a paper published in the *Annals of Surgery* a few months ago, had given a lucid account of the anatomy of the anus and had called attention to this special-sense apparatus whose function was to warn the person of the approach of fæces. When this apparatus was destroyed the consequences were likely to be unpleasant.

Dr. Syms said that he regarded the Allingham operation as a thoroughly good one, but believed that the clamp operation possessed certain advantages over it. In the first place, the wound made by the cautery was an absolutely aseptic one in the beginning, and the experience of those who had employed the method extensively showed that infection very seldom occurred. He had never seen any constitutional disturbance in any case after the first twenty-four hours of reaction. It was his custom not to operate exclusively by this method; in some instances he used one method on one part of the rectum, and the other operation on another part of the rectum in the same patient. He had not found in the case of tumors having a broad base that there had been unusually large ulcers and tedious healing after the clamp-and-cautery operation; indeed, he was of the opinion that this was more likely to occur with the other method. If care was taken to make the ablation in the line of the long axis of the rectum, if contraction took place the tendency would not be to narrow the lumen of the gut. While the loss of blood in the Allingham operation was slight, it was an important matter for these patients, because they were usually thoroughly depleted by frequent losses of blood from the hæmorrhoidal vessels. When cocaine first came into use he had employed it about the rectum, but as sudden deaths had been reported from the use of only three to five minims of a four-per-cent. solution of cocaine, he had abandoned cocaine in these cases. He had known of serious though not fatal cocaine poisoning in connection with rectal surgery. He had found the clamp-and-cautery operation exceedingly satisfactory, and it should be performed without loss of blood, either during the operation or after the removal of the clamps. The clamps should be applied deliberately and closed firmly, and then the cutting off of the superabundant mass should be done with great care. If it was done close to the clamp, there would be absolutely no control over the bleeding. A sufficient stump should be left, and this stump should be thoroughly seared, but not removed by the cautery.

Dr. S. ALEXANDER asked if Dr. Erdmann had found it possible to thoroughly dilate the sphincter under cocaine anæsthesia.

Dr. ERDMANN replied that he had never thought that it was necessary to absolutely paralyze the sphincter. He had used the method in cases in which there had been only two or three hæmorrhoids. Eucaine acted much better than cocaine, and so far as he had been able to ascertain there was no danger from it.

Dr. E. L. WILLIAMSON said that two months before he had assisted in an operation for anal fissure in which the sphincter had been thoroughly dilated under cocaine anæsthesia. The anæsthesia had been complete, although the patient was a nervous women. A further operation could have been done at that time if it had been required.

3

Meeting of December 1, 1897.

The President, Dr. ROBERT J. CARLISLE, in the Chair.

Paper.

THE HISTORIES·OF THREE MORBID SPECIMENS.

BY CHARLES PHELPS, M. D.

I. PERITONEAL HYDATIDS; LAPAROTOMY.

THE patient, an active business man, fifty-one years of age, had suffered previous to his final illness only from attacks of colic, which, though frequent and sometimes severe, were always brief. On an evening in June he rode upon his bicycle and fell, striking his abdomen upon some part of the machine without receiving appreciable hurt; indeed, it was only after some questioning that he remembered the fact of injury. After his return to his house he had a large movement from the bowels, which was followed by severe pain in the epigastrium; this pain was continuous and increased in severity. On the third day vomiting began; the temperature, which had been below 100°, rose to 102.8°, and the pulse to 110; the pain, tenderness, and abdominal distention were all more marked upon the right than upon the left side. I saw the patient at this time in consultation with his physician, Dr. Dan. H. Smith, who concurred in the opinion that operation should be immediate, and laparotomy was done without unnecessary delay. A perforation was discovered just below and a little to the right of the umbilicus, from which escaped a few bubbles of odorless gas and a seemingly endless succession of milky white gelatinous plaques and of cysts, mainly of minute size, but no fæcal matter. The almost invincible adhesions of the intestinal folds to each other and to the abdominal wall had prevented the invasion of the peritoneal cavity, if such could be said to exist, and at the same time made it impossible to obtain a clear conception of the conditions which actually existed. As the strength of the patient soon began to alarmingly fail, the perforation was closed by a purse-string suture, and further exploration was abandoned. Death occurred eighteen hours later.

Upon necroscopic examination access to the peritoneal cavity was found to be quite as difficult as during

life, and it became necessary to remove the thoroughly
and firmly agglutinated intestinal mass entire before
its parts could be separated and their pathic relations
determined. It was then discovered that three large
peritoneal cysts were attached to the greater curvature
of the stomach, and six to the ascending and transverse
portions of the colon, each containing from eight to sixteen ounces of turbid fluid in which floated a large
amount of disintegrated material, both in granular and
laminated form, and innumerable apparently living
cysts, varying in size from that of a robin shot to that of
a pigeon's egg. The perforation, recognized during life,
was in one which was attached to the cæcum. They
were all developed from the subserous tissue and none
communicated with the lumen of the intestine or with
the cavity of the stomach. The adhesions were mainly
of long standing and of exceeding strength. No pus had
been formed near the site of perforation, but three pock-
ets, each holding from half an ounce to an ounce, were
found in the left lumbar region. There were no cystic
formations or other evidences of disease in any of the
viscera or in other part of the body.

Subsequent examination in the laboratory proved
the hydatid nature of the disease, though no hooklets
were discovered in the fluid or in the few cysts which
were inspected.

I am unaware of any previously reported case in
which these parasites have remained in the subperito-
neal tissue, through which, after penetration of the
intestinal wall, they must first pass on their way to
more or less distant parts of election. Though no
tissue or organ is exempt from their lodgment and
growth, they seem in no recorded instance even by accident to have been halted at this first step of their progress. I am cognizant, however, of two unpublished
cases of somewhat similar character disclosed in post-
mortem examination; one of these only was in the
human subject. In this case, in which the morbid
condition was discovered by Dr. Ira Van Gieson in
the deadhouse of a suburban hospital, and without history, the small cysts which existed seemed to have been
derived from a previous invasion of the liver. The other,
which was noted by Dr. End. K. Dunham, was in a

monkey, and in this instance numerous cysts of the size of a marble floated free in the peritoneal cavity, or were connected with the mesenteric folds.

The case represented by the pathic specimen presented is noteworthy from the great size of the peritoneal tumors, which, with the extent and solidity of the peritoneal adhesions, indicate an amount and duration of serious disease remarkable in view of the history of the patient. He must have suffered, probably for years, from a chronic or recurrent peritonitis of considerable intensity which, with the gradually increasing morbid growths, had practically obliterated the peritoneal cavity, and yet remained of robust physique, a free liver, engaged in active outdoor pursuits, and without suspicion that his health was otherwise than perfect, his attacks of colic being no more severe or protracted than those which often attend simple indigestion.

II. RECURRENT SARCOMA; AMPUTATION OF BOTH LOWER EXTREMITIES ABOVE THE KNEE.

The patient, a girl, seventeen years of age, without hereditary predispositions, first noticed an enlargement of the right knee in October, 1895, which proved to be the result of sarcomatous disease, and led to an amputation of the thigh in February, 1896. Necrosis of the end of the bone was followed by an abscess and a sinus which was not healed till after the removal of the sequestrum, in April, 1897. In July, 1897, the left knee became the seat of a dull pain without swelling or other indication of organic change. I had removed the necrosed bone, and seeing the case at this time was inclined to refer the pain to some strain put upon the joint in an effort to get about without the aid of crutches. She was then treated by a physician with starch bandages for three weeks for supposed rheumatism, and on August 1st entered a hospital, where a diagnosis of synovitis was made and a plaster-of-Paris apparatus applied till September 1st. She was then sent home as cured, but without having been examined by the attending surgeon. At that time, however, she states that the knee was much enlarged, and that a small immovable tumor could be felt in the popliteal space. The enlargement of the knee was rapid, the popliteal tumor could no longer be isolated, and the nature of the affection was subsequently recognized by Dr. Martin Burke, who was called to attend her, and with whom I saw her early in October. The knee was then swollen, tense, and the seat of constant and severe pain, which was allayed only by the continued use of morphine. I advised immediate amputation, not with the hope of radical cure, but as the only practicable means of relieving pain with a possibility of some indefinite prolongation of life. The operation was done October 18th through the lower and middle thirds of the thigh, the growth being then in rapid progress, perceptible almost from day to day, the pain intense, and the patient anæmic and cachectic. The wound closed by primary adhesion, the constitutional condition at once improved, and recovery from the operation was complete.

The soft tumor, which has been lost by inexplicable negligence, apparently originated from the periosteum in the intercondyloid space of the femur, was of soft consistence, vascular, and from its gross characteristics evidently a sarcoma. The lower part of the femur, with which it was in contact, is roughened by the formation of a shell of new bone, and the cartilage of incrustation of the femoral condyles in great part destroyed. The tibia was not involved. An examination of a portion taken from the knee was made by Dr. End. K. Dunham and "proved to be composed of atypical hyaline cartilage so rich in cellular elements " that, in his opinion, " a diagnosis of chondrosarcoma was justified."

I am informed by Dr. Robert Abbe, who made the first amputation, that the primary tumor was a round-celled sarcoma which originated beneath the periosteum of the right tibia, and that its growth was exceedingly rapid. The knee joint was invaded, but the condyloid surfaces of the femur were unaffected, as was the tibial surface of the joint in the more recent instance. In a very careful examination of the left knee made by Dr. Abbe about the middle of August, no evidence of the impending recurrent disease was discoverable.

The rapid and painful growth of the tumors, in not more than two or three weeks in the first instance and in less than two months in the second, their histological characters, and the early recurrence of the disease in a distant part of the body, notwithstanding early operation, indicate in this case a type of extreme malignancy and profound constitutional implication.

It is possible that the first impression, both of Dr. Abbe and of myself, that the discomfort then felt in the left knee was from strain and overfatigue in the effort of getting about without crutches, was correct. This may well enough have determined the manifestation of the recurrent disease in that particular part.

Up to the present time the constitutional condition has continued to improve, and there is as yet no indication of the probably inevitable recurrence of the disease.

III. DEPRESSED FRACTURE OF THE CRANIAL VAULT; LATE TREPHINATION.

The patient, a man sixty years of age, sustained in July, 1895, a compound depressed fracture of the right parietal bone near its anterior superior angle. His history previous to his admission to Bellevue Hospital in September, 1897, is derived from his own statements, which seem sufficiently worthy of credence. The injury was occasioned by a blow, and he remained unconscious for a number of hours. On the fourth day he again lost consciousness, which was not regained until two or three days later. He was confined to the bed for seven weeks. After that time he suffered from constant vertigo and general headache, both aggravated at intervals, and the headache at times more severe in the frontal or in the occipital region. A discharge from the right ear, beginning two weeks after injury, persisted for several months, and deafness in that ear never has been relieved. In July, 1897, he began to have attacks of vertigo so severe that he fell unconscious in the street; these continued up to the time he entered the hospital, sometimes twice in the day, and sometimes with intervals of several days. He could give no further account of the paroxysms, and none occurred during the ten days which elapsed from the time of his admission to the hospital to the time of operation. A button of bone which included the entire depression was removed by a Galt trephine three eighths of an inch in diameter. The visible depression was confined to the external table which was driven into the diploe. The inner table had been fractured independently, and a fragment an inch wide by an inch and a fourth in length had been driven downward, but not detached posteriorly, and was now consolidated in its whole extent with the superincumbent calvarium. As the thickening of the bone was not limited anteriorly to the portion removed by the trephine, it was necessary to enlarge the cranial opening in that direction for five eighths of an inch in order to insure relief from osseous pressure. As the dura mater had been uninjured, and there was no indication of gross cerebral injury, operation was not carried further than this procedure.

The resort to operation in this case was not due to any confidence in its efficacy in general as a method of treatment in Jacksonian epilepsy. The beginning of the paroxysms, however, was so recent that there seemed a possibility that some good might be derived from interference, more especially if, as it actually happened, their obvious cause should be found to be confined to the osseous lesion.

The wound was closed by primary adhesion, and recovery was immediate. The time which has elapsed since operation is still too short to permit more than a statement of its direct results. There has been no recurrence of vertigo, not even when a stooping posture is assumed, and there has been no headache, except on rare occasions, when it seemed referable to constipation. Muscæ volitantes, to which the patient had called attention as a persistent annoyance, have disappeared. The patient makes much of his ability to open or close either eye independently of the other, which, since the accident, had been stricken from his list of accomplishments. There has been no epileptic seizure. The expression of his face remains somewhat pained from a retraction of the upper lip, which has existed since he first came under observation. Whether or not this general improvement will continue is, of course, problematical; pressure has been removed, but the nutritive changes which it has occasioned and the possibility of ultimate repair are unknown quantities in the equation.

The essential interest in this history of a case resides, not in the incident of late operation with its chances of ultimate failure or success, but in its illustration of the danger of neglect of early elevation of depressed bone in fracture of the cranial vault. As in this instance, the amount of depression of the external table of bone is never a guide to the extent of injury which is concealed; and the late results of unrelieved depression of the internal table are too serious to be left to the arbitrament of chance, when safety lies in immediate though possibly futile exploration. It is one of the mysteries of surgical practice that under the influence of tradition there should be any difference of opinion or procedure in a matter so well settled both in theory and by the teachings of experience. In a recent publication I have adverted to this still too common error in treatment.

Dr. JOHN W. S. GOULEY said that the surgeon might be almost certain of the recurrence of superficial or subperiosteal sarcomata. But if the disease had begun within the bone non-recurrence might have been almost certainly predicated. He had never seen a case of periosteal sarcoma which had not recurred sooner or later, generally within a year after an amputation.

Dr. J. B. MURPHY, of Chicago, being invited to take part, asked if there were a history of traumatism preceding the first sarcoma; also if the temperature had been elevated, and if a bruit had been present.

Dr. PHELPS answered that he had only seen the patient once prior to the amputation, and then the temperature was about 100° F. There had been no bruit.

Dr. MURPHY said that the rapidly growing sarcomata of bone that he had met with had been accompanied by an elevation of temperature, and most of them by a bruit. The first case in which his attention had been particularly called to this fact had been that of a man whose duty it was to carry lumber up a gangplank. While thus engaged the man had fallen and struck his knee. After remaining from work for three days he had been admitted to hospital. At that time he had been delirious, and had had a temperature of 103° F. for several days. The case had been looked upon as one of osteomyelitis; then a bruit and a large pulsating tumor had developed, and finally amputation had been performed. The case had proved to be one of aneurysmal sarcoma of very rapid growth. Amputation had been performed near the hip, and ten days later the patient had left the hospital and had not been seen since. He recalled another case, a sarcoma within the abdomen, in which a diagnosis had been made of acute appendicitis, with abscess. The patient had been sick for three weeks, and on admission to the hospital the temperature had been 102.6°.

Dr. GOULEY said that according to Bland Sutton's views elevation of temperature is most likely in any case of round-cell sarcoma—a growth which this ob-

server was disposed to regard as made up of leucocytes
in battle with microbia.

Dr. Gouley said regarding pulsating tumors, that
they had been first described in England under the name
of "fungus hæmatodes." These were the teleangiectatic sarcomata containing any form of cell, but having
many dilated capillaries. These growths in some parts
of the osseous frame had sometimes been called "aneurysms of bone." In the old days of Bellevue Hospital
there had been several operations performed on these
aneurysms of bone—teleangiectatic and pulsating sarcomata. It was only this subvariety that was endowed
with pulsation.

Dr. PHELPS said that without doubt from the time
he had first seen the patient up to the time of operation
a moderate temperature had persisted. He was quite
certain that there had been no pulsation at any time, nor
could it have been expected, as the tumor was quite solid
and did not contain vessels of much size.

Dr. JOSEPH D. BRYANT said that in the course of
the discussion he had called to mind four cases of the
kind. In two a marked elevation of temperature had
been noted. They were both sarcomatous growths of
the pelvis—one of the left and one of the right iliac
fossa. In these cases the temperature had been one to
two degrees above the normal, but there had been no
pulsation. No autopsy had been obtained. For the
last six months he had had under observation a case
which he regarded as one of sarcoma of the pelvis. In
this there had occurred an interesting manifestation
which had led him to doubt somewhat the correctness
of the diagnosis. Dr. Coley had seen this case, and had
used the erysipelas toxines in it without benefit. In
this patient the temperature had been still higher. Inasmuch as there had been manifestations of suppuration
on the surface of this tumor, followed by the escape of
pus and a fall of the temperature and diminution in
the size of the growth, it seemed more than probable
that much of this rise of temperature had been due to
the inflammatory action. He would like to inquire
whether any one present had seen in sarcomata superficial suppurative processes which had, directly or indi-
rectly, modified their growth. He recalled a case of
myxosarcoma of the pharynx. Not looking upon removal as a wise procedure, and wishing to observe the
effect of simultaneous ligature of the external carotids,
this operation had been done, and the growth had not
only ceased to grow, but had finally almost entirely dis-

appeared. The patient had been kept under observation
for several years. In his experience elevation of temperature in cases of sarcoma had been quite uncommon.

Dr. LOUIS A. DI ZEREGA remarked that suppuration
had been quite common following the treatment of sarcomata by the toxines.

Dr. GOULEY said that it was a well-known fact that
all tumors were liable to suppurate. He had repeatedly
found degenerative cysts in carcinoma and sarcoma,
sometimes as a result of violence and sometimes without
any known cause. Many cases of spontaneous cure of
sarcoma were on record. The so-called fungus hæmatodes had been known to slough out and the patient to
be cured. From a large number of cases on record he
would say that the occurrence must be quite common.
He had personally observed several dozen cases of suppuration in the course of malignant disease.

Paper.

A STUDY OF SEVENTEEN CASES OF A DISEASE CLINI-CALLY RESEMBLING TYPHOID FEVER, BUT WITHOUT THE WIDAL REACTION; TOGETHER WITH A SHORT REVIEW OF THE PRESENT STATUS OF THE SERO-DIAGNOSIS OF TYPHOID FEVER.

BY N. E. BRILL, M. D.

EVER since the discovery of the reaction of a pure
culture of the typhoid bacillus when brought into
admixture with the serum of a patient suffering with
typhoid fever, the diagnosis in many instances of typhoid fever has been made considerably easier and more
certain. Before this reaction, generally known as the
Widal reaction, came into use the diagnosis of this disease was established chiefly from the clinical aspect of
the case. Clinicians felt quite certain when a case presented the concomitant signs of headache, malaise,
epistaxis, coated tongue, loss of appetite, continuous
fever, delirium, enlarged spleen, roseola, and tympanites, with or without diarrhœa, extending over a period
of more than a week, that such a case was a case of
typhoid. A persistence of these symptoms would have
justified such a diagnosis, and especially if the symp-

toms had developed suddenly and were accompanied by progressive emaciation. In fact, up to the time that the epidemic of *grippe* swept over this country all cases adhering to the above-described symptom-complex were called typhoid, or typho-malarial, or continuous fever, and, in a few instances, ephemeral fever.

After the first appearance of *grippe,* a group of cases, similar in clinical features to the type just mentioned, were called intestinal *grippe,* and taxed the diagnostic acumen of the clinician in making a differential diagnosis between it and typhoid. After the disappearance of the last epidemic of influenza from this country these cases, whenever they appeared, whether they ran a two-weeks' or a four-weeks' course, were again called typhoid fever. When the course of the disease was short—that is, when the disease lasted for a period of ten to twelve days—we were apt to designate those cases presenting such symptoms as abortive typhoid. Every summer and autumn these cases have appeared, and have, up to the present year, been diagnosticated and treated as typhoid fever.

The use of the Widal test, however, must compel us to change or modify our diagnosis, and to entertain the suspicion that many cases of what was formerly diagnosticated as typhoid fever were, in reality, not typhoid.

It is generally recognized that agglutination and inhibition of the movements of the typhoid bacilli, occasioned by the admixture of either the blood serum or a watery solution of the dried blood of a typhoid-fever patient, in the proportion of one of serum or blood to twenty or more of the bouillon culture of the typhoid germ, is the standard test of the reaction; one may then expect the agglutination and inhibition to occur within fifteen minutes. In the vast majority of the cases this reaction is immediate, so that the resultant inhibition and agglutination have already occurred before the slide, on which the test is made, can be brought under the observing eye at the microscope. In some cases, however, a few minutes are necessary

after the admixture before the reaction is demonstrable.
In the former case the inhibition of movement amounts
to a complete arrest, and in the latter a slight, slow
wriggling motion of the bacilli may be present. Both,
however, are accompanied by the essential phenom-
enon of clumping or agglutination. When the reaction
presents these features, it is called a positive reaction.
Unless these results are obtained a reaction can not
be called positive. Our experience with this reaction
is based upon the results of an endemic of typhoid
fever at the Training School for Nurses of Mount
Sinai Hospital, on the cases of typhoid fever occurring
in the wards of the hospital during the past year,
and on cases in private practice during the same period. The blood examinations were made by the Pa-
thologists of the institution, Dr. F. S. Mandlebaum and
Dr. C. A. Elsberg, and by them alone, thus reducing
the error of personal equation to a minimum. I personally observed a large number of the results of the
test with these gentlemen, and in no case did we dis-
agree as to the nature of a reaction, whether it was
positive or not.

If a positive appearance of the Widal reaction, when
applied with the proper culture and in proper proportion of serum to culture, be an absolute test of typhoid
fever—and there is now very little reason to doubt it, as
I shall soon show—the suspicion mentioned above will
be fully substantiated. In my own experience of cases
of typhoid fever occurring in private and hospital practice in which the Widal test was applied (numbering
eighty cases during the past year) this reaction was
never absent during some period of the disease or convalescence. The experience of other clinicians is similar to mine.

The following analysis of the cases of typhoid during the past year, eighty in number, are from a report
furnished by the pathological laboratory of Mount
Sinai Hospital: Positive reaction in seventy-eight cases
(ninety-seven and three fourths per cent.) ; no reaction
in two cases (two and a half per cent.). Of the seventy-

eight cases which gave a positive reaction, two gave a reaction on the fourth day of the disease, four on the fifth day of the disease (seven and a half per cent.); forty-four gave a reaction from the seventh to the twelfth day of the disease, twelve from the twelfth to the fourteenth day of the disease (seventy-seven per cent.); ten gave a reaction from the fourteenth to the seventeenth day of the disease, six from the twenty-fourth to the thirty-second day of the disease (nineteen per cent.).

Seven hundred and forty-two examinations were made in all, of which two hundred and twelve were for diseases other than typhoid, and the latter, with the exception of one * case, at no time showed a reaction. The history of this case in the hospital gave no evidence of typhoid fever. The patient was a woman in whom the diagnosis of cholecystitis was made, and who, refusing operation, was discharged. She was a stupid, ignorant woman, from whom it was almost impossible to obtain a satisfactory history of her former illness. In her case, while the presence of a previous typhoid (she had been ill three months before she sought admission to the hospital with some other illness than the one for which she was admitted) could not be established, its presence at that time can not be denied. Deducing a judgment from the experience here cited, we are justified in concluding that the positive appearance of the Widal reaction in a case of supposed typhoid is diagnostic of the presence of the activity of the typhoid bacillus in the body. It still remains to be proved whether the reaction of the serum or blood of a patient with a culture of the typhoid bacillus occurs in other diseases. A few exceptional cases have been reported, but these cases have been so rare that we may be justly suspicious that they occurred in some of the instances in patients who had previously had typhoid, or that the observations were not made by competent observers,

* The Serum Diagnosis of Typhoid Fever. By C. A. Elsberg, M. D. *Medical Record*, April 10, 1897.

or were based on defective methods employed by the blood examiner.

In reference to these topics Dr. Wyatt Johnson * says: "I wish further to call attention to the importance of paying special care to the reaction of the test-culture medium. Bouillon cultures showing, after twenty-four hours' growth of typhoid at 37° C., a slight uniform cloudiness only, and quite free from scum and sediment, offer the greatest security against pseudo-reactions. . . . Cultures which give heavy bouillon growths are the ones most liable to give pseudo-reactions—*i. e.*, to clump in a deceptive manner spontaneously or with non-typhoid blood. If the culture is too acid, the reaction may be defective. With a proper culture I have never met with the typical reaction apart from typhoid fever. On the other hand, by employing certain incorrect methods of preparing the culture, I can obtain at will very perplexing pseudo-reactions with a large proportion of non-typhoid bloods. This may be the explanation of the number of anomalous published results."

It was stated that the experience of other clinicians supported the view expressed, that the Widal reaction was diagnostic of the activity of the typhoid bacillus in the body. Let us for a moment review the published results of a few of these individual experiences.

C. Fraenkel † never found a reaction in any but those suffering from typhoid fever.

K. Urban ‡ also found it present in all his cases of typhoid, and gives an interesting review of the work done in this field.

Perhaps the most voluminous collection of statistics as to the value of this test of typhoid fever is con-

* Wyatt Johnson. *Circular No. 4, Laboratory of the Board of Health of the Province of Quebec,* dated Montreal, October 6, 1897.

† C. Fraenkel. Ueber den Werth der Widal'schen Probe zur Erkennung des Typhus abdominalis. *Deutsche med. Wochenschrift,* 1897, No. 3.

‡ K. Urban. Blutuntersuchungen bei Typhus und die Gruber-Widal Sero-diagnosis *Wiener med. Wochenschrift,* 1897, pp. 1465, 1527, 1570, 1613.

tained in the article published by Dr. R. C. Cabot,* of Boston, who collected in various foreign and American journals the reported results of the experiences of other men. The total number of cases of typhoid fever which had been subjected to this test numbered 3,475. Of this number a positive reaction was obtained in 3,434 = 98.8 per cent. The number of non-typhoid cases examined was 1,649, of which 1,592, or ninety-six and a half per cent., showed no reaction. His own personal experience embraced 101 cases of typhoid, in which the reaction was positive in 96, and in 301 cases of other diseases, in but one of which he found the reaction.

Dr. W. H. Welch,† of Johns Hopkins University, also attests to the almost invariable presence of the reaction in typhoid and its absence in other diseases. He cites the statistics of Widal and Sicard of 163 cases, in which there was a positive reaction in 162; of Courmont, 116 cases, positive reaction in 116; of Chantemesse, 70 cases, positive reaction in 70; of Johnston and McTaggart, 129 cases, positive reaction in 128.

Since the above publication of Dr. Cabot's paper I have collected additional cases reported in the current journals, so that the total number of cases collected in which an examination for the reaction was made is 4,879, of which 4,781 gave a positive reaction (97.9 per cent.).

Considering this vast number of cases, and the error in diagnosis which might arise from so many examiners, the number of typhoid cases in which the reaction was not obtained is extremely small, and barely invalidates the statement that the test is an absolute diagnostic and pathognomonic sign of typhoid fever.

So generally accepted is the diagnostic test of this reaction that at a recent meeting of the American Medical Association, at Philadelphia. on August 14,

* R. C. Cabot. Clinical Report on Sero-Diagnosis. *Journal of the American Medical Association*, 1897, p 311.

† W. H. Welch. Serum. Diagnosis of Typhoid Fever. *Ibid.*, 1897. p. 395.

1897, the following summary of views * was expressed
in the discussion of serum diagnosis: " Without being
absolutely infallible the typhoid reaction appears to
afford as accurate diagnostic results as can be obtained
by any of the bacteriological methods at our disposal
for the diagnosis of other diseases. It must certainly
be regarded as the most constant and reliable sign of
typhoid fever, if not an absolute test." This statement is signed by the following men, whose names are
sufficient attestation of the reliability of the conclusions—namely: W. H. Welch, Wyatt Johnson, J. H.
Musser, R. C. Cabot, H. M. Biggs, J. M. Swan, M. W.
Richardson, and others.

Such being the generally recognized status of the
Widal reaction, the question arises, How shall we classi-
fy the following group of cases, which came under my
observation during the past summer, specifically during the months of July, August, and September, at
no time showing the Widal reaction (this test was made
daily in each), and having the following definite clinical history: A period of three to four days in which the
patients complained of loss of appetite, malaise, general weakness, headache, and general body pains, succeeded in many instances by either a distinct chill or
chilly sensation, and in a few by epistaxis. The patient is feverish, the temperature, as taken in the rectum, rapidly rising to 104° or even 105° F. The period
of temperature rise to its acme is within five days.
The morning and evening temperature of each successive day of this period being higher than that of
the preceding day. On the fourth or fifth day—that is,
when the patient's temperature is highest—the following objective signs are present: sensorium dull, the
patient apathetic, face flushed, cheeks reddened, there
being a zone of whiteness about the mouth; eyes dull
and expressionless, conjunctivæ congested, the tongue
in the greatest proportion of the cases moist and always
furred. The fur is thick, *white,* and covers the dorsum

* *Journal of the American Medical Association,* p. 313.

of the entire tongue, only the edges and tip of that organ being free from the coating.   There are contraction and wrinkling of the brow, owing to the intense headache of which the patient complains.   The skin of the body is hot and dry; that of the back, especially over the loins, and the skin of the abdomen are covered by an eruption of rose-red papules.   These papules have a diameter of two millimetres, are only slightly raised, disappear, as a rule, completely on pressure, and reappear when the pressure is removed.   The papules are not numerous, are lenticular in shape, sometimes acuminated, with a minute vesicle on top, and while present both over the skin of the back, chiefly between the scapulæ, and over the loins, they are, as a rule, more numerous over the abdomen.   Sometimes the eruption is absent.

The abdomen is slightly distended and tense, owing to a slight degree of tympanites.   There is usually abdominal pain, but little tenderness.

The spleen is enlarged, and its free border is palpable.

The bowels, as a rule, are constipated, and can only be moved by some laxative agent.   Diarrhœa is only exceptionally present.

The mental condition of the patient is disturbed. He is apathetic, he does not want to be molested, and lies in a state of drowsiness or semistupor the most of the time.   When the fever is highest, toward evening, a few patients become delirious.

The pulse is full and rapid, often dicrotic.

The temperature is continuously high, with morning remissions, as a rule reaching 103° to 104° F. in the evening, and falling off two to three degrees therefrom in the morning.   The temperature shows these exacerbations and remissions for ten to twelve days from the beginning of the disease, when it suddenly drops, in the large majority of cases, to normal.   In a few cases it shows a steplike descent, like the typical typhoid temperature of the fourth week, the descent to normal, however, not taking more than three days.   When the degradation of the temperature occurs the symptoms disap-

4

pear, and the patient feels well but weak. His appetite returns, his headache has disappeared, his tympanites has vanished, he regains his mental composure, and takes acute interest in his surroundings. The bowels now move regularly and without difficulty.

During the progress of the disease emaciation has developed, and, while not as extreme as it is in true typhoid fever, it is still considerable.

One of the earliest features of this group of cases is the prostration. It appears earlier than it does in unquestionable typhoid, and is often the subject of the patient's complaints. As a rule, these patients are unable, after they take to bed, to sit up without assistance.

The urine is high-colored and scanty. When subjected to Ehrlich's diazo reaction it responds in some cases, and in others not at all. Indican was not present in excess, and was sometimes entirely absent, and acetone and diacetic acid were absent in the cases examined.

The blood showed no leucocytosis, nor any change in the red blood-cells. *Plasmodium malariæ* was examined for and not found.

Hæmorrhage from the bowels did not occur, nor was there any trace of blood in the stools.

None of these cases presented any complications or sequelæ.

The course of the disease was not influenced in any demonstrable manner by any plan or method of treatment. All these patients were put on a strictly fluid diet, and were plunged if the temperature remained above 104° F. for any time. The bowels of some were thoroughly evacuated, while in others no attention was paid to them. Whether the bowels were moved thoroughly or not, the course of the disease remained the same in all, nor was the severity of the attack modified.

The following are a few histories abstracted from the more detailed histories taken by the house staff of the hospital, and are here presented simply to give a general idea of the clinical picture presented by the entire group. They make no pretension as to completeness, nor do they contain all the clinical observations made from day to day during the sojourn of the patients at the hospital:

CASE I.—Samuel S., aged thirty-eight years, Russian, cabinetmaker, was admitted on June 27, 1897. His family history is negative. He had gonorrhœa twelve years ago, never had syphilis, and abstains from alcohol and tobacco. Otherwise he was never ill to his knowledge.

He took to bed three days before, after complaining a few days of lassitude and inability to work. He had no diarrhœa, no epistaxis, but complained of loss of appetite and nausea. His sleep had been good. He gave no history of cardiac or pulmonary disease. His chief complaints are headache and pain in the back. General condition fair; well nourished; tongue is dry. Lungs: High-pitched note at right apex anteriorly; posteriorly, negative. Heart normal; pulse small and soft; liver normal; spleen enlarged and distinctly felt below costal margin; abdomen soft.

On admission his temperature was 102.6° F., his respirations were 24, and his pulse was 88. He was given a full bath, put on sterilized fluids, and treated as a typhoid. At 6 P. M. of this day (June 27th) his temperature was 104° F., which was reduced by a sponge bath to 103.8°, his pulse being now 82, and respirations 24. At 8 P. M. the temperature was again 104.2°, when he was given a plunge bath which reduced his temperature to 100.8°.

June 28th.—Temperature ranged from 100.8° to 104° F., at which point a plunge was given, when it fell to 99°.

29th.—Temperature was 103.8° F.; two plunge baths.

30th.—Temperature at 8 P. M., 102.8° F.

July 1st.—Temperature did not rise above 100° F. Tongue beginning to clear; no roseola has as yet been noticed either on back or abdomen. The general condition of the patient is improved.

2d.—Temperature normal; patient put on soft diet.

4th.—Patient discharged cured.

CASE II.—Arnold L., admitted to my service at Mount Sinai Hospital on August 8, 1897.

The patient was thirty-one years of age, a nurse by

occupation, and was born in Germany. His family history is negative. His previous history shows no venereal disease, and he indulged but slightly in alcohol.

His present history shows illness of ten days' standing, beginning with headache and pains in the legs, which continued for three days, whereupon he had to take to bed. He had entire loss of appetite, with nausea and some vomiting. His bowels had been constipated. On admission he complained of severe headache involving the entire head; it is quite continuous, with only slight remissions. Ocular pain is also complained of. General condition is fair; well nourished. His tongue is dry and coated down the centre with a white fur, red at the sides and tip. Lungs, anteriorly and posteriorly, negative. Heart not enlarged; apex beat in fifth interspace within the mammary line; slight blowing systolic murmur at the apex, but it is not transmitted. Pulse full and slightly dicrotic. Finger nails somewhat cyanotic. Liver slightly enlarged; extends from fourth interspace to one fingerbreadth and a half below the free costal margin. Spleen: Owing to the tympanites, the area of dullness is partly obliterated. The organ can not be felt. Abdomen somewhat tympanitic.

The temperature at 6 P. M. was 102.6° F., the pulse 120, and respirations were 32 per minute.

The headache is intense, necessitating the administration of a sedative. During the night the temperature ranged from 102.3° to 103° F.

On August 9th the morning temperature was 102.3° F.; the evening temperature, 103°; the pulse, 84, and the respirations, 28. At midnight the temperature had fallen to 101°.

On August 10th the morning temperature was 102.8° F.; the pulse, 96, and the respirations, 22; the evening temperature was 103.2°, which fell at midnight to 100.6°.

On August 11th the temperature was constant, there being but slight variations, and registered between 103.2° and 103.6° F.; still, at midnight, it fell to 101°.

On August 12th the morning temperature was 103.6° F. The headache is diminishing, the tongue has become moist, but it is still coated; the abdomen is soft and tympanitic, and the spleen can now be felt for the first time; the pulse is slightly dicrotic. A plunge bath was ordered, together with fifteen grains of salol, which reduced the temperature to 102.2° F.

In the evening the temperature again rose to 103.2°
F., the pulse being 82. At this time another plunge
was given, which reduced the temperature to 101.2°
F. and the pulse to 76.

On August 13th the temperature remained constantly lower, varying from 101° F. to 101.4° F. From this
day on the temperature fell gradually, and on the next
day, August 14th, in the morning, it became normal,
99° F., and 100° in the evening. The patient feels well,
but is very weak.

On August 15th the temperature was the same as on
the preceding day.

On August 16th the temperature is normal throughout, convalescence is established, all abdominal signs
have disappeared, though the spleen can still be felt, but
is much smaller.

On August 20th the spleen is no longer palpable.
The patient was discharged on August 25th.

In this case there was at no time a roseola. The duration of the disease was twenty days.

CASE III.—Felix H., nineteen years old, born in
Germany, a clerk by occupation. He was admitted to
the service of my colleague, Dr. Manges, to whom I am
indebted for the history. He came into the hospital
on August 12, 1897, giving a negative family history.
His previous history established that he had no gonorrhœa or syphilis, that he used neither tobacco nor alcohol, and that he never was ill before.

His present history is of one week's standing, and
began with malaise, headache, loss of appetite, and apathy
for usual employment. He had no epistaxis. He had
nausea, but no vomiting; diarrhœa was also present.
There were no cardiac, pulmonary, or urinary symptoms. The headache was constant. There was no abdominal pain.

The patient's general condition is good. He is well
nourished. His tongue is moist and coated. Lungs
normal. Heart's action slow; pulse slow, soft, slightly
dicrotic, and intermittent; liver extends from fifth
space to free border of ribs; spleen enlarged to percussion.

On admission his temperature was 102.8° F., his
respirations were 24, and his pulse was 100. He was
given a sponge bath and placed on sterilized fluids.
The temperature remained above 101° F. all day.

On August 13th the pulse dropped from 100 to 52.

the temperature varied between 100.6° and 99° F. The urine was acid, specific gravity 1.025, and contained no albumin. Diazo reaction was absent.

On August 14th the temperature became normal, and remained so from this time to the date of his discharge, August 21, 1897.

CASE IV.—Augusta L., aged thirty-three years, born in Germany, was admitted on August 23, 1897. Her family and previous histories are negative. Her present history is of one week's standing; it began with chill and fever, previous to which there had been lassitude, weakness, malaise. No epistaxis, no diarrhœa. Appetite gone, nausea, but no vomiting. There is headache, pain in back and over spleen. No cardiac, pulmonary, or urinary symptoms. General condition is fair and she is well nourished; tongue is dry, glazed, and devoid of epithelium. Lungs anteriorly, sibilant and sonorous râles; posteriorly, similar signs. Heart negative. Pulse weak, small, and thready. Liver extends from fifth space to two fingers below free border. Spleen enlarged to percussion and readily felt. Abdomen, numerous roseolar spots. Tenderness over bladder; right kidney situated very low and readily palpable.

Vaginal examination revealed the tissues all very lax. Cervix enlarged and lacerated. Uterus is enlarged; marked leucorrhœa.

On admission the temperature was 103.2° F., the pulse was 98, and the respirations were 26. A sponge bath was given, and the routine typhoid treatment ordered. Her urine was acid and showed no pathological conditions.

On August 24th the patient's general condition is poor; the tongue is glazed and red, but not coated. There was no abdominal tenderness nor tympanites. Her spleen can be readily felt.

On August 25th the urine is acid, specific gravity 1.014, and contains no albumin; it showed eight grains and a half of urea to each ounce. Her general condition is somewhat improved. Her temperature remained quite constant throughout the day, ranging from 102.8° F. to 103.2° F.

On August 26th the morning temperature was 100.1° F.; it steadily diminished, and at 11 P. M. it reached 99° F.

On August 27th the temperature was normal throughout; the patient felt well and wanted to get up. The spleen could no longer be felt. From this time on her temperature remained normal. She was discharged on September 4, 1897.

CASE V.—Abraham W., aged thirty-five years, born in Russia; occupation, tailor. The patient was admitted on August 27, 1897; the family and previous histories are negative.

Present history is of one week's standing; began with malaise and general weakness, with some fever and chills. On admission, diarrhœa; no epistaxis; appetite gone; digestion impaired. No cardiac, pulmonary, or urinary symptoms. Pain in abdomen, cramplike in nature. General condition is poor; he is fairly well nourished; the tongue is dry. Lungs anteriorly, negative, as well as posteriorly. Heart not enlarged, action slow and regular, slight impurity of second sound at apex. Pulse large, slow, slightly dicrotic. Liver extends from fifth space to free border. Spleen enlarged to percussion and very distinctly felt. Abdomen tympanitic; a number of *roseolar* spots here and on back. No œdema of legs.

On admission his temperature was 103° F., the pulse was 88, and respirations were 28. A sponge bath was given. Sterilized fluids ordered. At 5 P.M. the temperature was 103.8° F.; it came down without treatment.

August 28th.—Urine acid and clear, specific gravity 1.023; it contained a trace of albumin and a few pus cells and leucocytes. The first stool contained a little mucus.

29th.—Temperature came down gradually, and by night remained below 100° F.; the tongue was still moist and coated. Patient felt well and desired to go home.

On August 30th only a slight evening rise in temperature to 100.4° F.

31st.—Temperature was normal all day. Soft diet had been given on the 29th.

September 1st.—Full diet; no subsequent rise of temperature; patient discharged cured September 3, 1897.

CASE VI.—William G., aged twenty years, born in Austria; occupation, tailor. He was admitted on August 30, 1897. The family history is negative, as is the previous history. The present history is of two weeks' standing; during the last week he has been in bed. The acute attack began after an indiscretion in diet, with nausea, loss of appetite, but no vomiting. There is no headache. Bowels have been very much constipated for some time, are liable to be so often, and then these attacks come on in aggravated form. General condition is fair; he is fairly well nourished, but anæmic; the tongue is moist and coated. Lungs, anteriorly and posteriorly, negative. Heart: area not enlarged; systolic murmur over base, most marked at second right costal cartilage; pulse tense and regular. Liver extends from fourth space to free border. Abdomen: a number of atypical rose spots here, but on back typical spots. Spleen can be felt.

On admission the temperature was 101° F.; the pulse 86. A sponge bath was given. The patient was put on sterilized fluids. The temperature rose gradually to 103.8°. Urine is acid, contains a trace of albumin, and red and white blood-cells, epithelial cells, and hyaline and granular casts, with an occasional waxy cast.

September 1st.—Temperature at 4 A. M., 100° F., but rose at noon to 103° F., and at midnight rose again to 104.4° F.

On September 2d the temperature rose at 2 P. M. to 103° F., and was 102.8° at midnight.

On September 3d the morning temperature was 101.2° F., but came down during the afternoon and evening, reaching on the following day 99.4° F., from which time it did not rise again.

On September 5th the patient's general condition was excellent, and he was put on full diet. He sat up on September 7th and was discharged on September 12, 1897.

CASE VII.—Harris F., aged twenty-four years, born in Russia; occupation, carpenter. He was admitted to my service on September 1, 1897. His family history as well as his previous history is negative. There had been no gonorrhœa or syphilis. He indulged moderately in alcohol and tobacco, and had had no previous disease.

Present history is of ten days' standing; began with general body tenderness, pain in bones and head, fever and chill; no epistaxis; no diarrhœa; severe and constant headache; general feeling of lassitude; loss of appetite; nausea, but no vomiting; some cardiac palpitation; no cough; no urinary symptoms.

His general condition is poor, but he is well nourished; tongue moist and coated, with red tip and edges. Lungs, anteriorly and posteriorly, negative. Heart, marked accentuated second aortic sound. Liver ex-

tends from fifth space to free border. Spleen is enlarged to percussion and can be felt. Abdomen, numerous roseolar spots.

On admission temperature was 102.6° F.; the respirations, 36; and the pulse, 120, and slightly dicrotic.
A sponge bath was given; he was put on sterilized
fluids. The temperature rose gradually, and at midnight was 104.2° F. The urine was acid and contained no albumin.

September 2d.—Temperature, 103.8° F. at 2 A. M.,
gradually fell to 99.6° F. at 6 P. M.

4th.—Tongue moist, heavily coated, with brown centre. Numerous roseolar spots on abdomen, disappear-
ing on pressure, still present; no headache; complains
only of feeling weak.

5th.—Put on soft diet. Normal convalescence.
Temperature normal.

12th.—Patient discharged cured.

Case VIII.—Mrs. K., twenty-nine years of age,
married, born in United States, first came under my
observation on September 3, 1897, when I was asked to
see her in consultation with Dr. J. Brettauer. She was
spending the summer in the neighborhood of a place
on Long Island in which it was said a number of cases
of typhoid fever had occurred. She had been operated
on by Dr. Brettauer for a ruptured ectopic-gestation sac
on August 21, 1897. The post-operative history was uneventful, the operation disclosing a partly ruptured
tubal pregnancy of eight weeks' standing, the peritoneal
cavity of the patient containing about three pints of
fluid blood, which were removed, and the wound closed
without drainage.

The temperature after the operation was 102.6° F.
This varied for the next few days from this to 104° F.,
with a pulse varying from 130 to 150. From August
24th to August 27th the temperature varied from
100° to 102° F., with a pulse of constant rhythm of 98
beats. Her general condition was much improved.
She took nourishment well, and the wound was entirely healed by primary union. The sutures were removed
on the 27th. She was given solid food from this time
on. Her morning temperature next day was 100° F.,
and on the 29th it was 99° F. This day she had some
diarrhœa, her temperature rising in the evening to
101° F. For the next few days, up to September 2d,
her diarrhœa persisted, and she complained of headache, severe in character, her morning temperature

varying from 99° to 100.5° F., and the evening temperature from 101.5° to 102° F. On September 2d she awoke with extreme headache, and began to feel chilly, and at noon her temperature rose to 103.5°; pulse, 100. In the evening she was again chilly, and had a temperature of 104.5° F.; pulse, 100. On the morning of the next day she had a distinct chill, a t·¬perature of 103.2° F., which rapidly rose to 106.3° at 9 A. M., the pulse distinctly dicrotic.

At this stage I was called by Dr. Brettauer to see the patient. She was somnolent, apathetic, and indifferent to the fact that a stranger was examining her. Her face was flushed, skin hot. Her tongue was moist and thickly coated with white fur along the dorsum. Her conjunctivæ were congested. Examination of her chest revealed nothing abnormal in the lungs and heart. Her abdomen was concealed by the bandages which, upon removal, disclosed a perfectly united wound in the middle line. The abdomen was slightly tympanitic, and the spleen was distinctly enlarged and easily palpable. The liver was not enlarged. On her back a few red papules were seen over the left scapula. They were acuminated and did not disappear on pressure. The patient was greatly prostrated and had not the strength to move. Her temperature was 104.8° F., and pulse 106. The pulse was full, soft, and slightly dicrotic. The patient was placed on fluid diet. On the next day, September 4th, I saw the patient again and found, for the first time, a distinct roseola over the loins and on the abdomen. Her symptoms otherwise were the same as on the previous day. Owing to the fact that the patient was stopping at a summer hotel I suggested her removal to a hospital, which was done on the following day.

September 4th.—Her temperature, A. M., 102.5° F.; pulse, 100; P. M., temperature, 104.5°; pulse, 98. An examination of her blood failed to reveal *Plasmodium malariæ;* there was neither leucocytosis nor diminution in the number of red cells.

After entering the hospital on September 5, 1897, her pulse was 103, her respirations were 26, and her temperature was 103.8° F. She complained of chilliness. Typhoid-fever treatment was instituted. Her urine was acid, specific gravity 1.010, with a trace of albumin and with red and white blood-cells, epithelial and fat cells, a few pus cells, a few hyaline casts, but it did not show the Ehrlich diazo reaction. Her temperature on the evening of this day was 103.2° F.

On September 6th the morning temperature was 102.5° F.; the evening, 103° F.

On September 7th the temperature in the morning was 102.2° F., pulse 106, and respirations were 24; in the evening the temperature was 103° F.

On September 8th the tongue is moist and furred; the pulse of excellent quality, though dicrotic. The spleen is still palpable. The patient's mental condition is very good. The highest temperature was 102.6° F.

On September 9th the morning temperature was 101.2° F.; the evening, 102.6° F. An ice bag was applied to the left side, where she complained of pain.

On September 10th the temperature at no time went higher than 100.4° F.; the general condition of the patient was much improved.

On September 11th the temperature in the morning reached the normal. The tongue was moist and *clean;* there was no abdominal tenderness, and the spleen could still be felt. The urine was acid, specific gravity 1.010, and was otherwise negative, excepting the presence of a few leucocytes. Convalescence was now established.

On September 14th the spleen could no longer be felt.

On September 20th she was put on soft diet, which in two days was replaced by full diet.

The Widal test, taken every day, always proved negative.

She was discharged on September 30, 1897.

At no time were there any signs of sepsis. The pelvic cavity was perfectly free, and the presence of pus, while it may have been suspected, could not be demonstrated. In fact, the nature and character of her symptoms militated against the theory of sepsis. The temperature before and immediately after the operation indicated serum absorption (from the peritoneal cavity). Her subsequent disease dated from the day on which she complained of headache and chilly sensations.

Cultures were made from the fæces of this patient and showed *colon bacilli* only.

CASE IX.—Herman S., aged twenty years; nativity, United States; occupation, porter; was admitted on September 12, 1897. His family history, as well as previous history, were negative. The present history is of three days' standing; it began with headache, fever, chill, loss of appetite, malaise, and general weakness.

There was no epistaxis; there was nausea, but no vomiting; the bowels are constipated. He complains principally of general body tenderness and weakness. No
cardiac, pulmonary, or urinary symptoms. General
condition poor, but he is well nourished; tongue dry and
furred, with red tip and edges. The patient is very
somnolent. Lungs anteriorly, negative; posteriorly, a
few sonorous râles. Heart: dullness extends from lower
border of third rib to upper border of sixth rib, and from
midsternal line to just within nipple. Apex beat in fifth
space, regular and of ordinary force; rough systolic murmur over pulmonic area; pulse slow and regular.
Liver extends from fifth space to two fingers below free
border. Spleen enlarged to percussion and felt. Abdomen: a few typical spots here and on chest; no tenderness.

On admission the temperature was 102.2° F., the
pulse 104, and the respirations were 28. He was
given a sponge bath and was put on sterilized fluids.
An ice bag was applied to his head. The temperature
gradually rose to 104.4° F., which was reached at 8
P. M. It then began to fall and in the morning of
the following day was 100.8° F. His urine was normal.

On September 7th the morning temperature was
100.4° F., remaining at that mark during the whole
day, but declining at night to 99° F., which degree was
reached at midnight.

On September 8th he had diarrhœa; the temperature
was normal the whole day. His tongue was moist and
coated, the pulse was slow and slightly dicrotic. The
spots on the abdomen and chest have vanished. The
mental condition was clear and the appetite had returned. He complained of being hungry.

He was discharged on September 11, 1897.

CASE X.—Nathan B., aged twenty-eight years; born
in Austria; occupation, tailor.

September 7, 1897.—Family history negative; previous history, no gonorrhœa or syphilis.

Present history one week's standing; began with
headache, pain in left side, and, later, general body
tenderness. No epistaxis. One week previous to admission had diarrhœa (three or four stools daily).
Appetite gone. Nausea, no vomiting. No cardiac,
pulmonary, or urinary symptoms. At present complains only of an intense headache and of weakness.

General condition good, well nourished; *tongue*
moist and slightly coated. Lungs, anteriorly, negative;

posteriorly, sonorous and sibilant rûles. Heart extends from lower border of third rib to upper border of sixth rib, from midsternal line to just within nipple line. Apex beat in normal position, circumscribed, and of normal force; no murmur; pulse slow, soft, and very slightly dicrotic. Liver extends to just below free border of ribs. Spleen enlarged to percussion and felt. Abdomen: here and over chest are numerous roseolar spots; slight tympanites.

On admission his temperature was 102° F., his pulse 103, and respirations were 32. He was given a sponge bath and put on sterilized fluids. His temperature rose gradually and reached, at 8 P. M., 102.8° F.

The urine was acid, the specific gravity being 1.020; it contained no albumin.

On the following day his tongue was still dry and furred, but his headache disappeared. His spleen could still be felt, but the roseolar spots had become almost indistinguishable. The patient felt well and wished to get up. The temperature in the morning of this day was 98.6° F., and it rose to 100.2° F. in the evening.

On September 11th the temperature was normal throughout the entire day.

The patient was discharged on September 12, 1897.

CASE XI.—Jacob S., aged eighteen years; born in Russia; occupation, carpenter. Admitted to service of Dr. Manges on September 9, 1897. His family history is negative. The previous history shows moderate alcohol and tobacco habits; he never had any other disease, and denies having had gonorrhœa or syphilis.

The present history is of eight days' standing; it began with headache, prostration, and general malaise, also intense pain in the bones. Slight epistaxis two days ago. No chill, but continuous fever since onset; Appetite lost; no nausea; no vomiting; bowels constipated; no cardiac, pulmonary, or urinary trouble. The general condition is fair. The patient is fairly nourished; tongue dry and coated, with red tip, down centre, and around edges. Lungs, nothing abnormal. Heart: area normal, apex beat in the fifth space, just within the nipple line. It is diffuse, of fair force, and with slight systolic thrill. Second sound at apex prolonged. Vessels full, pulse of some tension. Spleen not enlarged to percussion nor felt. Abdomen: here and on back some *typical erythematous macular spots.*

On admission his temperature was 102.2° F., his respirations were 30, and pulse 110. An hour later his temperature rose to 103° F., and two hours after this it reached 103.4° F. During the remainder of the day it was around the 102.2° F. mark. Routine typhoid-fever treatment was ordered. The examination of the urine gave negative results.

On September 10th the urine is negative; the temperature ranging between 100.2° F. and 102.4° F.

12th.—Morning temperature, 99° F.; evening, 101° F. Pulse varied from 74 to 94 beats.

13th.—The morning temperature was 99.4° F.; the evening, 100° F.

14th.—Normal temperature throughout. The patient was discharged well on September 17, 1897.

CASE XII.—Herman G., Roumanian, admitted September 14, 1897, service of Dr. Brill.

Family history negative.

Previous history negative.

Present history of nine days' standing; began with headache, chill, and fever, attended by intense general weakness and malaise. During this entire time the symptoms have remained the same. Appetite is lost; digestion poor; nausea, but no vomiting.

General condition fair, and he is well nourished. Tongue somewhat dry, furred down centre with red edges and tip. Lungs anteriorly and posteriorly, a few sibilant râles; marked left scoliosis. Heart: dullness extends from upper border of third to lower border of fifth ribs, and from midsternal to just within mammary line. Apex beat in fifth interspace, is circumscribed and forcible. Slight roughening of first sound over pulmonic valve. Pulse regular, soft, and slightly dicrotic. Spleen enlarged to percussion and felt below free border of ribs. Abdomen, as well as back and on chest, *profuse roseolar eruption,* like typical typhoid roseola.

On admission this afternoon, temperature, 103.2° F.; respirations, 26; pulse, 118.

September 14th.—Given a sponge bath. 5 P. M., temperature, 102.2° F.

15th.—11 A. M., temperature, 101.4° F. 5 P. M., temperature, 101.4° F.

16th.—Temperature normal and convalescence established.

17th.—Spleen still palpable, pulse soft and regular. This morning the spleen was aspirated by Dr. Brill under most rigorous aseptic precautions. In the afternoon patient was permitted to sit up and was given full diet.

18th.—Normal temperature throughout.

19th.—Patient discharged cured. Duration of disease, twelve days. Length of time in hospital, six days.

A culture was made of the fæces of this patient and showed no typhoid bacilli. The blood which was aspirated from the spleen was also subjected to culture media, as was stated in the body of this paper, and showed colon but no typhoid bacilli.

CASE XIII.—Hyman F.; born in Russia; aged thirty-one years; occupation, peddler. He was admitted on September 19, 1897. His family history is negative; his previous history shows that he never had gonorrhœa or syphilis, and that he indulged moderately in alcohol and largely in the use of tobacco. He had typhoid fever sixteen years ago.

The present history is of eight days' standing; it began with pain in head, constant and severe; fever, chill, and general weakness. The bowels were constipated, the urine high colored, and there was pain in the abdomen over the region of the spleen. No cardiac, urinary, or pulmonary symptoms. No epistaxis. His general condition is poor; he is well nourished; the tongue is moist and very slightly coated. Lungs, anteriorly and posteriorly, negative. Heart normal; sounds full and strong. Liver extends from the fifth space to the free border of the ribs. Spleen enlarged to percussion and felt.

On admission his temperature was 102.6° F., respirations were 28, and pulse was 112. Typhoid treatment was ordered.

September 20th.—Patient complains of headache; tongue moist and coated. *A number of roseolar spots on abdomen.*

21st.—Tongue moist and glazed. A few spots on abdomen; pulse dicrotic. Spleen not felt. General condition good.

24th.—Full diet, out of bed.

26th.—Discharged, feeling perfectly well.

From September 19th to September 22d the temperature range was from 103.6° F. to 99.4° F. It reached the normal and remained there on September 22d.

CASE XIV.—Rosa M., aged twenty-five years; born in the United States; is a student at Mount Sinai Training School for Nurses, and was under my care during the end of December, 1896, January, 1897, and February of the same year, when she was suffering from an attack of typhoid fever. Her present attack began on September 16, 1897, when she complained of lassitude, headache,

and great prostration. These did not interfere with her
work at the hospital until September 18th, on the evening of which day she had to take to bed. I was called
to the training school to see her on the following day,
and found her with a temperature of 102.4°. The preceding history was then elicited together with the following:

She had complained of general malaise, nausea, but
no vomiting. Her bowels had been constipated for a
few days. She gave no cardiac or pulmonary symptoms.
Her headache is intense, and is her chief cause of complaint. Examination revealed the following: General
condition good; well nourished. Tongue moist, coated
with a thick fur. Face flushed, especially over malar
prominences. Brows drawn together and corrugated
transversely. Lungs, anteriorly and posteriorly, negative. Skin over the right shoulder is covered by a
localized hæmorrhagic eruption. Heart: normal area of
dullness; apex beat in fifth interspace, rapid, regular,
and forcible. Pulse, rapid, regular, and of varying
tension. Liver, normal area of dullness. Spleen enlarged and easily felt below costal margin. Abdomen
slightly tympanitic and very tender. Slight roseolar
eruption (five spots only) and none on the back. No
œdema of the legs.

On this day the morning temperature was 101.4°
F., the pulse was 94, and the respirations were 28;
the evening temperature was 103.2° F., the pulse 100,
and the respirations 28. A slight *epistaxis* occurred
during the day, and her menses put in their appearance.

On September 20, 1897, the morning temperature
was 101° F., and the evening temperature 103° F.

On September 21st the morning temperature was
101.8° F., and the evening temperature 103.4° F.

On September 22d the morning temperature was
100.8° F., the evening temperature 103° F.

On September 23d the morning temperature was
102.6° F., that of the evening being 101.4° F.

On September 24th the temperature ranged between
102° F. and 102.4° F. throughout the twenty-four
hours.

On September 25th the morning temperature was
100.6° F. and rose to 103.6° F., which it reached in the
evening.

On September 26th the temperature ranged from
the morning to the evening between 103.6° F. and 103°
F., respectively.

On September 27th the morning temperature was 100.2° F., that of the evening being 101.8° F.

On September 28th the temperature was again 100.2° F. in the morning, reaching 101.6° F. in the evening.

On September 29th there was a further diminution in the range of temperature, the thermometer registering 99.6° F. in the morning and 100.6° F. in the evening.

On September 30th the range of temperature was the same as on the preceding day.

On October 1st the temperature was normal throughout the entire day.

With the exception of the hæmorrhagic eruption on the right shoulder and a few papules on the abdomen, there was no other eruption to be noted anywhere.

This patient presented the Widal reaction throughout her previous typhoid up to and including some of the time of her second illness—*i. e.*, it disappeared during the second illness, and since then gives no reaction.

The most important abdominal symptoms in this case were tympanites and abdominal pains. Length of the disease, eighteen days. Length of time under observation, eighteen days.

It may be argued that this case was either a relapse of the original typhoid, with an interval of seven months between the original attack and the relapse, or that it was a second attack of typhoid fever occurring within seven months. Both views are untenable, however, if we accept the determined data relating to infection and immunity. In this connection it may be of interest to present our experience of the behavior of the Widal reaction in cases showing relapses from typhoid fever. Of these, there are in my notes five cases, four of which were reported by Dr. Elsberg, and the fifth was subsequent to this report admitted and treated in my wards at the hospital. In all these cases the reaction appeared very late in the disease—viz., one on the sixteenth day, one on the twenty-fourth day, one on the twenty-seventh day, one on the thirty-second day, and one on the thirty-seventh day.

I am at present inclined to believe that where the reaction appears very late one may expect that a relapse will probably develop. In all of these cases, excepting one, the reaction only persisted from twelve to sixteen days after its first appearance, when it disappeared entirely, to reappear again. In two it made its reappearance on the fourth day of the relapse; in two it did not disappear, but remained after convalescence

5

from the relapse, and in one it did not appear in the relapse, but on the fourth day of the second relapse from which this patient suffered.

CASE XV.—Samuel E., aged twenty-eight years; born in Russia; salesman. Admitted to service of Dr. J. Rudisch, to whom I am indebted for this history. He entered the hospital on September 22, 1897. He gave a negative previous history. His present history is of eight days' standing; it began with intense fever and general weakness. Patient had medical advice, was put upon fluid diet, and given antipyrine and quinine. Not getting better, he came to the hospital. He had no epistaxis; he had a slight hacking cough. Bowels regular. No cardiac or urinary symptoms. Complains principally of severe headache and pain in abdomen.

His general condition is fair, well nourished; the *tongue* is moist and heavily coated. His body is covered with pityriasis versicolor. On the abdomen, chest, arms, and lower extremities there is a well-marked " *tache bleuâtre.*" Lungs, anteriorly, a few sibilant râles; posteriorly, similar râles. Heart: a slight blowing systolic murmur over pulmonic area. The pulse is slow, soft, and slightly dicrotic. Liver extends from the fourth space to the free border of the ribs. Spleen enlarged to percussion and just felt. Abdomen: a number of typical roseolar spots present. Some tympanites. No œdema of legs.

On admission his temperature was 101° F., his pulse 108, and his respirations were 28. He was placed on sterilized fluids and given a sponge bath. In the evening his temperature rose to 103.2° F.

The urine was acid, of a specific gravity of 1.020, and contained no albumin.

September 24th.—Morning temperature was 101.2° F.; evening temperature was 102.2° F.

25th.—Morning temperature was 100.2° F.; evening temperature was 101.2° F.

26th.—Morning temperature was 98.2° F.; evening temperature was 100.4° F.

On September 27th the temperature remained normal all day. He was allowed to sit up, and on September 28th he was placed on full diet. He was discharged on the following day feeling perfectly well.

CASE XVI.—Hannah R., aged twenty-two years; born in Germany; domestic. Admitted to service of Dr. Rudisch on October 10, 1897. Her family history is negative; her previous history is that she had diphtheria six years ago, and that she suffers constantly with vertigo and headache.

Her present history is of two weeks' standing, previous to which she had been troubled with headache. Her attack began with excessive vomiting, nausea, constipation, palpitation, and slight dyspnœa; she had fever and chills at intervals. No sweating, or expectoration of blood. There was considerable coughing, and pain in abdomen on deep respiration. The appetite was lost, and there was inability to retain food. Headache constant and severe.

Her general condition is fair; she is fairly nourished; *tongue* moist and coated. Lungs normal. Heart extends from upper border of the third rib to the lower of the fifth, and from the right margin of the sternum to the nipple line. Action regular. Second aortic sound accentuated. Pulse slow, full, and regular, and of good quality. Liver extends from the fourth space to the free border of the ribs. Spleen slightly enlarged. Abdomen negative; no œdema of legs.

On admission the temperature was 99.8° F., but rose quickly, and soon registered 102° F., about which mark it remained.

On October 11th the urine is acid, specific gravity 1.024, and contains no albumin, but a fairly large amount of indican; no diazo reaction was elicited. The temperature range was the same as on the preceding day.

On October 12th the morning temperature was 99.8° F.; the evening, 101.6° F. The low temperature was probably due to the action of kryofin, which was twice administered to-day.

On October 13th the spleen is still enlarged, the headache is persistent, and the temperature range, from morning to evening, was from 99.8° F. to 100° F. Kryofin was again given.

On October 14th the temperature was normal throughout the day.

On October 15th convalescence is fully established; the patient feels perfectly well. He was allowed to get up on the following day, and was allowed to go home on October 21, 1897.

CASE XVII.—Max C., aged nineteen years; born in Russia. Admitted in hospital to service of Dr. Rudisch on October 24, 1897. He gives a negative family history as well as a negative previous history.

The present history is of one week's standing; it

began with headache, colicky pains in the abdomen, general weakness, and malaise. The bowels were loose—five movements daily—there was slight epistaxis. No cardiac or urinary symptoms; some cough. Pain is now severe in abdomen, and a feeling of distention is present. The appetite is gone. There is no nausea. He vomited once at the onset. The mouth is dry. The patient is very restless.

The general condition is fair; he is well nourished; the *tongue* is dry and devoid of epithelium. Lungs, anteriorly, sibilant râles over both sides; posteriorly, sibilant râles over both sides. Heart extends from the lower border of the third to the lower border of the sixth rib, and from the right sternal border to just within the nipple line. The sounds are of good force; no murmur; apex beat in normal position, forcible, and regular. Liver extends from the fourth space to the free border of the ribs. Abdomen held so rigid that an examination is impossible. Diffuse roseolar rash over body surface.

On admission the pulse, the respirations, and the temperature were 108, 24, 104.2° F., respectively. A sponge bath was given, and typhoid treatment ordered. The temperature fell gradually; at 11 P.M. it reached its lowest—viz., 101° F. The urine was negative. The temperature on the next day was 103° at 2 A.M., then dropped gradually to 100.4° at 11 P.M.

October 26th.—At 2 A.M. the temperature was 101.6°; fell slowly to 99.6° at 11 P.M. The tongue was still dry and glazed; tip red; the patient is dull and sick-looking. Pulse slow, regular, slightly dicrotic. A number of atypical spots appeared on abdomen. Only medicines given were whisky and salol. Respirations, 20 to 24.

27th.—The temperature was normal all day; pulse, 70 to 88. The tongue is becoming moist, though heavily coated. The atypical spots on abdomen still present. Spleen still enlarged to percussion. Headache gone, and general condition much improved. Pulse slow, regular, and still dicrotic.

28th.—The temperature was normal; patient stuporous and drowsy; the tongue moist, and still heavily coated; pulse soft and regular.

29th.—Normal.

30th.—Tongue coated; general condition better.

November 1st.—Full diet; out of bed this morning; urine negative; no Ehrlich reaction; no acetone reaction; no headache; patient comfortable, appetite good;

tongue moist and coated in the centre. Red cells, 4,200,000; white, 4,650.

6th.—Condition steadily improving. Discharged cured on the 6th.

On October 27th cultures were made from the fæces of this patient. These were demonstrated to be the *Bacillus coli communis.*

The prominent symptoms of these cases tabulated in the order of their constancy are as follows:

1. Headache .... in 16 cases.
2. Enlarged spleen............ " 15 "
3. Loss of appetite............ " 14 "
4. Prostration .... " 13 "
5. Roseola .... " 13 "
6. Nausea..................... " 12 "
7. Constipation .... " 11 "
8. Tympanites .... " 10 "
9. Abdominal pain............. " 9 "
10. Dicrotic pulse.............. " 9 "
11. Chill .... " 9 "
12. Pain in back and legs........ " 8 "
13. Vomiting .... " 4 "
14. Diarrhœa .... " 4 "
15. Chilly sensations .... " 4 "
16. Epistaxis .... " 3 "
17. Abdominal tenderness........ " 2 "
18. Roseola with *tache bleuâtre*... " 1 case.

None of these cases was fatal. It is therefore impossible to determine the morbid anatomy of this group.

That there may have been intestinal lesions of some sort may be inferred from the abdominal pains, the tympanites, the constipation in some and diarrhœa in others, and the abdominal tenderness.

Cases of typhoid fever have been reported in which there were no intestinal ulcerations either of the follicles or Peyer's patches. In one case of this kind, described by Cheadle,[*] cultures from the blood of the spleen and from the fæces showed typhoid bacilli. If the bacterio-

---

[*] Cheadle. A Case of Typhoid Fever without Ulceration of the Intestine. *Lancet,* 1897, ii, 254.

logical findings in this case are correct and the results are as stated, his case can not be confounded with any of ours.

In a diligent search of the literature I can find no cases reported even analogous to ours. This search was, of necessity, confined to the literature of the past year and a half, the period in which the Widal reaction was demonstrated to have diagnostic significance.

From the absence of indican, acetone, and diacetic acid in the urine in these cases, we may assume, if their presence indicates that decomposition is going on in the intestinal tract, that the toxic agent is not the result of a decomposition of the intestinal contents.

The blood of each of the seventeen cases here presented was examined for a reaction with a culture of the bacillus (coli communis) obtained from the fæces of two of the cases, and from the spleen (coli communis) in another case, and in no instance gave a reaction. In two of these cases the effect of the blood of the patient upon the bouillon culture of the coli obtained from the patients themselves was tried and showed no reaction.

From a general point of view these cases present almost the typical picture of typhoid fever, yet they differ in the following respects:

In typhoid fever there are premonitory symptoms of a few days' duration; in this group of cases there were none. Our cases show a history of from three to four days' standing before they come under the observation of the physician.

In typhoid fever there are lassitude and loss of energy; in the other cases there are general body pains of a severe type associated with these.

In typhoid there is no intense early prostration, as a rule, whereas such is common in these.

Typhoid is characterized by a gradually increasing daily rise in temperature. In the other group the rise is more sudden, and reaches its acme in from four to five days: In typhoid the highest temperature is reached in the second week of the disease. At the fastigium the temperature in typhoid makes but slight remissions, whereas in these cases there are excursive morning remissions of from two to three degrees Fahrenheit. In typhoid the temperature begins to fall at the end of the third or beginning of the fourth week, or later in protracted cases. The fall is then gradual, the descent, as marked on the chart, being steplike. In these cases the fall, in the largest proportion of those suffering, is sudden, and only in a few was the descent by lysis. In the latter the normal was reached on the third day after the fall began.

The tongue in typhoid is dry, brown, and furred, while sordes is not uncommon. In these the rule is that the tongue is moist and covered with a white coating. No sordes was observed.

Whereas all text-books have taught that the eruption in typhoid fever first appears on the abdomen, and is most extensively distributed there, such has not been my experience in the observation of this feature of the disease. I have found that the eruption appears first more frequently by far on the back between the scapulæ and over the loins than it does on the abdomen. In fact, so confirmed have been my observations in this respect that it is my custom now to look for the eruption first on the back. I usually find it there before it appears on the abdomen. Sometimes it never appears on the abdomen at all, while it is solely confined to the back. However, the distinctive mark of the typhoid eruption is its appearance in crops. No specific development in crops of roseola could be demonstrated in the group under discussion. In all other respects the eruption was identical with that of typhoid fever.

Abdominal tenderness is common in typhoid, and was not present in any marked degree in these cases. Nor is the tympanites as extensive, neither is it as distressing as in typhoid.

While the pulse in typhoid is, as a rule, dicrotic, this special quality of the pulse was observed in nine of these cases, and that not to a marked degree.

The most notable differences between the two classes of cases is the length of the disease. Typhoid fever, as a rule, runs its course in four weeks; ten to twelve days is the period consumed for this group of cases to run its course.

Emaciation is more extreme in typhoid fever than in this group.

Are we justified in calling these cases typhoid fever? To be so, two essential requirements must be filled: first, we must be able to find the typhoid bacillus in the patient's stools, in the intestinal tract, or in the blood from the spleen; secondly, the serum of these patients should show the positive reaction in a culture of typhoid bacilli. These requirements, it seems to me, are absolutely necessary to determine whether the patients have typhoid fever or not. In addition there is a third requirement: the clinical history must show a typical picture. It must not deviate from that, if we are to determine the nature of a disease alone from a recognized picture. We are not justified in making an absolute diagnosis of the presence of a disease where its clinical manifestations are modified, unless we bring to bear upon it the aid of pathology and bacteriology, so far as these sciences will aid in determining the nature of disease. We must, of course, rely for diagnosis on the clinical manifestations in those diseases whose pathology and bacteriology are unknown. But wherever the clinical manifestation of disease deviates from the standard clinical picture, a doubt will immediately arise as to the nature of the disease which presents itself, unless the disease can be determined and the diagnosis established by the aid of the other sciences referred to.

Applying these generalizations to the group of cases described, we find that these cases, while presenting a clinical picture similar to that of typhoid, differ in some respects from this picture.

Subjecting these cases to the examination of the laboratory, we find that they do not comply with any of the determined bacteriological features of typhoid fever in that, first, not one case showed the Widal reaction, which we have seen from our own experience was present in every single case of typhoid fever which was diagnosticated by its clinical manifestations, numbering eighty in the past year, and in 97.9 per cent. of nearly five thousand other cases reported by various authors. Daily tests for this reaction in this group of cases were made in the hospital. After the patients left they returned periodically to have the test applied. Secondly, the examination of the fæces of three of these cases by the most approved methods, and more recently by the method proposed by Hiss,* failed to reveal the typhoid bacillus. Thirdly, the examination of the blood aspirated from the spleen of another of this group failed to reveal the presence of the typhoid bacillus in that organ.

The objection may be raised that these cases do not constitute a definite type of a disease with distinct characteristics, but are cases of abortive typhoid fever. Such an objection would appear to me to be unjustifiable and illogical, on the grounds stated before—that none of the cases presented the Widal reaction at any period during the disease or convalescence; that no typhoid bacilli could be found in the fæces, and none in the blood of the three cases examined for them. It is a matter of regret to me that cultures were not made from the fæces of each case, and from the blood aspirated from the spleen of each, but the resources of the Mount Sinai Hospital laboratory, however, were not sufficient, and I hesitated to put such a stupendous amount of work upon the pathologist and assistant pathologist, who were engaged in the other pathological and bacteriological work of the hospital at the time. Had I been then acquainted with Hiss's differential culture medium, this material would not have been lost. However, to repeat,

* P. H. Hiss, Jr. On a Method of Isolating and Identifying *Bacillus typhosus*, based on a Study of the *Bacillus typhosus* and Members of the Colon Group in Semisolid Media. *Journal of Experimental Medicine*, November, 1897.

I wish to express my obligation to Dr. A. Lambert, who made me acquainted with Dr. Hiss's work and culture medium before they were published, which permitted me to corroborate, by this approved method of distinguishing the typhoid bacilli from the bacilli coli, the results obtained by the older methods.

not one of the cases showed the Widal reaction, and
no typhoid bacilli could be demonstrated in the blood
of the spleen and in the fæces of three of these cases,
either by the usual method of culture or by Hiss's method.   In addition, the clinical picture of these cases,
while closely approaching that of typhoid fever, dif-
fered materially from it.   On these grounds it seems to
the writer that we may fairly assume that the patients
under discussion were most probably not suffering with
typhoid fever.   The strongest evidence in favor of these
cases constituting a distinct disease entity is the case
of Miss M. (Case XIV), who was one of the training-
school nurses, attacked with typhoid fever in December, 1896, and who, convalescent in March, was seized
with an attack similar to the other cases in September
of this year, just six months after her convalescence
from typhoid fever.   We can not reasonably assume
that the last malady was a relapse of the original typhoid occurring seven months after convalescence, or
that it was a second attack of typhoid fever.

On the other hand, short typhoid, or so-called abortive typhoid fever, cases that have been admitted to
the hospital, and whose blood was examined (three in
number), showed the Widal reaction in every case.

It is almost a matter of supererogation to indicate
the points of differential diagnosis between *grippe* and
this group of cases.

The former occurs pandemically, and is ushered in
suddenly with intense backache and body pains.   The
prostration is the most important symptom.   The course
of the disease is shorter, the temperature ranges, as
a rule, lower, and the pulse rate is higher.   It is unac-
companied by roseola.   In the gastro-intestinal form,
vomiting and diarrhœa are the prominent symptoms.
It is, perhaps, this form alone with which this group
of cases might be confounded.   *Grippe* is the disease
par excellence of sequelæ and of slow convalescence.
While the spleen in cases of *grippe* is enlarged, it is
not so to the degree that it is in these cases.   The
catarrhal form is accompanied by involvement of the

respiratory tract, by the development of pneumonias, and of the sequelæ, otitis media, keratitis, etc.

We come now to a more important element in our consideration: If this group is not typhoid (we are only justified in saying that it does not conform to the essential clinical and pathological requirements of this disease), how shall the cases be classified? A careful analysis of the blood and of the excretions failed to reveal any specific germ beyond the presence of that ubiquitous bacterium, almost always found under non-pathological conditions in the human fæces, the *Bacterium coli commune.* I do not regard the presence of this germ in the fæces as the causative factor of this illness.

In the want of more definite knowledge, we are compelled to satisfy our desire to give a name to this class of cases by calling it intestinal toxæmia, or intestinal self-intoxication, although not justified in so doing because of our inability to define the toxic agent, or to prove that there was a toxæmia, in the strictest sense of the word, present at all.

However, the object of this paper will be realized if it will have called the attention of the profession to an anomalous class of patients, which may come under its observation, and which may lead some of our colleagues, who are better equipped for pathological investigation than your reader, to indicate the cause and character of the disease process giving rise to the symptom-complex which characterize each individual case of this group.

Dr. ALEXANDER LAMBERT said that in the very early days of bacteriology every disease had been supposed to have a specific organism, but it had soon become apparent that one germ might give rise to a great variety of clinical pictures. He could not share Dr. Brill's enthusiasm over the Widal test, because there seemed to him to be cases of undoubted typhoid in which this reaction was not obtained. In a given case, if the Widal test were negative, it could not be said that it was *not* typhoid. We did not yet know what caused the Widal reaction, or why in some very mild cases of ty-

phoid fever the reaction was marked, and in other severe
cases of typhoid the reaction was not so marked. Where
the test was positive and the dilution 1 to 100, 1 to 50,
or 1 to 40, there could be no doubt about the case being
one of typhoid fever. Another feature of typhoid fever
was that in a given epidemic there might be a lack or
a preponderance of some symptom considered as classical. For this reason, in a given epidemic, there might
be an unusual proportion of cases of typhoid fever in
which the Widal reaction was not obtained. That certain cases of typhoid fever ran a short and very mild
course was well known. He had with him the reports
of three cases of this kind sent by Dr. Root, of Hart-
ford. In these, the duration of the disease had varied
from nine to fourteen days, and the temperature from
104° to 107° F. They presented all the symptoms described in Dr. Brill's cases. The temperature had fallen
rapidly, and convalescence had been speedy. All three
cases had given a positive and marked reaction with the
Widal test. An analogy might be found, for example,
in tetanus. If tetanus toxine were injected into a hen,
an animal that could stand an enormous amount of this
toxine without a fatal result, it would be found that up
to a certain point these injections produced absolutely
no antitoxine reaction in the blood, and it was only when
the dose was still further increased that a decided
reaction was obtained. Similarly, in typhoid fever, it
might be supposed that the infection was not sufficient in a given case to give the Widal reaction.
The same might be observed in tuberculosis. In
the latter chronic disease the toxines were not thrown
into the system rapidly, and hence there was a slow
and feeble reaction. These facts made him hesitate
to accept the cases reported in the paper as being some
other disease than typhoid. In this connection, it was
of interest to recall the occurrence some years ago in
Paris of two sharp epidemics of what appeared to be
typhoid. In these cases the intestinal symptoms had
been mild, but the nervous phenomena had been intensely marked. But the specific germ had been found to be
one introduced with some parrots, and the disease occurred in parrot fanciers.

Dr. WILLIAM H. PARK said that the health department had examined over one thousand cases, yet out
of these definite information regarding the clinical diagnosis had been received in only about six hundred.
Of this number, only about two fifths had been consid-

ered to be typhoid. Of those considered by the clinician to be typhoid at the end of the disease, seventy-five per cent. had given a positive Widal reaction in 1 to 10 and 1 to 20 dilution. In the majority of these cases only one examination had been made. Of the cases in which repeated examinations had been made, probably ninety per cent. had given positive reactions, but in certainly ten per cent. no positive reaction had been obtained, even on repeated examination. While he agreed with Dr. Lambert regarding the negative value of the Widal reaction in a single case, yet if daily examinations were made, that negative value would be greatly enhanced. The fact that in all of the seventeen cases reported in the paper the reaction was negative was rather strong negative proof regarding the disease not having been true typhoid. He felt now that a positive Widal reaction in a 1-to-20 dilution positively indicated typhoid fever.

He recalled a case at the Presbyterian Hospital bearing upon the intensity of the infection. The patient had had fever for ten days, and pus in the urine, but none of the classical symptoms of typhoid fever. Examination showed the presence of the typhoid bacillus in the urine, though not in the fæces. Such a case taught us that although a case might not be typhoid fever clinically, it might still be a true typhoid *infection*. Dr. Hiss's method of isolating the typhoid bacillus revealed the presence of this organism, in the first few days, in about forty per cent. of the cases.

Dr. F. W. JACKSON called attention to the danger of teaching that the absence of the Widal reaction constituted a positive proof of the absence of typhoid fever. For example, it would be extremely dangerous to say that the cases reported in the paper were not typhoid fever, for such cases would then be treated by many as not typhoid, and hence a new danger would arise. It seemed a little premature at present to say that we had at last found a means of distinguishing between the perplexing borderline cases and those of unquestionable typhoid fever. So long as there was any doubt about a continued fever, it should be treated as typhoid.

The reader of the paper had presented very clearly a set of cases which were familiar to those on duty at the hospitals in summer. We had long been in doubt as to the exact nature of these cases, yet they were usually looked upon as typhoid fever, were treated as such, and the majority recovered. After studying these cases carefully with the aid of the Widal test for over a year, he still felt just as uncertain regarding their true nature.

Dr. C. A. ELSBERG said that it was only after observing the constant absence of the Widal reaction in this series of seventeen cases at the hospital that the suspicion had arisen that they might not be true typhoid. The cases had been examined for from three to five weeks, and also after leaving the hospital. It was unfortunate that we were not even yet in possession of an *absolute* bacteriological or other test for a given disease. We had no such test, even for diphtheria, for it was well known that the diphtheria bacilli had frequently been found in normal throats. The same was true of some cases in which the tubercle bacilli had been found. In one case, reported by a French author, of peritoneal effusion associated with Bright's disease, a considerable number of tubercle bacilli were found with absolutely no other change. A similar case had been reported by Dr. A. Jacobi—in a little girl who had died of multiple adenomata of the liver, and who had had ascites from pressure on the portal vein. Tubercle bacilli were found in this ascitic fluid. We could not, then, expect to have a test that would *always* respond in a given disease—indeed, the type of a disease was only determined by deductions from a large number of observations on similar cases. It was true that experimental work had shown that animals could be fed with typhoid bacilli without the development of any symptoms of typhoid fever, yet the blood would give the typhoid reaction. It would be more correct, therefore, to speak of the Widal reaction as a sign of infection with the typhoid bacilli. If marked symptoms of typhoid fever were present, in ninety-eight per cent. of the cases the Widal reaction would be obtained. It was, therefore, fair to assume that this test was a good indication of the presence of typhoid. Again, if in a carefully observed series of cases this reaction were not obtained, it seemed fair to assume that they were probably not typhoid fever. This conclusion had not been arrived at in the cases under discussion until the entire course of the disease had passed under observation. A few weeks ago it had been stated that an analogous reaction—*i. e.,* on the spirillum of relapsing fever—had been observed in the blood of persons suffering from relapsing fever, and that it had been noted that if the agglutination occurred in a short space of time this should be taken as an indication that the patient would not have another relapse. Possibly a similar condition might be found to obtain in typhoid, and if so, the reaction would prove to be of prognostic as well as of diagnostic value.

Professor MANDEL, speaking from the standpoint of a chemist, said that the present theory of bacterial disease was that these germs formed toxic albumins or albumoses. He thought, therefore, it would be advisable to examine the urine in order to ascertain the presence of a toxic albumin or albumose. Such a substance was found in typhoid fever. He thought it would have been possible to isolate the toxic agent from the urine in these seventeen cases, and thereby positively demonstrate that they were different from the ordinary cases of typhoid fever.

Dr. A. ALEXANDER SMITH said that if the members had listened to the history of one of Dr. Brill's cases, not knowing about the Widal reaction, hardly one would have concluded that the case was something else than typhoid fever, at least that type often seen in a given series or season. Certainly the type of disease varied greatly in different seasons. From a purely scientific standpoint, it was to be regretted that the treatment had been so exceedingly successful that there had been no opportunity to study the morbid anatomy. These cases had been seen at a time of year when typhoid fever was most prevalent here, and their clinical course certainly impressed him very strongly with the notion that at least a number of these cases were true typhoid. Almost every clinician could, without difficulty, recall similar cases. Personally, he had been inclined to look upon these as examples of auto-infection.

Dr. BRILL said that in his remarks introducing the subject-matter of the paper he had said that it was not improbable that clinicians had recognized in the past, as he had, types of fevers simulating typhoid and which they called typhoid, notwithstanding the symptoms were not all typical of the disease. They called these cases typhoid because they did not know under what other category they could be placed. He thought his paper had clearly defined his position, and on that account could not understand why the gentlemen who discussed the paper persisted in emphasizing the fact, to which he agreed, that the negative appearance of the Widal reaction could prove nothing. He had distinctly stated that he based his deduction that this group of cases was probably not typhoid on three grounds: (1) That the Widal reaction was absent in all of these cases; (2) that no typhoid bacilli could be found either in the fæces or in

the blood from the spleen in four cases examined, and
(3) that there was a notable departure in the clinical
history of these cases from that of typhoid fever.

He said he could not agree with Dr. Lambert in feeling that he was not sanguine about the value of the
Widal test, because the large majority of bacteriological
workers all over the world had come to the conclusion
that the Widal reaction was as positive a sign of typhoid
fever as was any other bacteriologic test at our disposal,
and that this belief could be well corroborated by the
fact that in about five thousand cases of typhoid fever
the reaction had been obtained in almost ninety-eight
per cent. of all the cases.

Here were, however, a group of seventeen peculiar
cases of a disease in which no reaction could be obtained
in a single case, and those cases occurred in a general
hospital in which the clinically pure cases of typhoid
fever gave the reaction. This occurrence might alone indicate a wide departure from the clinical typhoid group.

Meeting of January 5, 1898.

The President, Dr. ROBERT J. CARLISLE, in the Chair.

An Unusual Tumor in the Hypochondriac Region.—
Dr. W. J. PULLEY presented a man, twenty-four years
of age, a porter by occupation. He had had no serious
illness previously. Three years ago, while lifting a
heavy weight, he had suffered with pain in the right hypochondriac region. This had been followed by anæmia
and deterioration of the general health, and this had
been his condition on first coming under observation.
The patient had given no evidence of malarial disease.
The anæmia had been relieved by appropriate treatment,
and he had returned to his work. The diagnosis seemed
to lie between a hydatid cyst of the liver and distention
of the gall bladder from occlusion of the cystic duct.

Dr. JOSEPH D. BRYANT said that from the brief
examination he had been able to make he was not inclined to regard the tumor as due to a distended gall
bladder. If it was an enlargement of the gall bladder, one would expect the upper end of the tumor
to be opposite the costal cartilage of the ninth rib,
whereas it was much nearer to the costal cartilage of the

eighth rib. If the tumor was a gall bladder it should
descend markedly on inspiration, and move freely to
either side, and one would expect a history of accumulation of fluid, or of gallstones, or of inflammation of the
gall bladder. Moreover, the tumor had not been tender, and had, according to the history, grown rather rapidly and without inflammatory action. If it was a cyst
connected with the liver, it should descend more markedly and the base should be upward, which was not the
case. On turning the patient on his abdomen, he had
been surprised to find that the tumor became freely
movable. He was disposed to regard it as a cyst, probably connected with the liver or head of the pancreas.

Dr. ALEXANDER LAMBERT said that while the liver de-
scended on inspiration, the tumor varied hardly at all in
position, and its free mobility made him think that it
was connected with some portion of the peritonæum.
He would only venture the opinion that it was a hydatid cyst of the peritoneal cavity.

Cases of Ophthalmia treated with Argonin.—Dr.
HORACE BIGELOW reported some cases of this kind. He
said that his cases had not done well under the usual
methods of treatment—*e. g.*, cold applications and the
use of nitrate of silver. The former was disagreeable
to the patient, and required the constant care of a nurse.
The second method was painful and tedious. For some
months past, in the children's ward of Bellevue Hospital,
he had been using argonin, a plan of treatment that had
been introduced there by Dr. E. L. Dow. Thirteen cases
of purulent ophthalmia in infants had been so treated.
Three of these, developing in foundlings in the wards,
had been treated in this way from the earliest time of
the inflammation, and had been cured in seven days.
In the other cases. the average duration had been thirteen days. The first case subjected to the treatment
had previously resisted the usual methods, but had quickly improved under the use of argonin. A carefully prepared three-per-cent. solution of argonin had been used.
A minim dropper having been inserted deep under the
eyelid, enough of the solution should be instilled to thoroughly irrigate the eyelids twice and, later, once in the
twenty-four hours. Between these applications the lids
were kept constantly clean with boric-acid solution. Fifteen grains of argonin contained as much silver as a
grain of the silver nitrate. It was a white, amorphous
powder, easily soluble in warm water. It was not irritat-
ing, and it formed no slough on contact with the mucous
membrane, and, therefore, no neutralizing agent was re-

6

quired after its use. From his experience with argonin in these cases, Dr. Bigelow had concluded that it was a very valuable agent in the treatment of purulent ophthalmia, because of its mild but thorough and rapid curative action.

Dr. KALISH said that it was customary to distinguish two types of ophthalmia neonatorum. There was a mild form which under ordinarily good care ended in recovery. This type until recently had been considered as not being associated with a special micro-organism. The severe form was the dangerous variety, and was furnished with a special micro-organism, the gonococcus. In his service at the City Hospital there had been times when a long series of cases would prove amenable to treatment, while at other times the reverse would be noted. In this latter class the presence of the gonococcus was demonstrated by the culture test and Gram's method. He had used argonin in too small a number of cases to form an opinion, but a colleague had used it in a dispensary service, and abandoned its use because it seemed to him that the treatment with argonin was tedious and unsatisfactory. He was aware that comparison of the results obtained from treatment in hospitals with those in dispensaries would probably be unjust, since the unremitting care by trained nurses added a most important factor to any plan of treatment. In the City Hospital it was the invariable custom to detail a nurse for constant attendance in each case, and this unceasing care was largely responsible for the good results obtained. The chief damage to the eye arose from erosion of the cornea by the presence and contact of the acrid discharge, or from the swollen ring of ocular conjunctiva pressing upon the eyeball and shutting off the nutrient supply to the cornea. It was impossible in the majority of these cases to use nitrate of silver in the stage in which this ring or fold was found, as both the palpebral and ocular conjunctiva were dry and brawny, and early application of silver would aggravate the condition and perhaps destroy the eye. If argonin could be used in this stage, it would be a distinct advance in treatment. In gonorrhœal ophthalmia occurring in the adult, argonin had not been found so beneficial as the silver-nitrate treatment usually employed. He would like to ask Dr. Bigelow if the presence of the gonococcus had been determined in all the cases reported.

Dr. H. H. SEABROOK said that he did not remember having seen for some years past a case of ophthalmia neonatorum, with or without the gonococcus, in which the eye had been lost when the treatment with silver had been properly carried out. Some physicians had come to use weak solutions of silver—even one per cent. Ten grains to the ounce was strong enough for any case. The nitrate of silver caused a rapid exfoliation of the superficial cells. Such a solution was astringent and antiseptic. Perhaps the most important element in the treatment was constant cleanliness, which could be effected by a 1-to-10,000 solution of mercury bichloride, used two or three times a day, and for the rest of the time a solution of boric acid. Even after the disease had somewhat subsided—a week or ten days—he had, in former times, seen the cornea lost, because solutions of silver would set up circumcorneal swelling; hence his practice was to use ice cloths for at least an hour after the application of silver, after their constant use had been stopped. Dr. Wilson, of Bridgeport, had stated several years ago that in gonorrhœal ophthalmia he had found great benefit from the use of vaseline introduced into the eye. Whatever might be its action, it was unquestionably most beneficial. One effect of the nitrate of silver was to excite the secretion of tears, and this in itself would wash away more or less of the secretion.

Dr. BIGELOW said that the gonococci had been isolated in some, but not in all, of the cases. It was because the treatment had proved so eminently successful in those cases in which the presence of the gonococci had been demonstrated that he had thought the series worth reporting. The other cases had done fully as well under the argonin, and the diminished irritation and danger were the chief advantages of the argonin treatment.

Report on Lumbar Puncture in Cases of Alcoholic "Wet Brain."—Dr. CHARLES L. DANA reported the following case: A man, forty-one years of age, had been brought to the "cells" on the last day of September. He had been a hard drinker nearly all his life, and had had syphilis ten years before. He was suffering from acute serous meningitis, or "wet brain." He was semiconscious and in a state of muttering delirium. There were some tremor of the hands and tongue, general hyperæsthesia of the skin, slight retraction of the abdomen, coldness of the extremities, and involuntary evacuation of the bowels. On the second day the symptoms were somewhat more severe, and his temperature was 101° F. There were slight stiffness of the neck and some congestion of the conjunctiva. Dr. Dana said that he had first seen him on that day, and had looked

upon the case as a rather typical one of " wet brain."
On puncturing the spinal canal he had drawn off a few
drachms of fluid, and this had resulted in slight, tran-
sient improvement. The next day the man was much
more stupid and rigid; the retraction of the abdomen
had been increased, there was considerable rigidity of
the neck, and the urine and fæces were involuntarily
evacuated. His condition remained about the same
until the fourteenth day after his admission. During this time the temperature had risen at times to
104° F. in the evening, but was usually about 101° in
the morning. He had also had some hallucinations
of sight and hearing. On the fourteenth day nearly
two ounces of fluid were withdrawn by lumbar puncture. The improvement had been quite marked for the
next few hours, and the temperature did not rise after
that. The hyperæsthesia had diminished, the mind had
become clearer, and on the twenty-fourth day the patient had been practically well. Examination of the
fluid removed had shown that it had a specific gravity
of 1.020 and an alkaline reaction, and contained a trace
of albumin. Microscopical examination had shown uric-
acid crystals, a number of round cells, with one or two
nuclei, and some highly refractive substances collected
together in small and more or less granular masses.

Dr. Dana said that this was the third of about fifteen
cases of lumbar puncture in which the patients had recovered; in the other cases they had been practically
moribund when operated upon. Two or three years ago
he had tapped in this way in a case which had been
diagnosticated as tuberculous meningitis. The procedure had been followed by an improvement in the general condition, and the patient had eventually recovered.
It was, of course, possible that this was not a case of
tuberculous meningitis, but it certainly had presented
the clinical symptoms of the disease.

The condition " wet brain," the speaker said, was a
form of serous meningitis, in his opinion, the process
really being an inflammatory one. The cells of the
brain underwent a rapid degeneration from the poisons
brought to them in the blood; as a result, there was a
tremendous outflow of serum from the circulatory fluid.
This he believed to be a reaction of the organism to the
products of the cell's decay, the effusion being intended
to dissolve and remove the poisonous matter. This process was thus comparable to the leucocytosis and lymph
exudate in an ordinary vascular inflammation. As this
serous fluid absorbed the poison, if we could remove this

fluid it was reasonable to suppose that we should secure a quicker return to health—indeed, this was a familiar clinical experience in the treatment of pleuritic effusion.

In performing lumbar puncture the patient was laid upon the left side, with the trunk flexed a little, and a needle, about three inches and a half long (a veterinary hypodermic needle) was inserted between the second and third lumbar vertebræ. In children it could be inserted in the median line, but in adults it must be introduced half an inch to one side, and it must be directed slightly upward as well as inward. In his experience the puncture had proved absolutely harmless. In some cases he had removed nearly two ounces of fluid, but he did not think it was safe to exceed this quantity at any one time.

Dr. EDWARD D. FISHER asked Dr. Dana whether he regarded the symptoms as due to increase in the cerebro-spinal fluid in these cases or to the toxic condition of the cerebro-spinal fluid. If they were due to pressure, the fact that this fluid was known to increase so rapidly would make it seem improbable that puncture could have much effect. He would also like to know if the cerebro-spinal fluid had been injected into animals to determine its toxic nature.

Dr. DALY said that three months before he had done a lumbar puncture, and the fluid so removed had been injected into rabbits, but with a negative result. He had aspirated in a number of these cases of " wet brain," usually at a late stage, but always with temporary improvement.

Dr. DANA said that some relief was obtained by removing the pressure, but he did not expect benefit from this. If the procedure was of any value, it was apparently by its removal of the peccant matter. Sometimes as the puncture was made the fluid spurted out with force, but in ordinary cases it escaped drop by drop. The treatment to be of any value must be employed earlier and oftener.

Pure Infection with the Bacillus Aerogenes Capsulatus.—Dr. JOHN F. ERDMANN presented a boy showing the result of an amputation of the shoulder in a case of pure infection with the *Bacillus aerogenes capsulatus*. The child had sustained a compound fracture of both bones of the forearm on a Tuesday morning, and had had a chill on Wednesday night, at six o'clock. When he had seen the case on Thursday night, at nine o'clock, the boy was in a condition of profound coma, and there was crepitating gangrene up to the middle third of the arm, with crepitation along the inner aspect of the axilla and around the scapula. He performed a circular amputation of the shoulder as rapidly as possible, subcutaneous injection of salt solution being given, and kept the flaps covered with gauze thoroughly saturated with this solution. By eleven o'clock the following morning his delirium had subsided, and he was as bright as though he had had no such serious condition twelve hours previously.

Gunshot Wound of the Brain.—Dr. GEORGE D. STEWART reported such a case, in which he had followed a line of treatment suggested by Dr. Bryant. The patient, a man, thirty-nine years of age, had been admitted to the hospital on the morning of May 24th, after having shot himself in the right temporal region with a .22-calibre pistol. Examination showed a small penetrating wound, with powder stains close around its margin, and a little blood oozing from the wound. There was no wound of exit. The patient was rational, and showed no signs of paralysis. The reflexes were normal, and the pupils, though slightly and equally contracted, reacted to both light and accommodation. He was operated upon that afternoon through a tongue-shaped incision surrounding the wound. Exposure of the osseous wound, which was much larger than that in the soft tissues, revealed small fragments of bone broken from the inner table. These were removed, and the opening in the bone, which was half an inch above the external angular process and three fourths of an inch behind the temporal ridge, was enlarged, disclosing a small jagged wound of the dura, from which escaped a few long and slender blood-clots and a little cerebral tissue. With the patient's head on the opposite side, Fluhrer's probe was introduced, and it was found to pass almost transversely, without force, other than its weight, to a depth of three inches and seven eighths, and then to impinge on the bullet. Dr. Girdner's telephonic probe verified the position of the bullet. As the whole transverse diameter was only four inches and a half, it was decided that a counter-trephining would furnish the best drainage and the shortest route to the bullet. Fluhrer's probe, with a piece of silken string attached, was therefore passed to the bottom of the wound, and then this string was carried across the head at varying angles, keeping it parallel with the external portion of the probe, like the meridian lines of a globe. Where these lines intersected, on the opposite side of the cranium, an opening was made with a half-inch trephine. The localization was so exact by this device that no enlargement of the opening was needed. The probe was then made to emerge at the counter-opening, and the bullet, which was about half an inch below the surface, was easily removed with thumb forceps. This counter-opening was an inch above the left external angular process, and a fourth of an inch below the temporal ridge. Twenty strands of horsehair were carried through the frontal lobes directly, and the wounds were sutured on either side around the horsehair. On May 26th the wound was dressed. It was noted that at times the patient was quite noisy. On May 28th it was again dressed and the wound found to be healthy, but the patient was still restless. Two days later about half of the horsehair was removed, and in two days more most of the remainder. The patient was becoming more and more delirious and the temperature was about 101° F. On June 3d all drainage was removed. On June 4th the flap around the wound of entrance was opened and considerable inflammation found, with a fungous growth of cerebral tissue. Three days later the patient died.

Dr. STEWART, in commenting upon the case, said that ten years ago Dr. Bryant had written on this question of removing the bullet when it could be easily reached and had reported a hundred and forty cases. The percentage of recoveries in favor of removing the bullet was thirteen. He had also quoted three hundred and sixteen cases, with a percentage of seventeen in favor of interference.

Dr. L. W. HOTCHKISS asked what had been the source of infection in the case just reported.

Dr. STEWART answered that it probably came from the wound of entrance. In another case he would not attempt to close the wound of entrance so completely, but would use iodoform gauze in the entrance wound as well as through-and-through horsehair drainage.

Paper.

WHEN IS SURGICAL INTERFERENCE JUSTIFIABLE IN CEREBRAL DISEASE (*I. E.,* IN CEREBRAL GROWTHS, ABSCESS, EPILEPSY, MICROCEPHALUS, ETC.)?

BY EDWARD D. FISHER, M.D.

THE question of surgical interference in cerebral disease has been before the profession for some time. A few years ago, when it was found that with proper

antiseptic precautions the brain and spinal cord could be
handled with as little danger as the other organs of the
body, it was supposed that a great field had been opened
for cure in many cases hitherto regarded as hopeless.
Indeed, many operations have been suggested simply on
the ground that to do something, even if it was only the
opening of the skull, might prove beneficial, so that in
general paralysis, idiopathic epilepsy, etc., an operation
has often been advised.

The pendulum has swung in the other direction at
present.

As an operation had often been done in inappropriate
cases, with little if any result, and as also death was not
infrequent, either from inefficient methods or from un-
skilled operators, all operation was deplored. There has
always been a true middle course to pursue. In fact, in
certain cases a physician is culpable who does not advise
surgical interference, even although no positive promise
can be made of curative results, and even when only
relief can be hoped for. It must always, indeed, be remembered that these operations are capital, and that
therefore danger to life is always present. No inexperi-
enced surgeon should undertake them, at least without
careful study of the methods and indications. Another
side is also always to be remembered, and that is, that
life is often prolonged or made more endurable by operation, and this is important enough to take into consideration. I am glad that the conservative view of this operation has been generally accepted, and that men do not so
often rush in where angels fear to tread as was formerly the case.

Operations, therefore, for general paralysis, a disease
whose pathology shows it to be a widespread inflammation of the membranes and cortex of the brain, should
not be undertaken. There is no basis for operation in
these cases.

I would not have it understood that I am an earnest
advocate for surgical interference in cerebral cases, but
this much I would say, that knowing now that the brain
can be handled (indeed with caution) without injury to

its substance, we should no more hesitate to open into
it than we should to open up the abdominal cavity; indeed, there is usually less shock in these cases than in
abdominal cases. A certain number of cases, therefore,
urgently demand, all other conditions being favorable,
immediate operation—such as depression of the skull
from fracture; meningeal hæmorrhage, especially traumatic, but not necessarily only these cases. Rarely if ever
does intracerebral hæmorrhage indicate it, for from the
very condition of things it means that the brain substance itself has been destroyed, and the removal of the
blood could not restore the destroyed cerebral substance,
and, again, the situation of the blood in the region of the
internal capsule is too deeply placed to warrant removal.

The cause of the lack of success in these operations
lies mostly in the fact that we are dealing usually with
incurable conditions or irremovable complications. For
instance, tumors of the brain are only "operable" in a
small percentage of cases, say ten per cent., and out of
this small number only a possible ten per cent. can be
relieved. The explanation of this is, that the growth is
often situated so deeply that its removal would cause
such extensive ablation of the brain as to cause death;
or, again, it is so situated, as at the base of the brain,
that it can not be reached.

Accepting all these difficulties, there are certain
strong indications for operation. One case which has
been saved by operation demands that each case of that
nature should have like opportunities of relief. The
same may be said of localized epileptic seizures—whether
traumatic in origin or not. The knowledge of cerebral
topography is so accurate to-day that at least in these
cases we know where to look for the lesion, and if one
case can be recorded as benefited, although it is known
that the majority do not prove successful, it is our duty
to operate, provided other means have failed to bring
relief.

Some of the special indications for operation are the
following, therefore: 1. Fracture of the skull, causing
compression with resulting paralysis, epileptic seizures,

or coma. This would in no case be objected to, and was the practice long before the days of so-called cerebral surgery. 2. Meningeal hæmorrhages, traumatic or occurring in pachymeningitis hæmorrhagica. 3. Tumors of the brain when situated near the cortex of the brain or even in the cerebellum, but not when deeply situated or at the base. This last statement I would modify by saying that when the tumor is not thought to be a removable one a partial operation may be indicated, as the removal of a large area of the skull often relieves certain marked symptoms of tumor, as vomiting, headache, and convulsions. I have seen beneficial results of that nature in a number of cases in which that was all that could be attempted. 4. Localized epileptic seizures of the so-called Jacksonian type. I would include in this class cases, whether due to injury or arising from unknown causes—that is, so-called idiopathic epilepsy—if limited to special parts of the body, as the arm, leg, or face, or all three if only one side of the body is involved. In such cases I would advise the excision of these cerebral centres. This, indeed, results in paralysis, perhaps a permanent form; but in many of these patients we have already a certain degree of paralysis, and in that case we simply increase a previous disability. 5. The last indication which I shall mention for surgical interference is cerebral abscess, and especially in the form most commonly presented to us—that following otitis media. I will not include under this head operations in microcephalia or in infantile cerebral hemiplegia with epilepsy, although in some cases, owing to the otherwise hopeless character of these conditions, I am in favor of operative interference. It is too large a subject to take up on this occasion.

In conclusion, while not wishing to describe the methods of operation, I would urge that in cerebral operations a large area of the skull be removed. It both enables us to examine the brain better when exposed, and also, if benefit is to be obtained from relief of cerebral pressure, it surely increases that chance, and also it scarcely increases the danger of the operation. The removal of a mere button of bone with the trephine certainly exposes the patient to some danger, and rarely accomplishes much otherwise.

I will now relate in brief the history of a few cases, successful and otherwise, which have been under my care:

A. B., a boy, aged fourteen years, gave a history of a fall from a tree, injuring right side of head, causing some depression of skull. Five years later epileptic attacks ensued, for which a button of bone, somewhat anterior to the motor areas, had been removed without benefit. A large area of bone over the motor area was removed by Dr. George Woolsey. On the lower surface a spiculum of bone was found, which had extended into the hand centre. This was removed and the bone flap replaced, perfect union resulting. This boy was kept under observation and bromide administered. The attacks became less frequent, and when last heard from, three years following the operation, no seizures had taken place for a year, and the bromides had been long discontinued.

A second case was that of a Greek who came under my observation at the University College Dispensary. He gave the history of a blow on the left side of the head. This was followed by a localized convulsion of the right side of the body, commencing with a sensory disturbance—*i. e.*, tingling in the tongue and lips and fingers of that side.

This patient also had had a button of bone removed previous to coming under my care.

Dr. Woolsey removed a large area of the skull over the motor area by the bone-flap operation.

The dura at the site of the previous operation was found thickened and adherent, and was therefore removed. The bone was replaced. The patient was discharged improved and returned to his occupation in a circus. He returned some months later to the hospital and a second operation was performed, removing again a thickened membrane which was adherent to the skull Again improvement followed for a time only.

A third and a fourth operation was performed; in the last one the bone was not replaced, but a cap of celluloid was substituted. The result has finally on the whole been favorable, as the attacks are very infrequent and not severe, the patient being able to carry on his occupation.

There may be occasion for further surgical interference. Apparently no bad results from shock follow
the operation. A full report of this case will be made
at a later date.

The following case I shall merely refer to as showing how an extensive growth may present very few
symptoms, and as interesting also in that apparently the
shock of the operation, possibly owing to the size of the
tumor, resulted fatally. I will also pass the specimen
around.

A. B., laborer, about forty years old, was seen at the
clinic of the University Medical College for the first time.
He complained only of a slight headache, and said he had
convulsions, after which he had some weakness in his
hand, and dragged his leg in walking. He said he had
been in the Homœopathic Hospital for some months, and
there a button of bone had been removed from the skull.
He was sent to Bellevue Hospital for observation. Examination showed slight paresis of the right hand and considerable ataxia and exaggerated knee-jerk on the same
side. The patient was around the wards for some weeks,
and in that time only one convulsion was reported. The
eyes on examination gave no evidence of optic neuritis.
The headache was never severe.
The operation was badly borne, the pulse from the
first being weak.
The skull was removed over the motor area and the
large growth became evident. It would have been impossible to remove it entire.
The patient within a few hours succumbed.

This patient showed very few symptoms then or at
any time. The absence of paralysis can only be explained
by a gradual pressing aside of the fibres, and their thus
escaping destruction.
[The author then presented two other tumors and
gave brief histories of the cases. No operation was performed, and none was practicable.]

Dr. SEABROOK said that in a very large proportion
of cases of operation for brain tumor there was actual
relief of the choked disc; hence it was not unreasonable
to expect improvement in vision. Oftentimes there was

sufficient improvement of the vision and of what might be called pressure symptoms, it had been claimed, to justify operations on the skull, even though the tumor could not be removed.

Dr. JOSEPH D. BRYANT favored a liberal opening in the cranium, just as one-would make a free incision in removing a tumor from the soft parts. This had long been an accepted rule in surgery. Healing was better than where the incision was too small and the tissues were subjected to greater handling and roughness. Dr. Bryant referred to a case of cerebral tumor, regarded as inoperable, in which he had removed an area of bone, measuring three by two inches, along the line of the motor area. This had readily exposed the tumor and the motor centres near the fissure of Rolando, and had enabled the surgeon to determine that these centres were softened and destroyed. The patient had stood the operation well, and had recovered with a relief to the pressure symptoms. This was due to the removal of the bone, as the latter was not replaced.

Regarding operations in microcephalus, he said that these operations could not be regarded as trivial. In two instances in his practice the result had been disastrous. In one of these the patient had developed a high temperature within a few hours, and died on the fifth day. The discharges from the wound had been examined and pronounced by the bacteriologist to be entirely sterile. In isolated cases, therefore, no one could determine beforehand the amount of risk, and hence the friends should be informed of the possibility of a fatal termination. In cases of abscess there could be no question; all die without operation, while nearly half of the cases recover if operated upon.

Dr. N. E. BRILL said that he was not in sympathy with the radical views expressed by the previous speakers. He was inclined to be more conservative in recommending surgical interference in cerebral disease, because he could not assure himself that diagnostic localization of brain lesions was as absolute as the reader of the paper insisted. In fact, it was not an uncommon experience for neurologists of note to make a diagnosis of focal disease and fail to have the site of the lesion found either by operation on the brain *intra vitam* or by an examination *post mortem*. He did not think that our knowledge of the physiology of the brain was as yet sufficiently exact to warrant us in making positive statements as to the location of many lesions. While there could be no doubt that much progress had been made in our ability to localize in some areas of the brain, there were other areas in which as yet no sufficiently character- istic localizing symptoms had been observed.

He deprecated surgical interference, especially in many cases, because the operation was attended by shock of considerable degree and severity, and because the hæmorrhage from the scalp was quite extensive.

In his opinion operations in cases of microcephalia were unjustifiable, because he could not understand, and had been unable to learn, how an opening in the cranium could relieve a condition due to a defect in the embryo- logical or fœtal development of the brain.

The author of the paper had suggested that the skull be opened in cases of " inoperable " tumors of the brain on the ground that pressure symptoms would be relieved. Might not such pressure be relieved in a large number of cases by aspiration of the cerebro-spinal fluid, as sug- gested by Quincke? Lumbar puncture was much less serious than craniotomy.

Dr. GORHAM BACON said that he had understood the reader of the paper to say that there had not been many recoveries from brain abscess due to ear disease. He wished to correct that erroneous impression. Out of twenty cases at the New York Eye and Ear Infirmary, including brain abscess, sinus thrombosis, and suppura- tive meningitis, fifteen had ended in recovery after oper- ations. During the last three months there had been three recoveries in cases of thrombosis of the lateral sinus, and in two of them the internal jugular vein had been tied. These cases had led him to think there was a great field for such operative interference. He was very glad that the reader of the paper approved of making a very large opening into the bone, instead of removing merely a small button; this had been his own practice for a long time. We should always make the mastoid antrum the starting point of the operation, and cut away the bone upward toward the middle cranial cavity, if brain abscess was suspected. If the symptoms pointed to cerebellar abscess, the bone should be cut backward so that the abscess could be reached and the sinus explored. The operation should be done as quickly as possible, and at an early stage if we wished to meet with success.

Dr. ROBERT T. MORRIS thought the paper had pre- sented very well our present knowledge of brain surgery. Undoubtedly some unnecessary brain surgery had been done. Such things occurred in the history of advance movements. The reader of the paper had objected to operations for intracranial hæmorrhage because the clot had already damaged the brain. About two weeks before the speaker had operated in a case of apoplexy. The patient, who had been suffering from bronchitis, had ruptured a vessel in the left hemisphere in a paroxysm of coughing. This had been immediately followed by paralsis of the right arm, and five minutes later by paralysis of the right leg. Shortly afterward there had also been paralysis of the speech centres. When first seen by him, an hour afterward, the patient was entirely unconscious, and apparently dying. He was quickly taken to the hospital, and on his arrival there his pulse was 50 and weak, and the respirations were irregular. Dr. Morris immediately removed a large area of the skull over the ascending frontal and parietal convolutions, because there was some evidence of irritation along the motor arm area at first. On his opening the meninges a very large quantity of bloody serum escaped, and in a few seconds the patient's pulse and respiration became normal. Although the arm fibres were followed as far as the lateral ventricle on the left side, the clot was not found in that line of search, but near the island of Reil there was found freshly effused bloody serum, and small clots escaped from this point. The speaker provided for escape of blood externally to save further injury to the brain, and during the night apparently considerably more than a pint of blood and serum escaped. The case had progressed steadily toward recovery until the eleventh day, and the man was sitting up in bed and taking nourishment freely. At this time he was suddenly attacked with hypostatic pneumonia, which terminated fatally the following day. Dr. G. M. Hammond had made the postmortem examination, and the brain was now being hardened for careful examination. The autopsy had revealed the fact that the clot had been superficial in the left fissure of Sylvius and had extended as far as the lateral ventricle, but had not entered it. The free escape of bloody fluid had prevented that damage to the brain which would have resulted very quickly in death. He would report upon the specimen as soon as Dr. Hammond had completed his examination.

Dr. FISHER said that it was only the absolute hopelessness of cases of microcephalia that justified the surgeon in interfering. There were many cases in which the brain structure was not absent; there was simply a condition of atrophy, and in these it was proper to operate. Unquestionably these operations were occasionally fatal, but the cases were so hopeless otherwise that operation seemed to him justifiable. He had not been aware before of the fact that the proportion of recoveries after operations for otitis media was as great as Dr. Bacon had stated. He had never seen a case of intracerebral hæmorrhage, except those in which the hæmorrhage was considerably posterior to the motor areas, in which much could be expected from operation. The operation was not a new one. He thought that Dr. Morris had relieved the external compression, as in a case of meningeal hæmorrhage. Evidently some blood had penetrated into the substance of the brain, but it was certainly not in the motor area. The paralysis in this case had resulted from pressure on the convex surface of the brain under the dura; it was that form of paralysis found in cases of meningeal hæmorrhage or in fracture of the skull. In other forms of paralysis, as from destruction of a portion of the motor area of the brain, the paralysis could not be relieved, although it was true life might be preserved in some cases of intracerebral hæmorrhage. Dr. Morris's case was unique, but it did not open up, in his opinion, a field for operation in ordinary intracerebral hæmorrhage.

Interesting Röntgen Pictures.—Dr. JOSEPH D. BRYANT exhibited a life-size radiograph of a child of ten years who, while playing on the second floor of a house, had received a pistol wound, the pistol having been discharged from the floor below. The bullet had entered the posterior portion of the thorax, about opposite the ninth rib, and had lodged just above the crest of the ilium. With the aid of the Röntgen rays and the Girdner telephonic probe, it had been easy to make out the situation of the bullet and remove it by direct incision.

The second picture was that of a man, seen at St. Vincent's Hospital, in whom the diagnosis had rested between a dislocation outward of both bones of the forearm and a fracture running downward and inward between the condyles of the humerus. The picture showed it to be a dislocation of both bones outward, and illustrated in a very striking manner the valuable aid rendered by the Röntgen rays.

The third picture was from a case of twisting of the radius. The person had been injured by striking the arm against a revolving shaft, and the condition had been mistaken for a Colles's fracture.

Meeting of February 2, 1898.

The President, Dr. ROBERT J. CARLISLE, in the Chair.

Paper.

REPORT OF A CASE OF INTUSSUSCEPTION DUE TO A MECKEL'S DIVERTICULUM; ALSO REPORTS OF THREE ADDITIONAL CASES OF DIVERTICULA.

By JOHN F. ERDMANN, M. D.

THE history of the case of intussusception from which this specimen was obtained is the following:

F., aged nine years, male; was seized at four o'clock in the afternoon on a Friday in August of 1897 with colicky pain in the abdomen, limited to the right side and of rather severe character. During the night he vomited the contents of the stomach and some bile, and passed a large quantity of blood and clot by the bowel. There were marked tenesmus and frequent attempts to have a movement from the bowels throughout the following day, but with no further result than the passing of mucus and blood. His temperature was said to have been normal, while the pulse was slightly increased in number. On Sunday his condition showed all the evidences of severe shock, and upon palpating the abdomen a tumor rather elongated could be mapped out in the right side. In the absence from the city of Dr. Carl Beck the case was referred to me by the family physician. I saw the case at nine o'clock on Sunday night and found the following condition: Countenance anxious, temperature 101°, pulse 128, abdomen distended and tympanitic, painful to touch, and a sausage-shaped tumor extending from the right iliac fossa to the costal cartilage of the tenth rib. I had the patient transferred to St. Mark's Hospital, opened the abdomen at ten o'clock, about fifty-eight hours after the onset of the first symptoms, and found an intussusception of the enteric variety, the apex of which was within six inches of the ileo-cæcal junction.

The mass was irreducible and gangrenous, and the mesentery was gangrenous to within an inch of its attachment to the lumbar column. In addition, the intestines were deeply engorged and a quantity of pus was

found in the cavity. Resection of the mass and an end-
to-end anastomosis with the Murphy button was performed, the abdomen thoroughly washed out with salt
solution, and a gauze pack placed down to the anastomosis. The patient bore the operation very well and re-

Fig. 1.

acted well. During the two days following the operation
the patient was given sixty cubic centimetres of Mar-
morek's serum without any evidences of improvement.
The condition of sepsis increased, and the patient ex-
pired at the end of the fourth day following the operation.

Upon examining the specimen a mass about two
inches long was seen protruding at the distal extremity
(see Fig. 1), which was made out to be a Meckel's diverticulum that had become inverted and evidently was
the cause of the intussusception. Upon cutting the
specimen open it was found to measure thirty-three
inches in length; this extreme length was due to the tight
manner in which the intussusceptum was packed in the
ensheathing intussuscipiens (see Fig. 2).

Fig. 2.

In addition to the specimen of Meckel's diverticulum
in the case of intussusception, I present two other cases
of diverticula found upon operating within three months

of the foregoing case, and one specimen found in the anatomy room of Bellevue Hospital Medical College.

. Fig. 3 was drawn from the specimen which I show you of multiple (fifteen) perforating wounds of the intestines following a gunshot in an Italian who, while being pursued by an officer, was shot while in a stooping position; the ball, entering the right buttock, passed through the great sacro-sciatic foramen, then traveled up the posterior wall of the true pelvis behind the peritonæum, perforating this structure at the pelvic brim, then perforated the jejunum and ileum and the mesentery fifteen times in a length of twenty-one inches, and lodged under the skin to the right of the umbilicus. Owing to the extensive destruction of gut the entire twenty-one inches were removed. The diverticulum is situated between two perforations and is two inches long and half an inch in diameter.

Fig. 4 was drawn from a specimen that was obtained upon autopsy in the case of a patient operated upon by me

FIG. 3.   FIG. 4.

for multiple perforations by gunshot involving the stomach and intestines. The diverticulum was discovered at the time of operating, but not interfered with. At the time of the autopsy it measured three inches in length and three quarters in diameter, and was four feet and one inch from the ileo-cæcal junction.

Figs. 5 and 5*a* are drawings of a specimen obtained from the cadaver of a man about fifty years of age. Fig. 5*a* represents the specimen as it was when removed. It will be seen that there was a thin coat (peritonæum) extending from the main portion of the diverticulum to and across the intestine, and that upon dissecting through this coat of peritonæum the two projections, as seen in Fig. 5 marked 1 and 2, were found. These pro-

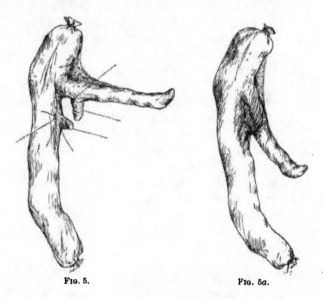

FIG. 5.   FIG. 5*a*.

jections were made of musculosa and mucosa only. Fig. 5*a* shows these accessory diverticula as they appeared under the coat of peritonæum, No. 1 having been folded upward and No. 2 projecting directly outward toward the main diverticulum, which measured five inches in length and half an inch in diameter. The specimen was situated seventy-nine inches and a half from the ileo-cæcal junction.

A Renal Calculus.—Dr. ERDMANN exhibited a calculus that had been passed by a young student who had first consulted him about one month ago for a pain in the lumbar region. The history obtained at that time had pointed to lumbago, and he had accordingly been placed on the usual remedies for that disorder. That afternoon, while riding in the cars, he had had a mild attack of renal colic, which had subsided under the use of morphine and hyoscine hydrobromide. The first urine passed had contained mucus and gritty detritus. He had then been put upon thirty drops of lysidine, and directed to take lithia water freely. After a week he had had another mild attack, but the examination of the urine at this time had been negative. During the fourth week of his trouble he had complained of uneasiness in the lumbar region. It had then been suggested that the stone might be located by an X-ray examination, and that operative interference seemed advisable. The following night, after a great deal of pain, the patient had expelled a calculus, fully an inch and a quarter long. It had been fractured in drying the calculus with a towel. It was composed of calcium carbonate and phosphate.

The Use of Extract of Suprarenal Capsule in Exophthalmic Goitre.—Dr. GEORGE W. CRARY made some remarks on this subject. He said that there were some well-marked cases of exophthalmic goître in which the exophthalmia and the goître were confined to the same side. In some instances the unilateral enlargement of the thyreoid and the other symptoms of the disease were crossed. It seemed to him inconceivable that the altered secretion of the thyreoid could possibly cause symptoms of exophthalmic goître on one side of the body only, and hence we must look further for the causes of exophthalmic goître. The thyreoid being a ductless gland, the attention of the profession had been called to other ductless glands. The extract of thymus gland had been used by a great many observers in the treatment of exophthalmic goître. It had been begun accidentally, the thymus having been used by mistake for the thyreoid gland. Those who had used extract of thymus had agreed that it was not a specific. The essential symptoms of the disease had not been very much benefited, but the general condition had been decidedly improved. Very large doses must be used, and, personally, he was of the opinion that the benefit was due to the nuclein which necessarily existed in the thymus extract. He had had six or eight cases of exophthalmic goître on thymus-gland extract for periods varying from a few months to two years or more. The improvement had not been constant, and the essential symptoms of the disease had not disappeared.

Another of the ductless glands that had been used in the treatment of exophthalmic goître was the extract of the suprarenal capsule. It was not a specific for the disease. The suprarenal gland, on section, was shown to be composed of a cortical and a medullary portion. In the former were found the arteries, veins, and lymphatic spaces. The medullary portion was made up mostly of a large plexus of veins, but also contained a great number of nerve fibres and nerve cells connected with the solar and renal plexuses of the sympathetic, and with the plexuses of the phrenic and pneumogastric nerves. It was only from the medullary portion of the gland that the active principle was obtained. This substance had been shown by a number of observers to exist normally in the blood of the suprarenal vein (Dreyer). This vein, on the right side, opened into the vena cava, and on the left side into the left renal vein. This active substance had been investigated by Abel and Crawford, among others, and had been classed by them with the pyridine bases, or alkaloids.

A watery extract, containing this substance, could be easily prepared by drying the chopped glands over a water bath and powdering the residue. The desiccated preparations on the market had been found to contain the alkaloid. A watery extract could be made from these by placing a quantity of the preparation in cold water for a few minutes, filtering through paper, and evaporating to dryness. Sixteen ounces of the fresh gland and eight ounces of the desiccated powder would yield one ounce of the watery extract. The evaporation was best done at a temperature of 105° F., but the solution might be boiled repeatedly, for fifteen minutes at a time, without the extract losing its toxic properties (Bates).

An extract containing the active principle of the adrenal had been found to be toxic, even to a lethal degree, when injected into the veins of animals, and the death of the animal had been preceded and accompanied by paralysis of the hind limbs, convulsions of the anterior limbs, opisthotonus, and suffocation. A marked rise of blood pressure had also been noted. Examination after death had revealed pulmonary œdema, extravasation into the pleural cavity, the heart in diastole, and acute parenchymatous nephritis. The rise in arterial pressure was a constant result of the administration of suprarenal extract, both in the lower animals and in man, whether the drug was introduced endermically, hypodermically, by intravenous injection, or by the mouth. Associated with this rise in blood pressure were a contraction of the capillaries and small arterioles and a slowing of the heart's action through the sympathetic. It should seem, therefore, that in suprarenal extract we had a therapeutic agent whose physiological action might be used to antagonize some of the symptoms of exophthalmic goître.

One case that had impressed him a good deal was that of a girl of twenty-three years, who had first come under his observation on February 28, 1896. She had been poorly nourished, and had had a very large goître, with marked exophthalmia and a loud systolic murmur. Her pulse had been 126 to 144, and the heart action irritable. The tremor, muscular weakness, sweating, flushing, and general nervousness had been very marked indeed. Under the use of tonics and thymus, kept up until January, 1897, there had been slight improvement in the essential symptoms, and marked improvement in the general nutrition. The administration of the extract of the suprarenal gland had then been begun, and the improvement had been quite progressive until, in May, 1897, the patient had considered herself well. She had ventured then to take to bicycle riding. Notwithstanding this improvement, the pulse would, at times, run up to 136. The goître had almost entirely disappeared, the tremor was not very marked, and she had gained considerable flesh. She had not had any extract of the suprarenal for about two weeks before this examination, which perhaps had accounted for the rapidity of the pulse. It seemed to him quite remarkable that she had improved so much more under the extract of suprarenal gland than under the thymus extract. The great improvement in the muscular strength had been especially noticeable. The patient had ceased taking the suprarenal capsule for some time, and this had been followed by a rapid deterioration in her condition. This "see-sawing" had been observed on three different occasions. She was by no means well now, but her improvement had been so decided that he had been favorably impressed with the treatment. The speaker said that unfortunately a good deal of unfavorable criticism had been made regarding the use of animal extracts because of certain ridiculous statements that had been made for them. His object in reporting the case was to encourage a further trial of the treatment. Any quantity of the thymus gland could be administered to a patient without giving rise to any symptoms whatever, but it was very different with the extract of the suprarenal capsule,

which was far from being inert. In marked cases of
conjunctivitis, or in other eye affections causing injection of the cornea, the application of a little of the
watery extract of the suprarenal gland would at once
cause a blanching of the part. This action had been
made use of in various eye diseases to reduce the hæmorrhage in cases in which cocaine had been used (Bates).
The injection of a large dose of suprarenal extract into
the vein of a small animal would cause death in a few
minutes.

Dr. ALEXANDER LAMBERT asked if the chemical con-
stitution of the pyridine base had been made out, because the symptoms produced in animals were similar to
those caused by the application of nicotine to the tongue.
The substances having a pyridine base were those which
caused the toxic symptoms observed in excessive pipe-
smoking. Last year Dr. Dana had had in Bellevue Hospital a young woman with a very marked and typical
exophthalmic goître. He had given her tablets composed of the pituitary body, and she had improved very
rapidly, and had been discharged apparently in excellent health. She had returned to the hospital last week
for observation. The exophthalmia and the goître had
remained away, but the tachycardia had returned, and
the pulse was 146. She was apparently in good health.

Three weeks before a man had come into the hospital
with tremor, attacks of dizziness, and marked exophthalmia. He had had Stellwag's and von Graefe's sign to
a slight degree. There had been no goître, but moderate tachycardia. He had placed this man on the use of
pituitary extract as an experiment. He had now been
on the remedy only about one week. The pulse ranged
between 80 and 90; the Stellwag's and von Graefe's signs
had almost disappeared; the exophthalmia had been reduced, and the dizziness and anæmia had disappeared.
Small doses of iron had also been given. Apparently the
use of the adrenal extract was more scientific, because it
was founded on a certain physiological action of the
gland.

The PRESIDENT asked Dr. Crary if the extract had
made any impression on the urine, and also for more
specific statements regarding the dose.

Dr. CRARY replied that he had not heard before of
the use of the extract of the pineal gland in cases of
exophthalmic goître. He supposed it had been used on
the general principle that the other ductless glands had
proved of some service. The action of the extract in
Dr. Lambert's case had apparently been much more rapid

than with the other extracts. He would not ordinarily draw any conclusions from one or two cases, and his only reason for reporting a single case was because of the instructive contrast afforded by the different methods of treatment that had been employed.

The essential symptoms of exophthalmic goître he believed to be the tachycardia and the tremor, and if in a supposed case of exophthalmic goître there was tachycardia but no tremor, he would be inclined to think that it was some other disease, or else that the tremor had not yet developed. He had been unable to make examinations of the urine in the case reported by him, because the patient had been a girl living out of town, and it had been difficult to keep her under observation

fine tumor which had disappeared under tonic treatment. This had been followed immediately by an attack of erysipelas and a disappearance of the tachycardia. Both tachycardia and tremor had returned after four weeks.

Acute Intestinal Obstruction simulating Meningitis. —Dr. WALTER C. WOOD presented a specimen of Meckel's diverticulum in connection with the report of a case that illustrated the statement made by Mr. Treves, that sometimes acute intestinal obstruction was diagnosticated as acute meningitis. The specimen had been removed by him from a girl of eight years who, after having freely indulged in cheap candy on November 15th, had had an attack of vomiting and abdominal pain. On November 17th the attending physician had given enemata, with small but unsatisfactory results, and as the vomiting and abdominal pain had continued he had been asked to see her on November 19th. At that time she had been delirious and had had frequent convulsions in the face and arm muscles; the pupils had been equal, the neck rigid, and the abdomen slightly distended and apparently tender near the umbilicus. The pulse had been 130 and the temperature 99° F. On rectal examination, a small quantity of fæces had come away. The clinical picture had been that of acute poisoning or of cerebral irritation. An opium suppository had been given to quiet the nervous symptoms, but the obstruction having become complete, an operation for its relief had been done the next day. The cause had been discovered to be a Meckel's diverticulum, which was adherent by the tip to the mesentery, and compressing an underlying coil of small intestine. Since the operation the child had been remarkably quiet and free from nervous symptoms. The clinical picture certainly had pointed very strongly to meningeal irritation, and if the case had been seen only at this time, and there had been no history, it would have been almost impossible to have detected the abdominal condition.

Dr. WILLIAM J. CHANDLER, of South Orange, N. J., thought it was a well-recognized fact that in many autopsies in cases of acute meningitis intussusception was found, so that it was quite possible for such an error in diagnosis to be made.

Paper.

GONECYSTITIS.

BY WINFIELD AYRES, M. D.

INFLAMMATION of the seminal vesicles is of quite common occurrence in a large genito-urinary practice. Of one thousand and fourteen cases applying for treatment in my class at Bellevue Dispensary between March 1 and November 1, 1897, thirty were cases of seminal vesiculitis, while thirty-five were cases of epididymitis. Many of these cases were of long standing and had gone the rounds of the dispensaries trying to get rid of their symptoms. Of these thirty patients I have been able to cure twelve, two are still under treatment, and the rest disappeared after the pain and discharge had been relieved.

Anatomy.—I shall not give a complete description

of the anatomy, simply stating that the vesicles lie at the base of the bladder, the posterior extremities being opposite the entrance of the ureters. The ampullæ of the vasa deferentia lie to the inner side. The duct of the vesicle joins that of the vas at an acute angle at the posterior border of the prostate to form the ejaculatory duct, which empties into the sinus pocularis. The vesicles are about two inches and a half in length, half an inch in width, and a quarter of an inch in thickness. To the finger they feel firm and are easily outlined in some subjects. It is impossible to reach the top of the vesicle with the ball of the finger in a muscular or fat subject, but in a thin subject the whole vesicle may be mapped out.

Pathology.—Normally, the vesicle contains a thin, mucous fluid, holding the spermatozooids in active motion. This fluid can not be expressed by the finger except in an occasional case where the vesicle is much distended. When the vesicle becomes inflamed it increases in size, is much softer, and is often not distinctly felt, owing to the surrounding infiltration. The contents of the vesicle become much thicker and often contain large masses of inflammatory exudate.

Ætiology.—The most common exciting cause is gonorrhœa. Stricture is often the exciting cause; the subacute inflammation of the posterior urethra, which so often accompanies stricture, extending to the vesicles. Other exciting causes are tuberculosis and syphilis. Excessive venery and masturbation are said to be a common cause, but where the disease occurs in a masturbator who has never had gonorrhœa there is always a stricture at or near the bulb, and the cause of the affection is the stricture and not masturbation. Gonecystitis occurs most frequently between the ages of twenty-five and thirty-five years. I have found it more frequently on the left side than on the right.

Classification.—Acute, subacute, and chronic.

Acute gonecystitis is almost always due to gonorrhœa, yet the tuberculous may take on acute symptoms. The inflammation may be on one or both sides, and may or may not be accompanied by epididymitis. In my thirty cases three were of the acute variety.

The subacute and chronic forms are very much alike in their cause and symptoms, so I shall describe them together. They are due in the great majority of cases to gonorrhœa. Of the remaining twenty-seven cases, twenty-four were due to gonorrhœa or stricture, two were due to syphilis, and one was due to tuberculosis.

Symptoms.—In the acute form the general symptoms are quite well marked. The patient feels weak and rapidly loses in weight. The temperature usually rises, sometimes as high as 103° or 104° F. The appetite is disturbed and the bowels are constipated. Evacuations are painful. There is usually considerable pain referred to the back, to the suprapubic region, or to the groin. Sometimes the pain takes the form of a sciatic neuralgia. There is a burning sensation at the end of the penis on passing water. Frequency with but little urgency of urination is usually present. The urine contains a large amount of pus in both specimens, and often pus or blood clots. These clots are sometimes in the shape of a cast of the vesicle. In cases in which the inflammation has lasted from a week to ten days there are apt to be frequent seminal emissions. Rectal examination will show one or both vesicles to be enlarged, tender, hot, and often pulsating.

The subacute and chronic forms usually begin by the slow extension of inflammation from the posterior urethra, but they may follow an acute attack. The symptoms are very varying and indefinite. There are usually the morning drop, a burning sensation in the end of the penis on urination, and indefinite pain in the groin, in the back, and over the suprapubic region. These symptoms may one or all be absent, the only thing complained of being a frequently recurring discharge. In other cases the patient may complain of occasionally passing very muddy urine, which often contains large pus clots. The urine is very characteristic. If there is considerable pus present, it will be in both specimens and have a more flaky appearance than in urethritis or cystitis. If the urine is comparatively clear, the shreds are apt to float near the surface and have the appearance of being diffuse, often looking, as one patient expressed it, "like chewed-up strings." The glairy mucous shred of prostatorrhœa is often present.

Sexual intercourse is often disturbed. In many cases ejaculation occurs almost as soon as, sometimes before, the penis is introduced into the vagina. A second erection is often impossible. In these cases there is a hyperæsthesia of the posterior urethra, often with oxaluria. In other cases ejaculation is much delayed, and in neither is there much satisfaction. Often copulation causes pain in the back, groin, or suprapubic region. In a few cases there is functional impotence; but in many there is an increased sexual desire. Following erection, after a hard movement of the bowels and at the end of the stream, there occasionally appears a glairy mucous discharge. This is usually prostatic, but may contain spermatozooids.

On examining the urethra with the endoscope, the pendulous portion will be found perfectly healthy unless there is a purulent discharge; while the posterior urethra is usually hyperæmic and hyperæsthetic. Rectal examination will show one or both vesicles enlarged, somewhat sensitive, and boggy.

The general symptoms are not well marked. There are often anæmia, constipation, and intestinal indigestion. In cases of long standing there are usually extreme nervousness, insomnia, and sometimes melancholia.

Diagnosis.—Gonecystitis must not be mistaken for spermatorrhœa. This condition presents many of the same symptoms, but the trouble is due rather to a stricture of the urethra, together with a congestion of the posterior urethra and prostate, and irritable vesicles.

Acute gonecystitis sometimes resembles cystitis. If the urine passed is muddy, while that drawn by the catheter is clear, then cystitis may be excluded.

I have seen gonecystitis mistaken for pyelitis, for stricture, for posterior urethritis, and for granular patches. The finger in the rectum will determine at once if there is any inflammation of the vesicles.

Prognosis.—For recovery this is good, except in tuberculous cases. In acute cases the time is from two to eight weeks; for the subacute, three to six months; for the chronic, six to twelve months. In cases of long standing, say eight to ten years, the prognosis is not so good; yet many of these are amenable to treatment.

Treatment.—Acute gonecystitis should be treated by rest in bed, together with hot applications to the perinæum of flaxseed poultices, cloths wrung out in hot water, or preferably, by hop poultices. Internally, diuretics and anodynes should be given, with no local treatment to the bladder, urethra, or vesicles. Under this mode of treatment the inflammation usually subsides in the course of from three to ten days and the vesicles regain their normal condition in two or three weeks, or the inflammation may take on the subacute form.

In the subacute and chronic forms, except those of the tuberculous and syphilitic varieties, the only treatment that is of any service is the stripping or milking of the vesicles. The method is as follows: The patient is made to flex the body on the hips by bending over a chair, and the finger, well lubricated with vaseline, is passed into the rectum. The prostate is first mapped out and then the finger is passed upward and to either side, the other hand making pressure above the pubes to force the contents of the pelvis downward. The healthy vesicles may be mapped out easily. They feel like flattened cylindrical bodies, about half an inch in width, with numerous irregularities. A little to the inner side may be felt the ampulla of the vas deferens. If the vesicle is inflamed it will feel much softer than normal, and is considerably increased in size. If the vesicle is found enlarged, it is stripped slowly and gently toward the prostate, the tip of the finger only being used. The patient is then allowed to empty his bladder. If the stripping has been successful, the fluid voided will be found to contain large masses of inflammatory exudate, a flocculent precipitate, or it may have a milky appearance. In some cases the result of the stripping appears at the meatus. I have stripped out in two cases perfect casts of the vesicles and, in several, masses which, floating on the surface of the water, were fully an inch long by three quarters of an inch wide and a third of an inch thick. These under the microscope are found to be composed of fibrin and a few white blood-corpuscles and spermatozooids.

That this fluid stripped out is vesicular and not prostatic I have proved to my own satisfaction in a number of instances by first stripping the prostate, allowing the patient to pass water, then stripping the vesicles, having thrown into the bladder a non-irritating solution, and having him urinate. There will be in the first water passed some shreds and many bodies, nearly round and glistening, of about the size of No. 1 shot; while the water passed after stripping the vesicle will be like that described above. Also, stripping produces a marked diminution in the size of the tumor felt above the prostate.

There is no medicine that will have much effect in aiding the cure. Sodium bromide will often relieve the burning at the end of the penis. Phytolacca and hydrastis sometimes have a sedative action. I have used phenalgine with great benefit to relieve the seminal emissions. Usually a tonic is indicated and the bowels need regulating. A moderate amount of exercise is of benefit, but overexercise and bicycle riding should be prohibited. Excessive smoking irritates an inflamed vesicle.

Local treatment to the urethra is of no benefit and often does harm. It is true that the shreds will be eradicated in some cases, but the improvement is only temporary.

I have selected a few cases to show how varied may be the symptoms.

CASE I.—F. Mc., aged twenty-six years; occupation, clerk; applied for treatment at the dispensary February 23, 1897, with the following history: He had had a discharge for five days, which began on the eighth day

after connection. This ran the usual course for three
weeks, when he began to have great frequency and passed
some blood. He had some fever and chilly sensations,
with pain in the back and suprapubic region; also pain
at the end of the stream on passing water. His urine
contained pus in both specimens, with some blood and a
few diffuse pus clots in the second. The left vesicle
was much enlarged, hot, and tender. To exclude cystitis I passed a catheter and the water drawn was perfectly clear. I ordered him to stay in bed and apply
hot poultices to the perinæum. Internally, I gave him
an alkaline diuretic. In three days the pain and frequency had disappeared, and the vesicle was much reduced in size. In one week he had entirely recovered
except for a slight gleety discharge, which responded
later to the usual treatment.

CASE II.—C. W., aged thirty years, mechanic, applied at my office for treatment May 29, 1897. He had
contracted his first gonorrhœa three years previously
and had had a constant discharge since, in spite of constant treatment. Two years later he had typhoid fever,
at which time he occasionally passed very muddy urine
containing many large pus clots. About three months
after this he had to wear a leather cot on the penis to
keep himself from masturbating in his sleep. When I
first saw him he complained of pain over the pubes on
movement of the bowels and of a sticky discharge from
the penis. Copulation was not satisfactory and was
followed by pain over the pubes and a feeling of melancholia. I found the left vesicle enlarged and soft, and
was able to strip a large amount of fluid from it. I
stripped him once a week for five months, and at the
end of that time he was perfectly well. His discharge
had disappeared in the first month of treatment and his
other symptoms during the second. I saw him again
last month and found that his vesicles had remained
perfectly healthy and that he had had no return of his
symptoms.

CASE III.—J. Q., aged twenty-three years; occupation, clerk; came to the office March 20, 1897. He had
a gonorrhœa which I treated with argonin. I succeeded
in stopping the discharge in nine days, but could not
clear the urine of shreds. He occasionally noticed a
morning drop. I enlarged the meatus, which was very
small, and searched for stricture but found none. On
April 2d he complained of pain in the groin. I found
both vesicles very much enlarged and soft, and was able

to strip out large masses of inflammatory exudate. I stripped him every sixth day for two months. At the end of that time the vesicles were perfectly normal to the touch and very little could be stripped from them. I continued stripping him once in ten days for two months longer and then discharged him. He has had no symptoms of any trouble since.

CASE IV.—G. M., aged thirty years; occupation, laborer; applied at the dispensary February 20, 1897, with the following history: He had contracted gonorrhœa three months previously and was apparently cured in four weeks. For four weeks previous to coming to the dispensary he had noticed that his urine was occasionally very muddy and at other times perfectly clear. He had no pain or discharge. The urine passed at the dispensary was perfectly clear, but his morning urine, which he had brought with him, contained a lot of pus and numerous large pus clots. His left vesicle was found very much enlarged and a large amount of fluid was expressed from it. He was stripped every week for four months and then disappeared, not having had any return of his symptoms in three months. He came back in December complaining of a pain over the heart. I examined the vesicles and found them perfectly normal, the pain being due to indigestion.

In conclusion I may affirm:

1. That gonecystitis occurs with about the same frequency as epididymitis; the acute form much more rarely than acute epididymitis; the chronic form more frequently than chronic epididymitis.

2. That in my opinion masturbation or sexual excesses can not cause it, unless they have first produced a stricture in or near the bulb.

3. That stripping the vesicle is the only treatment that is of any service in chronic non-tuberculous and non-syphilitic gonecystitis.

4. That the vesicle can be reached and emptied in spite of the fact that it seems impossible from measurements made on the dissecting table.

5. That we have by this method a treatment whereby we are able to cure a large number of the so-called "incurable gleets."

8

Dr. LOUIS A. DI ZEREGA asked for a more minute description of the method of stripping the vesicles.

Dr. AYRES replied that the patient stoops over a chair and flexes his legs. The examining finger is then passed well upward in the rectum, first on one side and then on the other. A person with a long finger can readily reach the parts. The finger in the rectum is aided by the outer hand pressing down over the pubis. But little pressure is used in the stripping.

Dr. ERDMANN said he felt confident that three cases in the last few months had been markedly benefited by this treatment, although he had not been able to reach the tip of the vesicles. In each instance he had succeeded in obtaining some of the peculiar exudate spoken of. One specimen had come from a man whose vesicles had been stripped at intervals of three days for about two months. He had come to him with a "morning drop." The endoscope had revealed no lesion in the urethra, but on stripping the vesicles he had obtained some of this exudate. The man had made a speedy recovery from the morning drop. In another case of persistent morning drop, which had lasted for over three years, he had first dilated up to No. 32, and then stripped the vesicles. Recovery had been rapid. With the bladder distended so as to facilitate counter pressure the vesicles could be easily manipulated in thin subjects.

Dr. C. E. QUIMBY said that a few years ago he had had a patient who had been distinctly gouty and of a decidedly nervous temperament. There had been no morning drop, and he had not been able to detect a stricture, but there had been more or less irritation in the deep urethra and frequent urination at night. A leading specialist in this city had stripped his seminal vesicles, and had displayed a milky fluid, and had thereupon made a diagnosis of chronic seminal vesiculitis. For several months he had continued the strippings with this specialist without any relief, and had then been compelled to go abroad on business. While in Europe he had gone to Carlsbad and taken a thorough course of treatment there. On his return to this city his vesiculitis had apparently disappeared and there had been little local irritation. The speaker said that he had all along looked upon the condition as largely due to the gouty diathesis and the nervous temperament. He raised the question of the possibility of this so-called inflammatory exudate being frequently a physiological exudate, due to an excess of nutrition produced by sim-

ple congestion. He thought some of these subacute
cases might be found to depend upon other sources of
irritation than gonorrhœa, stricture, syphilis, or tuberculosis.

Dr. AYRES, in closing the discussion, admitted that
he believed a good many cases in which the milky fluid
could be obtained by stripping were not cases of vesiculitis. He had had such a case only yesterday. Neither
vesicle had been much enlarged, yet, as an experiment,
he had stripped them and had obtained this fluid in considerable quantity. A vesicle the seat of chronic inflammation was nearly as large as the index finger. He
had never been able to draw the exact line between a
congested and an inflamed vesicle from the appearance
of the products of stripping. If on a second stripping
very little of the fluid was obtained he thought vesiculitis could be excluded. Considerable experience was
necessary to determine whether the vesicle was inflamed
or simply enlarged. A great many cases of painful and
frequent micturition were due to oxaluria and lithuria,
and in these a little of the fluid would be obtained only
on the first stripping. He did not advocate stripping
cases of oxaluria and lithuria, but if the vesicle was considerably enlarged, and from it a considerable quantity
of inflammatory exudate could be stripped, it was safe
to say that it was the seat of inflammation.

Meeting of March 2, 1898.

The Vice-President, Dr. S. ALEXANDER, in the Chair.

A Clinical Report upon the X Ray in Fractures.—
Dr. GEORGE W. CRARY presented this report. He said
that he had been struck with the fact that a well-marked
fracture might be present without showing in the X ray
at all. A Röntgen picture was presented from a case of
Colles's fracture, in which the fracture could not be discovered even in the negative. Four surgeons had examined the case, and all had obtained easily the most definite evidence of such fracture. Where there was no displacement, and the fractured ends were in contact, the
picture might not show a fracture at all. This fact was
of some medico-legal importance.

Another fact that had impressed him was that the callus would not always be shown in an X-ray photograph. Röntgen pictures were presented from a case of non-union, which had been brought to him two months after the injury. He had succeeded in getting union, but had been unable to reduce the deformity. It had been a case of fracture of both bones of the forearm. Four months after the receipt of the injury, while there had been distinct and firm bony union, the Röntgen picture had appeared to indicate that union had not taken place. Apparently, these pictures would not prove that union had occurred unless the callus was old. Another Röntgen picture was shown, that of a case of fracture of the femur, with angular deformity, taken five months after the injury. Although the bony union had been perfect by callus, the appearance of the picture indicated that union had not occurred.

The next Röntgen picture was exhibited to prove that a plaster-of-Paris dressing did not always immobilize the fractured bones. The case had been one of fracture of both bones of the forearm in the lower and middle third, treated under one plaster dressing. The reduction had been effected under chloroform anæsthesia. One picture showed that the deformity of the ulna had not been reduced. Another, taken five weeks later, showed that the radius had slipped out of place. Bony union had, however, taken place. This same defect in plaster-of-Paris dressings was still further emphasized by pictures from a case of fracture of the ulna very near its lower end. The first one, taken at the time of the application of the plaster dressing, showed overriding of the fragments; the second, taken the next day, showed that this overriding had disappeared. In this case the slipping of the bones had happened to be in the right direction.

The speaker said that the value of X-ray photography depended largely upon the interpretation placed upon the picture. In illustration of this, photographs were exhibited from a case in which a fracture of the forearm had resulted from direct violence. There had been no crepitation, but the false motion had been so marked that there could be no doubt about the diagnosis, and there had been no overriding. Nevertheless, the line shown by the photograph was not that ordinarily seen in cases of fracture; it was a dark and not a white line.

The next Röntgen picture shown was from a case in

which a diagnosis had been made of Colles's fracture. The peculiar course of the fracture and the outline of the styloid process of the ulna were very well shown in the picture. Another picture was shown from a case of fracture of the styloid process of the ulna which had come under observation two weeks after the injury. It had been impossible to make out anything more than a rupture of the internal lateral ligament by the usual methods of examination, but the X-ray photograph showed that, in addition, the styloid process had been torn off.

The next photograph was instructive because it had failed to throw any light upon the diagnosis. It was from a case in which a man had struck a blow with his fist closed. He had struck the carpo-metacarpal joint of the thumb. The photograph had been taken a few weeks after the injury. Attention was called to the apparent prominence of the metacarpal joint of the thumb. Dr. Crary said that when the thumb was held closely opposed to the hand this extreme prominence of the carpo-metacarpal joint was always shown in photographs of normal hands.

The next Röntgen picture was of a compound fracture of both bones of the forearm, and was of interest as showing that the apparent deformity which had existed in the forearm was greater than the real deformity. The radius was perfectly straight, but there was a slight bowing of the ulna. The deformity was largely due to the prominence of the proximal end.

The last of the series of photographs was from a case of sarcoma of the carpal bones, with dislocation forward of the entire carpus.

Dr. H. M. SILVER presented in connection with this exhibit three additional photographs. He said that last June he had been called to see a young lad of sixteen, who had been thrown from his bicycle a few hours before. He had already been seen by a physician, who had almost completely reduced the deformity of the wrist. The next day photographs had been taken of both the uninjured and injured sides. They had shown, on the injured side, an epiphyseal separation of the lower end of the radius, and also a fracture of the base of the styloid process of the radius, and a fracture of the styloid process of the ulna. The latter was carried down toward the pisiform bone. The patient had been anæsthetized and the hand carried forcibly inward to overcome the slight outward displacement. Eight months and a half afterward, a second photograph had been taken, and this had shown that the carrying of the hand to the inner side had completely restored the epiphysis to its normal position. The fragment at the base of the styloid process of the ulna had seemed to have united, and there had been some slight thickening of the lower extremity of the radius.

Dr. ROBERT T. MORRIS referred to a case of impacted fracture of the head of the humerus which had been seen by a number of surgeons, none of whom had been able to make the diagnosis by the usual methods of examination. The Röntgen picture had shown that there was an impacted fracture of the head of the left humerus, and that the greater tuberosity impinged upon the acromion. In another case, one of disability of the elbow, the photograph had disclosed only a separation of the cartilage of the head of the radius.

Paper.

A CASE OF PULSATING EXOPHTHALMUS: RUPTURE OF THE LEFT CAROTID INTO THE CAVERNOUS SINUS. CURED.

BY J. H. WOODWARD, M. D.

Mrs. M., thirty-nine years of age, was brought to consult me by her physician, Dr. La Belle, of Lewis, New York, on November 23, 1893. She stated that in May, 1893, after working hard all day, she had noticed a noise like the puffing of a locomotive at a considerable distance. She was standing in her doorway at the time and supposed that it was a locomotive that she heard. Very soon, however, she discovered that the noise was in her head. Since then it had been continuous, and it had become very distressing, especially at night. Not long after the noise began she noticed that her left eye was becoming more prominent than the right. She had not noticed any double vision. In September, 1893, the vision of her left eye became less acute than it had formerly been.

Her mother had died of some affection of the lungs; her father was still living. She had had seven children, of whom five were living still and in good health. The youngest child was five years old. From her replies to my questions, and from my examinations of the patient,

I was not able to detect that she was suffering from any constitutional dyscrasia whatever. Her heart and the blood-vessels were normal. Her pulse was full and strong and regular. She was well nourished. Her skin was somewhat bronzed.

She complained of a continuous noise in her head, which annoyed her very greatly. Her left eyeball was displaced forward, downward, and outward. This exophthalmus was very marked, but the patient was still able to close her eye completely. She did not complain of pain in the eye or its vicinity. The veins of the left superior eyelid were dilated, and those of the bulbar conjunctiva were engorged with blood. A slight exfoliation of the epithelium of the cornea had occurred, and the consequent failure in the transparency of that structure rendered it impossible for me to make a satisfactory ophthalmoscopic examination at that time. The pupil was normal. The movements of the eyeball were restricted in every direction. The supraorbital and the infraorbital blood-vessels were greatly dilated, and in these, especially in the supraorbital vessels, an aneurysmal thrill was distinctly perceptible. On applying the stethoscope above the eyeball, an aneurysmal bruit was very plainly heard, and also, from time to time, the *bruit de piaulement*. The aneurysmal bruit could be heard also above the *right* eye. Compression of the left common carotid artery checked the pulsations and put an end to the noises.

Rest in bed, iodide of potassium, and occlusion of the affected eye were tried for about two weeks, without producing any effect upon the disease. But the abrasion of the cornea was healed by the treatment, and I was able then to make a satisfactory ophthalmoscopic examination. I found that the retinal veins were tortuous and dilated, and that there were several small retinal hæmorrhages. There was no visible pulsation in the retinal vessels. Intraocular tension was normal. Vision was ⁵. Inasmuch as the treatment had produced no effect upon the various bruits, the exophthalmus, or the other symptoms, the patient was now ready to submit to any operation that might put an end to the noises in her head.

On December 11, 1893, I ligated the left common carotid artery. On the 21st the wound was healed and all dressings were permanently removed. At this time there was no abnormal pulsation in or about the left orbit. Since the operation she had not heard any bruit or other sound in her head. The exophthalmus had diminished very much already. The bulbar conjunctiva still presented some dilated veins. The cornea, the other refracting media, and the retinal vessels were normal; the retinal extravasations had disappeared. Vision was $\frac{5}{5}$. With a stethoscope applied to the left orbit, however, one could still hear an aneurysmal bruit, and from time to time a buzzing sound. But these noises were very much less intense than they had been prior to the operation, and they could not be heard, at this time, in the region of the right orbit. The patient returned to her home on the 22d of December. Her condition improved in every respect, and she remained apparently cured for two months, when she again heard the noises in her head.

In May, 1894, she came to see me again. The exophthalmus was much less marked than it had been before the ligation of the carotid. The supraorbital and the infraorbital vessels were only slightly dilated. With the stethoscope one could perceive the aneurysmal thrill, the aneurysmal souffle, and the *bruit de piaulement*. The patient had discovered that she could stop the sounds in her head by pressing upon the side of her nose near the inner canthus of her left eye. My friend, Dr. W. W. Seymour, called my attention to this fact. I had intended to ligate the right common carotid; but, inasmuch as compression of the arteries of the collateral circulation at the root of her nose put a quietus to my patient's symptoms, I ligated those vessels instead. After those arteries had been tied, no abnormal noises of any sort could be heard about the patient's head. All pulsation had ceased about the left orbit.

The wounds healed under the first dressing. The exophthalmus had by that time subsided in a marked degree, and all subjective and objective sounds had ceased in the region of the aneurysm. The patient was cured, and she has remained cured ever since. I saw her physician in October, 1897, and he reported that the patient had not suffered any relapse whatever since the last operation; that the exophthalmus had completely disappeared, and that the patient's vision was as acute as it had ever been.

Ligation of the arteries of the collateral circulation has never been done in any other reported case of this affection. I must confess that I had very little confidence in its permanent utility in my case, but the sequel has been perfectly satisfactory in every respect.

The clinical aspects of this case indicate conclusively that a rupture of the carotid artery into the cavernous sinus had occurred. Such lesions are not common. They have been caused by traumatisms, such as fractures of the base of the skull, penetrating wounds of the orbit, etc., while in other numerous cases the rupture has occurred spontaneously. In the idiopathic cases about eighty per cent. of the patients were women. The greater number of the traumatic cases have occurred in men. In my patient I could find no reason for the existence of the lesion.

It is needless to say that the course of the disease is toward a fatal termination, and that the most satisfactory method of treatment consists in ligating one, and sometimes both, of the common carotid arteries; or, as in my case, ligating one carotid and subsequently, if feasible, tying the arteries of the collateral circulation.

A CASE OF CEREBELLAR ABSCESS: DEATH, AUTOPSY.

BY J. H. WOODWARD, M. D.

JOHN D., an Irish boy, about fourteen years old, was brought to my clinic at the Mary Fletcher Hospital in May, 1892, to be operated upon for an abscess behind his left ear. A large quantity of pus was evacuated from it through a long Wilde's incision, and a large aperture through the external wall of the mastoid process was found opening into a large cavity in the bone. The suppurating area was curetted, irrigated, and drained, but neither the mastoid antrum nor the tympanum was invaded by the operation.

On the following day the boy was removed to his home, and I did not see him again for more than a year. I was told, however, by his physician that he had not only made a rapid and complete recovery from the mastoid abscess, but that the purulent discharge from his ear had also been checked by the treatment.

In July, 1893, this patient consulted me for a recurrence of the otorrhœa, and because the wound in the mastoid had opened and was discharging. I found a fistulous tract running into the process toward the antrum, and was readily able to determine the presence of carious bone at the end of it. I advised an immediate and radical operation. Owing to other engagements, I could

not operate upon him myself, and recommended that
another surgeon be secured for the work. When I returned in the autumn, I was told that the boy had recovered without an operation. He had been treated with
antiseptic douches and dressings.

On April 17, 1894, I saw this patient for the third
time. His ear was discharging again. The attack had
begun about three weeks earlier, and he had suffered
from very severe pains in his left mastoid region
over the left side of the base of the skull. The pain had
ceased some days before he consulted me, but the ear
was still discharging very freely. Neither swelling nor
tenderness was found in the mastoid region, and the
scar was normal. He was pale and thin, but said that
he felt well. His skin had a peculiar yellowish tint.
He was admitted to the hospital and remained there
until he died.

The morning temperature, April 18th, was 98.5°.
During that forenoon the boy had a prolonged chill, and
in the afternoon his temperature had risen to 103.5°.
The morning temperature on the 19th was 98.5°; the
evening temperature was 102.5°. On the 20th, the morning temperature was 98.5°; the evening temperature was
100.5°. On the 21st the temperature in the morning
was 104°. I opened the mastoid cells, but did not find
much excepting eburnated bone. I did not trephine the
skull, because my patient's condition was very unfavorable.

During the evening of the 21st he complained, for
the first time, of very severe pain in the middle of his
forehead. On the morning of the 22d, his mind being
perfectly clear, he assured me that he was feeling very
well. The otorrhœa had already diminished. His temperature was 99°. His pulse was irregular in rhythm
and also in force. The variability in the strength of his
pulse was sufficiently marked to attract immediate attention. The evening temperature was 102.5°. During the
evening he had a second attack of pain in the middle
of his forehead. On the 23d the morning temperature
was 99.5°; the evening temperature was 100.5°. On the
24th the morning temperature was 99.5°.

About 4 P. M., April 24th, I saw him alive for the
last time. The otorrhœa had ceased. The wound showed
no signs of repair. The boy was irritable for the first
time, and wished me to let him sleep in peace. He was
passing into a state of stupor. Still, he was easily
aroused and replied rationally without hesitation to my
questions. He was able to sit up in bed without help.

I examined him with great care at this visit, as I had done at all preceding visits, for motor and sensory symptoms, and, as before, the result was negative. With the ophthalmoscope I found that the media were clear and the fundus normal in each eye. His pulse was irregular in rhythm and in force, and its strength was failing steadily. In the evening he had a short attack of pain in his forehead. About three o'clock in the morning of the 25th he was found dead in his bed.

At the autopsy, which was made by Dr. H. C. Tinkham, professor of anatomy in the University of Vermont, we found a purulent pachymeningitis over the posterior surface of the petrous portion of the left temporal bone, extending from near the internal auditory meatus to the sigmoid groove, which it invaded. The bone under this area of inflammation was carious. The sigmoid sinus was empty. Numerous small openings into the sinus were found, through which pus might have entered the blood stream. The cerebellum, where it was in contact with the area of pachymeningitis, was discolored and softened, and, adjacent to the sigmoid sinus, it was necrotic. Continuous with this necrosed cortex of the cerebellum was a large abscess cavity full of foul-smelling pus. The boundaries of the abscess consisted of softened and necrosed cortex. *The entire white matter of the left hemisphere of the cerebellum had broken down into an abscess.** The remainder of the cortex and the membranes covering the cerebellum, excepting the area of pachymeningitis already described, were perfectly normal in appearance. About an inch behind the superior extremity of the left fissure of Rolando a very small fibrous nodule was found in the pia mater. In other respects the cerebrum and its membranes were normal. Further examination of the body was forbidden.

The pain at the base of the brain and in the left mastoid region, which had ceased before the boy was brought to me the third time, the three attacks of pain in the middle of the forehead, the irritability and tendency to stupor, which I observed on the last afternoon of his life, were the only symptoms referable to his nervous system that this patient ever had. His intelligence was normal, *he was not troubled with vertigo,* and he showed no paralysis of motion or sensation, not even paresis, at any time, although I examined him repeatedly with great attention. It is somewhat singular that I

---

* Macroscopic appearance. No microscopic examination was made.

did not find even a slight change in his eyes, but I am
certain that there was not the faintest tendency to optic
neuritis, or to paresis of any of the ocular muscles.

The abscess was complicated by pyæmia, I think.
The temperature range, which in uncomplicated cases of
abscess of the brain seldom rises above 100°, and the
jaundiced skin were, however, the only symptoms indicating it.   Further evidence might have been found,
perhaps, if we could have made a more complete autopsy.

My first operation upon this boy was apparently
thorough enough, if one considers only the immediate
results.   In similar cases I had effected a permanent
cure by far less radical measures.   However, the relapse,
although occurring fourteen months after the operation,
was due to the fact that a focus of germ life had not
been removed from the ear.   Observation of the course
of this case, and that of other fortunately not fatal cases,
has convinced me that inflammation in the mastoid
division of the middle ear should be treated in the most
radical way.   The disease must be pursued to its farthest
ramifications and thoroughly eradicated, *if possible.*
Many cases of chronic suppurative otitis, in which, *apparently,* the mastoid has not been invaded, should be
submitted to the same treatment.   By bringing these
two sets of cases under such radical management, the
possibility of the occurrence of otitic abscess in the brain
will be materially diminished.

Since the date of my last operation upon this case
I have regretted that I did not search the cranial cavity.
If I were to be confronted with similar conditions again,
I would risk the chances of the operation; possibly, because we are able to control shock much more surely
now than we were then—a circumstance of considerable
importance in cerebral surgery.   Exploratory operations
upon the brain, if the wounds do not become infected,
are not harmful, even though the result be negative.   It
seems to me, therefore, that it is imperative in all cases
where cerebral abscess is suspected to search the brain
for it, provided that the patient may probably endure
the shock of the operation.

Dr. EDWARD D. FISHER, referring to the case of cerebellar abscess, said that the localizing value of occipital or frontal headache was not great. A lesion in the cerebellum very frequently expressed itself by pain in the forehead. Whether or not the gait was staggering depended somewhat upon the actual destruction in the cerebellum. It was not exceptional to find lesions in the cerebellum, such as hæmorrhage, in cases in which the diagnosis could not be made out by the symptoms. Naturally, one would not look for sensory disturbances, and paresis or paralysis would not be expected, except that form, associated with considerable incoordination, occasionally found on the same side as the lesion. The cases just reported were very interesting, as showing how destructive a lesion might be without any distinguishing symptoms.

Dr. C. L. DANA said that he had always found in cases of cerebral disease (*e. g.*, tumor, abscess, or sclerotic disease), if the tract going from the labyrinth to the cerebellum were injured, there would be some disturbance of equilibrium. It was possible in the case reported that this symptom might have been present and not observed. In a case of gummy tumor that he had recently seen, he had noticed that when the patient was nearly well the staggering movements had disappeared, and that the only evidence of cerebellar disease had been brought out by making the patient close his eyes and endeavor to walk straight; he invariably walked toward one side—the same side toward which he would fall when the lesion was more marked. That this had not been observed in the case under discussion might be because the abscess had been in the upper part of the hemisphere, and had not involved this tract, or the fibres had been actually destroyed by softening so that there was no irritation, as from active inflammation. A symptom of cerebellar disease which had been noted very often was loss of the knee-jerks, although it was by no means constant. The presence of an old abscess in the brain without any particular symptoms was not very rare. He had had a patient at Bellevue Hospital who had gone around and attended to the work of the ward, and had shown no symptoms except occasional staggering and vertigo. He had died quite suddenly, and the autopsy had revealed rupture of a blood-vessel into an old brain abscess. It was known that lesions of the hemispheres of the cerebellum did not necessarily cause any symptoms.

Dr. H. V. WILDMAN recalled having seen at one time, with Dr. Starr, a case that had been under his observation for two years. The diagnosis had been tumor of the anterior lobes of the brain. The patient had afterward become insane, and had died in the Pavilion for Insane, Bellevue Hospital. The autopsy had disclosed a tumor on the superior portion of the cerebellum. The diagnosis of cerebellar tumor had not been made, simply because of the absence of staggering. There had been constant and severe headache but no incoordination. The tumor had been of about the size of a walnut.

Dr. WOODWARD said that the boy, whose case he had reported, had been going about the ward in spite of chill and fever until the operation, and there had been incoordination, but not afterward. There had been pain in the mastoid region before his admission. The irritability and stupor had appeared to be due to failing strength. He had been wonderfully clear mentally until the last afternoon of his life.

Paper.

RADICAL CURE OF FEMORAL HERNIA, WITH PERSONAL EXPERIENCE OF THE INGUINAL METHOD.

BY HENRY MANN SILVER, M. D.

THE surgeon who is interested in the operative treatment for the radical cure of hernia, and who may have occasion to look up the literature of the subject, will be astonished to find, first, such an enormous number of papers on hernia, and second, that such a very small number treat of the femoral variety.

Although surgeons had been working for some years on the treatment of inguinal hernia for radical cure, it was not until 1890 that they really began to devote any attention to the radical cure of the femoral variety. Quite recently gynæcologists have turned their attention to this subject, as a considerable number of their patients suffering from retrodisplacements of the uterus also suffer from femoral hernia, a condition much more frequent in women between eighteen and forty than in men. I was very much surprised, in looking over Coley's (9) statistics, to note that six of the twenty-five patients operated on for femoral hernia were under ten years of age.

Before giving my own experience it will be interesting to study the work of others, classifying it under the head of that thought which dominates their treatment in securing a radical cure.

I. Methods which deal with the sac alone: Socin (45), Mitchell Banks (2), and my own cases.

II. Methods which have in view the closure or obliteration of the internal ring and canal by relaxing Poupart's ligament: Fabricius (18), Fowler (19), Delagénière (14).

III. Methods which have in view the restoration of the femoral canal to its normal relations: Bassini (3), Raffa (38), Deneffe (16), Coley (9), and many who follow Bassini.

IV. Methods which make an attempt to close the rings or canal with some substance that will plug the canal or act as a barrier at the internal or external ring: Salzer (40), Watson Cheyne (8), Moullin (31), Schwarz (42), Poullet (37), Trendelenburg (49), Hackenbruch (20), Körte (25), and Wolff (52).

Before speaking of the different operations for radical cure of femoral hernia, a short review of the various methods of managing the sac used by the most prominent surgeons will be of interest. Haidenthaler (21) states that if the sac was no larger than a hen's egg, the chance for radical cure was three to one; if larger than a hen's egg, the chance of a relapse was two to one.

According to Macewen (29), McBurney (28), Fowler (19), De Garmo (54), Braisted (5), and others, the ideal management of the sac has in view the restoration of the peritoneal cavity to its normal size and shape, in order that pressure of the abdominal contents may be evenly distributed over every part of the peritoneal surface, and not at a single point. Braisted states the case clearly as follows: "We must remove the tissue forming the wedge itself—that is, the infundibulum sac—which, if left behind, either after being returned to the abdominal cavity or left as a plug in the femoral

canal, results in the one case in destroying the normal
symmetry of the peritoneal surface, and in the other
prevents the walls of the crural canal from coming in
direct apposition," and really aids in the formation
of a new hernia. To meet the above indications, Berger (6), O'Hara (32), Delagénière (14), Deldalle
(15), Deneffe (16), and Lockwood (27) ligate the sac
high up and suture the stump to the abdominal wall
above Poupart's ligament.

Kocher (24) twists the sac while still in the canal,
then passes it through an opening in the abdominal
wall, and fastens it to Poupart's ligament, but more recently he carries it outward toward the anterior superior
spine of the ilium and fastens it to the aponeurosis.

Greig Smith (43) twists the sac and sutures it just
above Poupart's ligament, or directly above the ring.
Bassini twists sac, ligates high up, cuts it off, and returns it within the abdomen.

Macewen (29), Lauenstein (26), and Kellogg (23)
fold the sac into a pad, and stitch it against the opening of the femoral canal. Moullin (31) places it just
above the ring.

Fabricius (18), Banks (2), Coley (9), and the
larger majority of operators ligate the sac high up and
return the stump to the abdominal cavity. Recognizing
the fact that high ligation of the sac does not completely
meet the indication, as a little dimple is formed, the
apex of which presents in or at the femoral ring, and
which may, under pressure, enlarge into the infundibulum mentioned above, Fowler (19) and Stinson (44)
cut away the sac entirely, the edges of the peritonæum
being brought together in such a manner that when sutured a smooth surface will be presented.

In order to accomplish the same result with the
addition of a buttress, Davis (13) and A. M. Phelps (34)
pass purse-string sutures around the neck of the sac
where it joins the peritonæum, invert the sac, and
tighten the suture. Davis, in order to strengthen that
part where the ligature was tied, draws down on a catgut
ligature previously placed and thus folds the sac on

itself in a mushroomlike form on the interior of the peritoneal cavity.

I. *Methods which Deal with the Sac Alone.*—Socin (45), 1879, really began the radical operation. He believed that the sole cause of relapse of a femoral hernia was to be found in the omental fat, which was generally adherent. If this plug of fat was removed by excision the hernial opening would close spontaneously. As a contributory cause for relapse, he reckoned the loose tissue which was allowed to remain in the femoral canal, helping to keep up its patency. His operation deals with the sac alone, which is isolated, drawn strongly outward, ligated, resected, and replaced within the abdomen, and clears the femoral canal of all *débris*.

Mitchell Banks (2) isolates the sac, ligates the neck high up, resects it, and cuts it away, making no attempt to close the canal.

I have four cases to report later, treated by rolling the sac from above Poupart's ligament, and suturing the rolled sac over the femoral ring.

II. *Methods which have in View the Closure or Obliteration of the Internal Ring and Canal by relaxing Poupart's Ligament. Operation of Fabricius* (18).— He first exposes Poupart's ligament, then the femoral canal by separating the superficial layer of the fascia lata at its insertion into Poupart's ligament. The femoral vessels are pushed beyond the ileo-pectineal eminence and held there with a blunt hook while the first stitch is taken to unite the ligaments of Cooper and Poupart from a point opposite the femoral vessels up to the spine of the pubes. The suture, threaded in a strongly curved needle, is passed first through the pectineal fascia, through the muscular fibres and periosteum to the bone, and then transfixes Poupart's ligament. Five or six sutures are required in all. In order to attach Poupart's ligament as closely to the bone as possible without tension, he nicks the edge of the lesser falciform process and even the ligament at its insertion to the spine of the pubes. The loosened superficial layer of the fascia lata is then sutured to the deep layer and the wound closed.

9

This operation fulfills what Fabricius thinks are the necessities for a true radical operation—viz., first, to do away with the funnel-shaped space; and, second, to attach as closely as possible Poupart's ligament to the horizontal ramus of the pubic bone. At the suggestion of Weinlechner (51), and to avoid a possible inguinal hernia, the external abdominal ring in males was narrowed by the insertion of two or three sutures, and completely closed in females. Fowler (19), in a recent article on the radical cure of femoral hernia, in which he advocates the method of Fabricius (18), goes farther and completely separates Poupart's ligament from the spine of the pubes and then the superficial layer of the fascia lata from it. He passes the sutures through the aponeurosis of the external oblique muscle about three eighths of an inch from its edge, so as to secure a good hold, then through the periosteum at the point of origin of the pectineus muscle, emerging about half an inch from the point of entrance upon the upper margin of the bone. Five or six sutures are placed, the suture material being kangaroo tendon.

Delagénière (14), in an interesting article, described an operation devised by him which carries out this same idea—viz., obliteration of the femoral ring and canal by relaxing Poupart's ligament. Through a vertical incision directly over the femoral canal Poupart's ligament is exposed and divided midway between the pubic spine and femoral vein. The vein being drawn to the outside, two or three strong catgut sutures are passed from before backward through the aponeurosis of the pectineus and the periosteum over the ileopectineal line. The posterior part of each suture is passed through Poupart's ligament near the point of division, some from the front, some from the back part of the ligament. As the ligatures are tightened the divided ligament is drawn down to the horizontal ramus of the pubes, transforming in this way the vertical incision into a triangular one, with the apex at the upper part and anteriorly. The triangular space is closed progressively by strong cicatricial tissue. After reconstructing the crural canal with catgut the external wound is closed. He reports three operations with complete success.

Method III. Those Operations which have in View the Restoration of the Femoral Canal to its Normal Relations.—Bassini (3) lays great stress upon the necessity for the surgeon to restore the original anatomical relations of the parts to be operated on, and proceeds as follows: With a strongly curved needle of medium size, and with a firm thread, three sutures are placed which draw together the lower posterior part of Poupart's ligament and the pectineal aponeurosis at the level of the pectineal crest. The sutures are close together and extend outward from the pubic spine. The first stitch is passed through the inner and posterior part of Poupart's ligament, then through the pectineal aponeurosis high up. Then half a centimetre externally the second suture is placed, and similarly the third and last. This one remains about a centimetre removed from the vein. These sutures are not yet tied, but three or four more are introduced to embrace the falciform process above and the pectineal fascia below, the lower suture entering just above the saphenous vein. The sutures are now tightened, beginning with the one introduced first. He reports fifty-four successful operations in fifty-one subjects; forty-one remained cured from two to three years, and twenty-seven from three to nine years. Trusses not worn, even at hard labor.

Coley (9) reports ten cases of operation by this method; no relapses.

Bassini (3) has many followers with his method.

Cabot (7), in order to prevent tension and cutting of stitches, which he thinks is a weak point in this operation, makes a semicircular incision through the fascia lata just beneath the saphenous opening, the vein having previously been cut away. The lower wall of the canal is now readily attached to Poupart's ligament. One case, no return after a year. Billroth (4), Czerny (12), and Schede (41) suture the middle third of Poupart's ligament to the adductor fascia. Wood (53), Berger (6), Deldalle (15), Piechaud (35), Raffa (38), and Thibaudet (47) attach Poupart's ligament to the pectineus muscle and fascia.

Marcy (30) closes the external part of the canal with a loop stitch of kangaroo tendon.

Coley (9) has had success with the purse-string suture suggested by H. W. Cushing (11), of Boston. He introduces the suture as follows: A curved Hagedorn needle threaded with kangaroo tendon is passed through Poupart's ligament; then, going down the pectineal fascia, some of the muscular fibres are picked up; the needle, being brought out, takes a second or third hold in the same tissue (forming floor of canal); then the needle is carried through the fascia overlying the femoral vein, and finally comes out through Poupart's ligament a quarter to half an inch to outer side of point of entrance. On tying this suture the floor of the canal is brought up against the roof and the opening is obliterated.

IV. Methods which make an attempt to Close the Rings or Canal with some Substance that will Plug the Canal or act as a Barrier at the Internal or External Ring.—1. Salzer (40), in one case, used sterilized glass wool to block up the femoral canal; he abandoned this for a flap of pectineal fascia stitched with silk to the middle of Poupart's ligament. Two cases reported.

2. Watson Cheyne (8) plugs the crural canal with a flap of pectineus fascia and muscle, being held in place with stitches passed through canal and abdominal wall just above Poupart's ligament and tied without tension. Two cases, results perfect some months after. Stoneham (46) performs same operation. Reports four cases, three being perfect cures.

3. Moullin (31) uses a flap taken from the pectineus and adductor longus for the same purpose, holding it in place with two silk ligatures passed from before backward through the periosteum covering the pectineal surface of the pubic bone behind and Poupart's ligament in front, and traversing the flap so as to hold it in its place. Results: Five cases showed no sign of yielding after eighteen months; eight others doing well, but eighteen months had not elapsed.

4. Schwarz (42) placed a flap of the adductor longus muscle in front of the femoral ring, holding it to the crural arch and pectineal aponeurosis with silk sutures.

5. Poullet (37) uses a portion of the tendon of either the rectus femoris or adductor longus muscles, holding it in place with silver-wire sutures, which are removed in a few days. It would seem as if these barriers were placed at the wrong end of the canal to prove efficient and lasting.

6. Trendelenburg (49), Hackenbruch (20), Körte (25), and Wolff (52) do an osteoplastic operation. A long oblique incision opens up the hernial region. Portions of the recti, gracilis, and adductor magnus muscles are divided, and the anterior surface of the pubes cleaned. Then with a broad chisel a piece of bone is removed from the anterior surface of the pubes and symphysis. The segment made up of bone, cartilage, and periosteum, about two centimetres in breadth and several millimetres in thickness, is pried up, turned backward, so that its cut surface is in front and the periosteum behind, and fitted into the femoral canal, its upper extremity being placed behind Poupart's ligament and fastened with catgut. Free drainage provided. Five cases reported, three successful.

7. Thiriar (48), of Brussels, places a disc of decalcified bone against the femoral ring within, the disc being larger than the ring, the soft tissues being sutured to it. He claims that the disc is replaced little by little with a fibrous, thick, solid tissue, which will become adherent to the surrounding tissue, closing completely the hernial orifice.

In 1887 I operated on my first case of femoral hernia. It was a small, irreducible entero-epiplocele. The sac was exposed by a vertical incision, opened, and the contents returned after the adhesions were divided. The sac was ligated well up in the canal, cut away, and the superficial wound closed. The wound healed without suppuration. I was very much disappointed on examining the patient a year after operation to find that the hernia had returned. A second operation was refused.

At this time the radical cure of hernia, especially the inguinal variety, was beginning to occupy the attention of surgeons, when the able and remarkably clear paper of Macewen (29) on the management of the sac and closure of the inguinal canal appeared and seemed to give a new impetus to the subject. A careful examination of the tables given shows that the sac in femoral hernia was managed on the same principles as in the inguinal variety.

My second case, three years after, was a strangulated femoral hernia, the sac containing a small knuckle of intestine, with a considerable amount of adherent omentum. The constriction at Gimbernat's ligament was relieved, the knuckle of intestine drawn down with difficulty, inspected, and, as it seemed to be in good condition, was returned, the strangulation having been present but a short time. The neck of the sac was ligated high up, excised, and the external wound closed. Unfortunately, the patient developed peritonitis and died. A careful review of the technique of the operation impressed me that the cause of the failure was due to imperfect examination of the constricted intestine.

. After reading Macewen's article on the radical cure of inguinal hernia, and while giving the courses on operative surgery at the Woman's Medical College of the New York Infirmary, I was deeply impressed with the ease with which the femoral ring could be exposed while applying a ligature to the external iliac artery. The thought occurred to me, Why not open the neck of the sac above Poupart's ligament, withdraw the intestine, make a careful inspection, meet the indications for treatment, and, after returning the intestine and omentum, make a pad of the sac and suture it against the abdominal aspect of the femoral ring, *à la* Macewen?

After the death of my second patient I did not see another case of femoral hernia, with one exception, for six years, although actively engaged in emergency hospital practice. Then four followed within a year.

CASE I.—Mrs. D., aged forty-two years; married; mother of one child. Had a swelling in left groin for thirteen years, which gave but little trouble until a month ago, when it became strangulated and was replaced with difficulty. Before this it could, as a rule, be replaced with ease, but would return with any great exertion. Examination revealed an entero-epiplocele as large as a hen's egg in the left groin. On March 27, 1896, the following operation was performed: The usual incision, four inches in length, for ligating the external iliac artery was made half an inch above Poupart's ligament, but carried a little nearer the spine of the pubes than usual. The aponeurosis of the external oblique muscle was opened, the inner fibres of the internal oblique were cut, the underlying transversalis fascia divided, and the vessels and femoral ring easily reached. The deep epigastric vessels were drawn to the outer side. The neck of the sac was isolated and seized with the left hand, which made gentle traction, while the fingers of the right manipulated the sac at or just within the femoral opening; it was soon loosened and drawn out of the canal. The sac was opened, a small quantity of omentum reduced, and the opening closed with a fine catgut. The fundus was then grasped gently with a clamp and the sac was rolled like a scroll, longitudinally, in order to avoid traction on the bladder, until it pressed against the peritonæum. As the clamp was withdrawn a suture of catgut was passed through the folds of the roll and tied, in order to prevent the scroll from unrolling. Three sutures of chromic catgut were then passed through Poupart's ligament above and Cooper's ligament below, then through the rolled sac; when these sutures were tightened the mass was brought down over the internal femoral ring, no attempt being made to close the tendinous structures of the ring. The divided fibres of the internal oblique muscle were carefully united with silver sutures, the aponeurosis of the external oblique with chromic catgut, the skin with subcutaneous suture. No drainage. For three or four days after the operation the patient was very hysterical and restless, a condition quickly relieved by hypodermic injections of sterilized water. During this time it was necessary to use the catheter to empty the bladder. She complained of no pain about the wound, which was found to be perfectly healed when the dressings were removed ten days after operation. Remained in bed three weeks.

Result: Have been unable to trace this case.

CASE II.—M. B., aged thirty-five years; married; mother of nine children; suffered much from prolapsus uteri, also from pain in left side, especially when lifting heavy weights.

Examination revealed a small, firm, irreducible mass just below and to the outside of the spine of the left pubic bone. Operation, July 9, 1896. An incision four inches long and parallel to Poupart's ligament exposed the aponeurosis of the external oblique, which was opened the length of the inguinal canal.

The round ligament was drawn to one side, the floor of the canal opened, and the deep epigastric vessels drawn to the outside. The technique of the remainder of the operation was the same as in Case I. No drainage.

On the fourth day after operation patient complained of some pain in wound, also in bladder during micturition. Ice bag placed over site of wound. On the ninth day the dressings were removed for the first time and the wound was perfectly healed, but the distress in the bladder continued for two weeks more, when it disappeared. Patient remained in bed three weeks.

Result: No return of hernia twenty months after operation.

CASE III.—A. L., aged forty-one years; married; mother of sixteen children.

On December 7, 1896, I was called in consultation by my friend, Dr. Francis Huber, to see this patient at her home. She was suffering severe pain in her right groin, where there was a hard, tender swelling about the size of a lemon. There was no impulse on coughing, and the swelling could not be reduced. Bowels constipated, but have moved daily with enemata. There was no tympanites or abdominal tenderness. The swelling had not been noticed until the pain began three days before. A diagnosis of femoral epiplocele, somewhat constricted, was made, and I advised removal of the patient to the infirmary for operation, she seeming to suffer not from strangulation, but sepsis. Patient was operated on December 9th, a vertical incision being made over the swelling. When this was reached and isolated it was found to be a mass of softened, greenish, congested properitoneal fat, protruding from the femoral canal. After a thorough washing with hydrogen peroxide, an incision was made above and parallel to Poupart's ligament, the neck of the sac exposed, opened, and its contents proved to be a hard and congested appendix epiploon; this was ligated and removed. The fatty tissue about the sac without the canal was removed, and the

sac was isolated with some difficulty from the canal.
The bladder was adherent to the neck of the sac, and
separated by careful dissection without injury. The
sac and upper wound were treated as mentioned above,
the lower wound was packed with iodoform gauze.
Dressings changed on third day: upper wound perfect,
dressings in lower wound stained with blood; cavity
washed out with hydrogen peroxide and repacked. For
the next three days patient's temperature steadily rose,
pulse grew weaker, and she had a drowsy, septic look,
with red, dry tongue. Dressings removed on eighth
day. All sutures removed from upper wound and its
edges separated down to the aponeurosis of the external
oblique muscle. There was no suppuration or discharge,
but the fat presented a grayish look with a few small
grayish sloughs in depth of wound. The lowest deep
suture was removed, and a strip of gauze carried down
to drain the deeper tissues. Both wounds were packed
with iodoform gauze. Patient's general condition improved at once, and after frequent dressings and a slow
convalescence she returned home a month afterward
with wounds just about closed.

Result: Hernia remained perfectly cured fifteen
months after.

CASE IV.—A. W., aged thirty-five years; married;
mother of six children, the oldest being eight. Admitted to the New York Infirmary February 22, 1897.
About two months after last confinement, nearly two
years ago, a small lump, the size of a marble, appeared
in the left groin. This continued to increase in size
slowly and always gave some pain, but no constipation.
It seemed a little smaller in the morning. Three weeks
before admission, while carrying a pail of water, she
slipped, giving herself a severe strain; immediately the
swelling in groin became as large as a hen's egg and she
was seized with cramplike pains, beginning in the groin
and radiating to the umbilicus, then over whole abdomen. After suffering agonizing pain for five hours
the hernia was reduced by a physician, giving instant
relief.

Examination after admission to the hospital revealed
a reducible entero-epiplocele. Glands in groin somewhat
enlarged. Patient was operated on February 23d, with
the same technique as in previous operation, excepting
that catgut sutures instead of silver wire were used.
Just a word about the sac, which, after gentle but prolonged traction, was drawn from the ring surrounded

by a considerable amount of properitoneal fat. The sac
was found to end in two blind pouches, the neck of the
smaller one being more constricted, with vessels engorged. In both, the serous lining was smooth and glistening. Patient's convalescence was rapid, and after remaining in bed three weeks she was discharged from
the hospital.

Result: No return after a year.

Three of the patients were operated on by me in the
New York Infirmary, and I was fortunate in having the
assistance of Dr. Gertrude B. Kelly, the visiting surgeon; the fourth was operated on by Dr. Kelly with my
assistance. In reviewing the histories of these cases, it
will be seen that after the first case the incision for
ligating the external iliac artery was abandoned, as it
seemed to weaken the abdominal wall unnecessarily by
dividing the fibres of the internal oblique muscle. In
two of the cases the bladder was found adherent to the
neck of the sac and was separated only after a careful
dissection, without injury to the bladder. Pouchet (36)
mentions a similar case, but the bladder was opened,
then sutured with silk. A month after she was discharged she returned with a vesical calculus; on its surface was a piece of silk. Other cases are mentioned by
B. Farquhar Curtis (10) in his exhaustive article on
injuries to the bladder during operations for hernia.
In isolating and withdrawing the sac from the canal
great care was taken not to strip off its covering of
fascia and vessels; these were allowed to remain to provide nourishment and prevent atrophy of the sac. It was
loosely rolled, in order not to interfere with its circulation, and for the same reason no ligature was placed
around its neck. No ill effects resulted from the closure
of the wounds without drainage, except in Case III; here
the trouble was due to too tight suturing of fatty tissue; just as soon as the sutures were removed and the
fatty walls separated there was no further trouble. I
always regretted removing the lower deep suture, as it
was unnecessary, and had the wound been septic it
would have infected the deeper tissues. Great care was

taken in closing the wound: the floor of the inguinal
canal was sutured, the canal itself was reconstructed by
Bassini's method, in order to avoid weakening of the
canal and formation of an inguinal hernia at some
future time. Too much stress can not be laid on this
point. The ease with which the sac and its contents
could be inspected and treated,* and the simple manner
by which the internal opening and upper part of the
femoral canal could be reached and treated, impressed me
greatly.

The results in the four cases mentioned uphold, as
far as any cases can that have been operated a year or
two, the views of Socin (44) and others. As yet this
method of operating has not received a large amount of
attention.

Annandale (1), in 1876, was the first to mention
this method, speaking of the originality in his operation as being the situation and direction of the incision,
it being one which gives free access to the neck of the
sac close to the general peritonæum. His first case was
one of inguinal and femoral hernia on same side; he
tried to cure the femoral variety by suturing the sac
of the inguinal in the femoral canal; the femoral relapsed. The disadvantages of doing this have already
been mentioned, and Annandale himself speaks strongly
against it.

Tuffier (50) carries out the ideas of Ruggi (39) and
Parlevecchio (33), but in a simplified manner. He
opens the floor of the inguinal canal, ligates sac, and
sutures the crural ring by uniting the aponeurosis of the
pectineus muscle to Poupart's ligament in the middle of
the superior part of the crural ring.

Cushing (11), in one case, being unable to separate
the sac by the usual incision, reached the neck of the
sac through an incision in the inguinal region without
difficulty, folded the sac on itself, and fixed it within
the abdomen, closing the femoral canal with purse-string
suture, inclosing pectineal fascia and Poupart's liga-

---

* Keen (22), Cushing (11), and Lockwood's (27) cases.

ment, with closure of the saphenous opening *à la* Macewen.

Edebohls (17), in an able review of the inguinal method for radical cure of femoral hernia, gives his personal experience with four cases, a relapse taking place in one case after six months. This patient was unmanageable, removed the dressings, and infected the wound, with consequent suppuration.

His conclusions are: The classical operation from below Poupart's ligament should be the operation of choice for femoral hernia, the inguinal operation being performed upon special indications—the special indications being (1) the coexistence of complete or incomplete inguinal hernia, with femoral hernia of same side; (2) in women, the coexistence with femoral hernia of a retrodisplacement of the uterus, which can be corrected by shortening the round ligaments. The histories of the four cases given constitute my experience with the inguinal method of treating femoral hernia.

I do not wish to be understood as advocating the radical cure of this variety of hernia by treatment of the sac alone; to it I would add some method, preferably Bassini's, only the sutures, three in number, being placed on the abdominal side of the internal opening of the femoral canal, and the rolled sac sutured to the closed opening. If the sac is large, the neck can be exposed above Poupart's ligament, opened, and contents returned if the intestine is not adherent, the omentum being ligated and divided. The internal ring and stump of sac are now treated as just mentioned, the sac and omentum being removed through an incision made below the ligament, or allowed to remain and gradually contract.

General Conclusions.—I. That it is not wise to attempt to obtain a radical cure of femoral hernia by treatment of the sac alone.

II. That the methods which have in view the closure or obliteration of the internal femoral ring and canal by relaxing Poupart's ligament are open to the serious objection of relaxing the tissues about the external abdominal ring, and thus possibly aiding in the formation of an inguinal hernia.

III. That those methods which have in view the restoration of the femoral canal to its normal relations are near approaches to the ideal method, but fail in that they act upon the wrong end of the canal and do not absolutely obliterate the depression at the internal ring.

IV. That the use of foreign bodies, osteoplastic flaps, and sections of neighboring fascia and muscles to plug the femoral canal renders the operation much more serious, and is open to the same objection as given above, while the results show no advantages over simpler methods.

Conclusions on the Inguinal Method.—I. That in all cases of suspected or small femoral hernia the ring, sac, and contents should be examined and treated from above Poupart's ligament, as it adds to the safety, ease, and celerity with which the case can be handled.

II. That by so doing only are the indications for permanent and complete radical cure met—viz., the high treatment of the sac, and closure of the canal at its highest point, the internal ring.

III. That in case an inguinal hernia is present on the same side, or a retrodisplacement of the uterus, amenable to relief by shortening the round ligaments, exists, the treatment is greatly simplified by performing two operations through one incision.

NOTE.—Since this paper was read I have had an additional experience with three cases, in two of which the intestine was strangulated.

CASE I.—H. S., aged thirty-four years; single. Mother died of strangulated hernia. About six months before the operation the patient accidentally discovered a swelling of about the size of a walnut in the right groin. Remembering the cause of her mother's death, she sought surgical aid. She was operated on April 12, 1898, in the New York Infirmary, by Dr. Kelly, with my assistance. The usual incision above Poupart's ligament was made, the inguinal canal opened, and the neck of the sac exposed, and, as it was impossible to separate the sac, it was opened, a small quantity of omentum reduced, and then was cut off within the canal and the abdominal end closed. Two sutures were then passed through Poupart's ligament and the pectineal fascia and periosteum and tightened. The sac was then rolled and sutured to the closed ring, the wound being closed as usual. It was noticed that the obturator artery arose from the deep epigastric artery, passing in front of and to the inner side of the femoral ring. The convalescence was uneventful; the dressings were removed on the ninth day, and the wound was completely healed. The patient was kept in bed for three weeks, and was discharged on the twenty-sixth day.

CASE II.—W. O., aged forty years; iron worker. On the 17th of April, 1898, I was called by my friend Dr. S. P. Leveridge to see this case. Three years ago the patient first noticed a swelling in the right groin, which was easily reduced and never caused any pain or inconvenience. The day before I saw him he was seized with severe pain in the vicinity of the swelling, which quickly became colicky, spreading over the abdomen, and accompanied with obstinate constipation, retention of urine, and frequent vomiting. When I examined the patient there was tenderness on pressure over the lower part of the abdomen, with constant vomiting of a dark fluid with a fæcal odor and a very weak pulse. I advised an operation, which was accepted by the patient, and he was at once removed to Gouverneur Hospital.

The neck of the sac was exposed by the usual incision, opened, and the loop of the small intestine entering the femoral ring easily discovered by its congested appearance. Considerable turbid serum escaped when the neck of the sac was opened. As it was impossible to reduce the prolapsed intestine with ordinary traction from above, a vertical incision over the tumor was made below Poupart's ligament. A considerable quantity of properitoneal fat covered the sac, which, when opened, contained a dark fluid, clotted blood, and four inches of intestine. The sac was washed out with hydrogen peroxide, the contents of the intestine were returned, and the intestine itself was pushed through the femoral ring with gentle manipulation without difficulty, gauze sponges having been placed about the opening within the abdomen. The intestine was deeply congested, but under the influence of warm towels the circulation was soon reestablished. The properitoneal fat and sac were cut off below Poupart's ligament. The stump of the sac was drawn within the abdomen, closed, rolled, and sutured against the internal femoral ring. The upper wound was completely closed, the lower wound partly closed and packed with iodoform gauze. The stomach was washed out before the patient left the operating table. The patient's convalescence was without interest; the wounds healed rapidly and he was discharged from the hospital three weeks after the operation. Immediately after he returned home a small deep fistula formed in the upper cicatrix and discharged a few drops of pus for about three weeks, when it closed. This I think was due to imperfectly sterilized chromicized catgut.

CASE III.—M. L., aged forty-three, widow, laundress. Admitted to the New York Infirmary, June 20, 1898. Three days before she had been suddenly seized with severe colicky pain in the abdomen, which was soon followed by persistent vomiting. On her admission a tumor of the size of a large walnut was found in the right groin, and the patient was vomiting a yellowish-colored fluid with a strong fæcal odor. With the assistance of Dr. Kelly and Dr. Wakefield, I exposed and opened the neck of the sac above Poupart's ligament. An opening into the sac was also made below the ligament; it contained an inch and a half of gangrenous intestine, the mesentery not having entered the ring. The sac and intestine were washed with hydrogen peroxide and the intestine was returned by very gentle manipulation, the peritonæum having been protected with sponges placed within the abdomen. With all the care taken there was a slight perforation of the intestine. Three inches of the intestine were resected and a Murphy button was inserted. The internal femoral ring was closed with three sutures and the rolled sac was sutured against it. The upper wound was closed as usual; one half of the lower wound was closed and the remainder packed with iodoform gauze. The patient's convalescence for the first few days was uneventful, her nourishment consisting of broth and white of egg. On the fifth day the dressings were changed; the upper wound was found to be completely closed and the lower wound was repacked. After a week had passed, the patient began to complain of pain in the upper wound, which on examination looked red at the lower portion. Two days afterward the external wound was opened throughout its entire extent, as a considerable quantity of pus was escaping; two sutures were also removed from the deeper tissues for the same reason, and the wound was cleansed with hydrogen peroxide and packed with iodoform gauze. After this nothing of interest occurred in the history of the case, except that the button was passed twenty-eight days after the operation. I think the cause of the trouble in this case, as in the second one, was imperfectly sterilized chromicized catgut.

The experience gained from these cases forcibly emphasizes the first conclusion under the inguinal method —viz., that in all cases of suspected or small femoral hernia, the ring, the sac, and the contents should be examined and treated from above Poupart's ligament, as it adds to the safety, ease, and celerity with which the case can be handled. It also emphasizes the necessity of using absolutely sterile chromicized catgut.

Bibliography.

1. Annandale. *Edinburgh Medical Journal,* 1876, xxi, p. 1088.

2. Banks, W. M. *British Medical Journal,* 1893, ii, p. 1041.

3. Bassini, E. *Archiv f. klin. Chir.,* 1894, xlvii, p. 1.

4. Billroth. *Ibid.,* 1890, Bd. xl.

5. Braisted, W. C. *Physician and Surgeon,* Ann Arbor, Michigan, 1890, xii, p. 14.

6. Berger. *Bull. et mém. de la Soc. de chir. de Paris,* 1892, N. S., xviii, p. 340.

7. Cabot, A. T. *Boston Medical and Surgical Journal,* 1895, cxxxiii, p. 510.

8. Cheyne, Watson. *Lancet,* London, 1892, ii, p. 1039.

9. Coley, W. B. *Annals of Surgery,* Philadelphia, 1897, xxvi, p. 246.

10. Curtis, B. F. *Ibid.,* 1895, xxi, p. 631.

11. Cushing, H. W. *Boston Medical and Surgical Journal,* 1888, cxix, p. 546.

12. Czerny. *Wiener med. Wochenschrift,* 1877, pp. 21–24.

13. Davis. *Annals of Surgery,* Philadelphia, 1896, xxiii, p. 32.

14. Delagénière. *Ann. de chir. et d'orthop.,* Paris, 1896, ix, p. 133.

15. Deldalle. *Journal de la Soc. méd. de Lille,* 1897, i, p. 502.

16. Deneffe. *Ann. de la Soc. de méd. de Gand,* 1895, lxxiv, p. 156.

17. Edebohls, G. M. *Postgraduate,* New York, 1897, xii, p. 75.

18. Fabricius, J. *Centralblatt für Chirurgie,* 1894, xxi, p. 12.—*Wien. klin. Wochenschrift,* 1895, viii, p. 553.

19. Fowler, G. R. *Brooklyn Medical Journal,* 1897, xi, p. 728.

20. Hackenbruch. *Beiträge zur klin. Chir.* (Bruns), 1893–'94, xi, p. 779.

21. Haidenthaler. *Archiv für klin Chir.,* 1890, Bd. xl.

22. Keen, W. W. *International Medical Magazine,* Philadelphia, 1892, i, p. 25.

23. Kellogg, J. A. *Transactions of the Michigan Medical Society,* Grand Rapids, 1896, xx, p. 246.

24. Kocher, T. *Correspondenzblatt für schweizer Aerzte,* 1892, No. 18.

25. Körte. *Deutsch. med. Wochenschrift,* Leipzig, 1895, xxi, Vereins Beilage, p. 63.

26. Lauenstein. *Archiv für klin. Chir.,* 1890, p. 639.

27. Lockwood, C. B. *Lancet,* London, 1893, ii, p. 1297.

28. McBurney, C. *Medical Record,* New York, 1889, xxxv, p. 312.

29. Macewen, W. *British Medical Journal,* 1887, ii, p. 1263.

30. Marcy, H. O. *Anatomy and Surgical Treatment of Hernia,* New York, p. 405.

31. Moullin, C. W. M. *Lancet,* London, 1896, i, p. 479.

32. O'Hara. *British Medical Journal,* 1892, ii, p. 1279.

33. Parlevecchio. *Riforma medica,* 1893, i, pp. 496 and 507.

34. Phelps, A. M. *Postgraduate,* New York, 1897, xii, p. 267.

35. Piechaud. *Bull. et mem. Soc. de chir. de Paris,* 1894, N. S., xx, p. 92.

36. Pouchet. *Gaz. méd. de Picardi,* Amiens, 1897, xv, p. 252.

37. Poullet. *Atti d. XI. Cong. med. internat., 1894,* Roma, 1895, iv, p. 526.

38. Raffa, A. *Clin. chir.,* Milano, 1897, v, p. 49.

39. Ruggi. *Bull. della Soc. med. di Bologna,* series vii, vol. iii.

40. Salzer, F. *Centralblatt für Chir.,* 1892, No. 33, p. 665.

41. Schede. Volkmann's *Samml. klin. Vorträge,* 1886–'87, No. 360.

42. Schwarz, E. *Ass'n franç. de chir.,* Proc. verb., Paris, 1893, vii, p. 689.

43. Smith, Greig. *Bristol Medico-chirurgical Journal,* 1890, viii, p. 1.

44. Stinson, J. C. *Medical Record,* New York, 1896, i, p. 807.

45. Socin, A. Langenbeck's *Archiv,* 1879, Bd. xxiv.

46. Stoneham, C. *Lancet,* London, 1892, ii, p. 1198.

47. Thibaudet. *Jour. de la Soc. méd. de Lille,* 1890, i, p. 137.

48. Thiriar. *Ass'n franç. de chir.,* Proc. verb., Paris, vii, p. 318.

49. Trendelenburg. *Verhandl. d. deutsch. Gesell. f. Chir.,* 1893, xxii, p. 76.

50. Tuffier. *Rev. de chir.,* Paris, 1896, xvi, p. 241.

51. Weinlechner. *Centralblatt für Chir.,* 1894, xxi, p. 12.

52. Wolff, J. *Deutsche med. Wochenschrift,* 1895, xxi.—*Beiträge zur klin. Chir.* (G. Bruns), 1890–'91, Bd. vii.

53. Wood, John. *British Medical Journal,* London, 1885, i, p. 1280.

54. De Garmo, W. B. *International Clinics,* Philadelphia, 1896, 6 S., ii, p. 43.

Dr. GEORGE M. EDEBOHLS was invited to open the discussion. He said that he was glad that the reader of the paper, in so ably presenting the operative treatment of femoral hernia, had included not only the operation as performed by incision through the inguinal canal, but also the operation as done through any incision above Poupart's ligament large enough and low enough to enable one to reach the crural ring from within the abdomen. The main distinction between the two types of operation for the radical cure of femoral hernia was, that in one we endeavored to reach the crural ring, the objective point of the operation, from above, and in the other from below, Poupart's ligament. The crural ring, as we all knew, was situated immediately behind Poupart's ligament. Personally, he was of the opinion that the operation below Poupart's ligament should be the operation of choice, except under certain special indications. The operation, whether done from above or from below, should have the same object in view: to close as effectually as possible, or to obliterate, the crural ring. To close the external saphenous opening and the crural canal was not sufficient; the crural ring, the opening between Poupart's ligament anteriorly and the horizontal ramus of the pubes posteriorly, the true gateway of a femoral hernia, must be closed. All methods of dealing with the sac were good which obliterated the sac to a point well up above the crural ring.

Regarding the closing of the highest point of the crural canal, the crural ring, he said that the efforts which promised greatest success were those which approximated most thoroughly Poupart's ligament to the structures forming the posterior boundaries of the ring. Fabricius had gone so far as to detach Poupart's ligament from the spine of the pubes, so as to relax it and enable it to be brought firmly against the posterior wall of the crural ring. This method, however, he felt was entirely unnecessary, and even harmful, by weakening the external inguinal ring, whose external pillar was thereby detached. The formation of osteo-periosteal flaps from the anterior surface of the pubes, and their transplantation across the crural opening, as practised by Trendelenburg, was superfluous, and constituted a severe operation involving a tedious convalescence.

In a paper on The Inguinal Operation for Femoral Hernia, published in the *Post-Graduate,* February, 1897, the speaker had detailed his views upon, and his experience with, the operation as done from the abdominal side —*i. e.*, from above Poupart's ligament. In his cases of femoral hernia operated upon from below Poupart's ligament, he had also always made closure of the crural ring the essential of the operation. He had found that the crural ring could be readily exposed from below by the proper use of retractors. When the crural ring was but moderately dilated, its closure was readily effected by a few sutures passed through Poupart's ligament anteriorly and the periosteum covering the horizontal ramus of the pubes posteriorly, and drawn taut. In cases in which the crural ring was very patulous, he had practised incision of the periosteum forming the posterior boundary of the ring, stripping off a narrow periosteal flap from above downward, leaving the flap attached by a base as broad as the full width of the posterior wall of

the ring, and sewing the free edge of the periosteal flap
to Poupart's ligament with forty-day catgut.   He even
felt that the latter procedure—*i. e.*, sewing a small periosteal flap across the ring—could be applied with advantage even in case the crural ring was found but moderately dilated.   In his opinion the periosteal irritation
produced by suturing either the attached periosteum or
the periosteal flap tended to close the crural ring by bone
proliferation, that most effective of all barriers.

As already stated, the classical operation for femoral
hernia from below Poupart's ligament should be the
operation of choice, and should always be performed in
the absence of special indications for operating from
above Poupart's ligament.

The speaker's first inguinal operation for femoral
hernia had been performed in December, 1893, with no
special indication for operating from above except the
supposition that the crural ring could be more effectually closed from above than from below Poupart's
ligament, a supposition which further experience had
proved to be unwarranted.

The special indications for the inguinal operation for
femoral hernia might be enumerated as follows:

1. Whenever an indication, or indications, for opening the abdomen above the pubes coexisted with a femoral hernia. The speaker had operated twice upon this
indication, in the first case performing, at the same sitting, curettage of the uterus, trachelorrhaphy, excision of
painful annexa stumps, removal of a diseased vermiform
appendix, ventral hysteropexy, and radical femoral herniotomy.   In a second case the patient had been operated upon three years previously by another surgeon
for an acute strangulated femoral hernia. Two weeks
ago the speaker had had occasion to operate upon her
for the cure of a ventral hernia following an operation
for acute perforative appendicitis. Introducing his finger into the crural canal from within the abdomen, he
had found the crural ring quite patulous, constituting
a direct invitation to the redescent of a femoral hernia.
He had closed the crural ring by sewing Poupart's ligament to the periosteum of the pubis and had finished by
operating for the radical cure of the ventral hernia.

2. The coexistence of a complete or incomplete inguinal hernia with a femoral hernia of the same side.
The speaker had operated once upon this indication, an
additional reason for the inguinal operation—retroversion of the uterus—coexisting. In this case he had

performed, at the same sitting, curettage of the uterus, amputation of the cervix, shortening of the round ligaments, and radical inguinal and femoral herniotomy.

3. In women, the coexistence, with femoral hernia, of a retroversion or retroflexion of the uterus which could be corrected by shortening the round ligaments. In addition to the case just mentioned, he had operated for this indication on a patient upon whom he had performed, at the same sitting, curettage of the uterus, cœliotomy for multiple papillomata of the tubes and peritonæum, inversion of the vermiform appendix, inguinal shortening of the round ligaments, and radical femoral herniotomy.

In conclusion, the speaker said he felt certain that the inguinal operation for femoral hernia, when once the above indications were accepted, would be performed more frequently in the future than in the past, especially in women.

Dr. W. B. Coley was invited to continue the discussion. He said that he had been struck with the multiplicity of operations described in the paper. He was strongly opposed to any method of treating femoral or inguinal hernia by folding or rolling up the sac, or by making periosteal flaps; the canal should be filled with normal tissues. The method of Macewen, it was true, had proved a great success in the hands of its originator, but at the Hospital for Ruptured and Crippled they had seen many relapses after this operation. These had been undoubtedly due to the suppuration of the poorly nourished sac. He did not think one was as likely to obtain primary union where the sac was folded up, either within the canal or outside of it. The ideal operation seemed to be to ligature the sac on a level with the peritoneal cavity, remove the lower portion of the sac, and, if possible, close the canal as well. In his opinion, osteoplastic flaps were entirely unnecessary. He had now employed the method of Bassini in thirteen cases of femoral hernia. The first of his operations for femoral hernia had been done in 1891 on a girl of nineteen years, with an irreducible femoral hernia. Since then he had done thirty-three operations on thirty-one patients and, with two exceptions, he had been able to trace the entire number and determine the ultimate results. In twenty cases he had carefully dissected the sac beyond the femoral ring, and had practised high ligation with excision and closure by a purse-string suture of kangaroo tendon.

The suture had been introduced through the roof of the canal at the outer portion of Poupart's ligament, and had passed downward through the fascia overlying the pectineal muscle, and outward through the fascia lata over the femoral vessels, and upward again through Poupart's ligament, ending about a quarter of an inch from the point of entrance. On tying this suture, the floor of the canal had been made to come in close contact with the roof, completely obliterating the crural opening. Before doing this the sac had been dissected carefully from the crural canal. Primary union had been secured in every instance, and so far there had not been a single relapse. He had used Bassini's method in thirteen cases, with no mortality. In one case a stitch-hole abscess had developed ten days after operation, and had not healed for several weeks. After fourteen months there had been a small relapse. Fourteen of the operations had been in children under fourteen years of age, and nineteen in patients between the ages of eighteen and forty-three years. No cases had been refused operation on account of the size of the hernia, and no selection had been made. Either method, he thought, gave results so nearly perfect that they should receive preference over operations having a more complicated technique. It seemed to him that there were some important disadvantages connected with the inguinal method, particularly where there were strong adhesions. In such cases the inguinal method alone would be insufficient. His own experience, and the greater experience of Bassini, would seem to show that it was possible to obtain practically perfect results by the simpler methods. Of his thirty-three cases, one had been well at the end of six years, two after five years, two after four to five years; one had been well between three and four years after operation, six had been well after two or three years, twelve had been well after an average period of two years; two were still well after six months; two had not relapsed when seen between three and six months after the operation; two could not be traced; one had relapsed; and two had been quite recent cases. The cases that had gone beyond two years had been the only ones that could be fairly considered as cured. Some of Bassini's cases had been known to have remained cured at the end of nine years. These results went far toward proving that the simpler methods were the better. In exceptionally complicated cases, in which the abdomen had already been opened, there might be an advantage in the inguinal method, but in ordinary femoral hernia, the simpler methods of radical cure, which could be performed in fifteen or twenty minutes, met all the indications and seemed to be in every way preferable.

Dr. L. W. HOTCHKISS said he had had no experience in the method described by Dr. Silver, but it seemed to him that the inguinal method was unnecessarily complicated, and was hardly the one to be chosen in ordinary cases in view of the excellent operations of Bassini and Halsted. The method of high ligation or excision, he thought, gave a more nearly flush peritoneal surface at the site of the internal ring than any extraperitoneal bolster by a rolled-up or twisted sac. In the one case there was usually a good flush surface at the site of the original hernial opening; in the other, there was liable to be a slight depression on either side of the elevation, caused by the bolster, which might become a starting-point of another hernia.

Dr. SILVER, in closing the discussion, said he thought that the purse-string suture was an excellent one. Regarding the depressions on either side of the rolled-up sac, it seemed to him that the pressure would come upon either pubic bone, or on Poupart's ligament above, and that these structures being sufficiently strong there would be no tendency to the formation of a new hernia.

Meeting of April 6, 1898.

The President, Dr. ROBERT J. CARLISLE, in the Chair.

A Case of Paralysis of the Musculo-spiral Nerve following Fracture of the Humerus.—Dr. LUCIUS W. HOTCHKISS presented a boy of nineteen years, affected with musculo-spiral paralysis after a multiple fracture of the shaft of the humerus. The injury was received in July, 1897, and, although the patient said he had noticed loss of power in the extensors of the wrist immediately after the accident, the diagnosis of injury to the musculo-spiral nerve was not made until some time later. The fracture was treated by the plaster-of-Paris splint, and after the bone had united the paralysis was complete. As no improvement took place, and as the site of fracture was such as to lead to the belief that the nerve had been included in the callus, an operation was done for its relief. The nerve was exposed by the usual incision on the outer side of the arm, beginning at the elbow, and supplemented later by an incision high up on the inner aspect of the arm, in order to fully expose the musculo-spiral nerve. This was found flattened, shrunken, and deeply imbedded in the callus around the seat of fracture, to the extent of about two inches. The nerve was released and stretched, and the wound closed. Healing by first intention followed. The humerus was accidentally refractured about two weeks later, as the union was still soft; but this did not interfere in the slightest degree with the result. Sensation began to return in about six weeks, and subsequently the boy slowly regained the power of extension. At the present time the patient showed perfect restoration of both motion and sensation.

A Case of Thyreoid Fever.—Dr. Robert T. Morris reported a case of thyreoid fever. The patient was a woman about twenty-six years of age, and had had a slowly developing tumor in the region of the thyreoid gland for seven or eight years. During the past two years it had increased quite rapidly and had become distinctly pulsating. It was feared that it was becoming malignant. On January 3d Dr. Morris had removed this right half of the thyreoid gland and had found a degenerating mass simulating, according to the pathologist, sarcoma at several points. All of the structures of the neck that had been divided were sutured again in their normal anatomical relations, and the wound was closed without drainage. The nurse noted that the patient did not rally properly from the ether, but remained in an apathetic condition. At midnight the temperature was 96° F. and the pulse 80. The face was markedly swollen. During the next twenty days the changes in the vital signs were interesting. The temperature at midnight on the first day was 96° and the pulse 80. The highest temperature on the next day was 99.8° with a pulse of 80. On the third day the temperature nearly reached 104°, with a pulse of 140. The temperature then ranged between 102° and 104° until the seventh day, when there was a very distinct rigor, followed by a rise of temperature to 105.8° and a pulse of 150. This occurrence, it should be noted, was very rare in a case of thyreoid fever. After this the temperature ranged between 100° and 102° for the next week. It reached about the normal point at the twentieth day after operation. Most of the time during the two weeks succeeding the operation the patient was apathetic, but she smiled when spoken to. When the temperature was 104° and the pulse 140 the patient had not given any evidence of discomfort. She frequently had a mild type of delirium for a few hours at a time. There had been almost constant and, at times, bloody vomiting. There had also been bleeding from the gums, and involuntary evacuations from the bladder and rectum. There had been no swelling of the fingers or toes, or other symptoms of myxœdema except the swelling of the face, which was very marked, and had persisted for three weeks after operation. An erythema appeared on the right side a few days after operation, and extended successively to the arms and knees and various parts of the body. The eruption was of a very bright color, but was not associated with any marked pruritus. The condition of the pupils had been very variable, they being at one moment widely dilated, and shortly afterward markedly contracted. By the twentieth day there had been sudden improvement, and in the course of a few hours the patient's apathy had gone and her appetite had returned. After this there was desquamation over all the skin. The examinations of the blood and urine were negative. On the night on which the temperature was so high, following the rigor, knowing that this was not an ordinary feature of thyreoid poisoning, Dr. Morris feared that there was some septic infection, and accordingly opened the wound. It was found entirely united by primary union. A small blood-clot was found, but this proved to be sterile. He sutured the wound in such a way as to allow of drainage of the thyreoid secretion, but this had no effect on the symptoms. The wound did not granulate as usual, but repair took place mostly by the lymph coagulum being replaced by connective tissue.

Dr. Morris said that the case appeared to be one of those in which, a part of the thyreoid having been removed, the remainder continued to furnish its internal secretion, which, escaping perhaps too rapidly, caused the poisoning of the patient. The history of the case would seem to bear out this view.

Dr. GEORGE W. CRARY said he looked upon the case as one of special interest because there were symptoms of myxœdema as well as of thyreoid poisoning. The bleeding from the gums, the hæmoptysis, and the desquamation were all found in myxœdema. When thyreoid extract was given in myxœdema one of the first

things noticed was desquamation. It was for this reason that the case just reported was so peculiar, for,
instead of there being a lack of thyreoid, there seemed
to be an excess? The theory had been advanced that the
symptoms were caused by absorption from the cut surface of the thyreoid, and it had been found that drainage usually caused a cessation of the symptoms. In this
respect also Dr. Morris's case was unusual. It seemed
evident that the symptoms had resulted from the absorption of a true internal secretion.

Dr. MORRIS said that, recognizing the presence of
some symptoms of myxœdema, he had begun the administration of thyreoid extract on the sixth day, and it had
been continued for five days without affecting the symptoms.

Primary Gumma of the Epididymis.—Dr. SAMUEL
ALEXANDER reported this case.

Dr. EUGENE FULLER said that the specimen was exceedingly interesting, and was the first of the kind that
he had ever seen. Late syphilis in the epididymis, not
in the form of gumma, was occasionally seen. It was
an infiltrating lesion of the epididymis, which generally
extended into the parietal layer, giving rise to the feel
of a " clam-shell " configuration. This condition was
almost always associated with hydrocele. It had been
described as " *pachyvaginalitis hæmorrhagica syphi-
litica,*" because it was considered that the lesion was in
the tunica vaginalis associated with bloody hydrocele.
In the cases that he had seen he had not noted blood in
the hydrocele. In these cases one tapping of the hydrocele usually caused it to disappear, because there was an
obliteration of the layers of the tunica vaginalis due to
adhesive inflammation. He had seen such a case last
year in a man who had given a history of syphilis. The
hydrocele had been tapped, and obliteration of the tunica
vaginalis found except in one small spot. The fluid
had been drawn off from this portion, and had not returned. The infiltrated portion in this case had disappeared under antisyphilitic treatment.

Dr. Fuller then referred to a case which he had
seen, which simulated a late case of syphilis of the epididymis. He tapped the mass, and spent about ten days
in antisyphilitic treatment. The man then became impa-
tient and insisted upon an operation. The testicle was
therefore removed and submitted to microscopical examination, which showed the tumor to be an endotheli-
oma. Had the growth not simulated a syphilitic lesion

so closely, a much more extensive operation would have been done, and this would probably have prevented the early recurrence of the disease.

An Unusually Large Fibromyoma of the Uterus; Absence of the Cervix.—Dr. CHARLES CLIFFORD BARROWS presented a tumor which, at the time of its removal, had weighed eighteen pounds. It had been removed from an unmarried woman, about sixty-six years of age, who had been sent to him by Dr. Jeffries with a history of having been in good health up to the time of the menopause, which had occurred about eight years before. At this time she had begun to have some pain about the pelvis, and the abdomen had become enlarged. On vaginal examination he and several others were unable to find the cervix uteri, even under anæsthesia. He then opened the abdomen and removed the tumor, which shelled out without trouble. The top of the vagina ended in a blind pouch, and absolutely no opening corresponding to the os could be discovered, either from above or from below. The patient made a satisfactory recovery.

Removal of a Hairpin from the Uterus.—Dr. BARROWS also exhibited a hairpin which he had removed from the uterus of a woman weighing at least three hundred pounds. She had presented herself at the dispensary with the story that she had been suffering for some time from endometritis, and that she had been accustomed to make applications of iodine to the interior of her uterus. She had used a hairpin for this purpose, and it had finally escaped from her grasp and had been retained within the uterine cavity. Examination revealed a slightly enlarged uterus, from which issued a fœtid discharge. With a forceps he succeeded in seizing the round end of the hairpin, but the points were deeply buried in the tissue of the uterus. By slipping in a pair of scissors he succeeded in snipping off a portion of one leg of the hairpin. This permitted of its removal. Examination showed that the woman had been pregnant, for some decidua was present. The subsequent history of the case was uneventful.

Appendicitis associated with Abortion and the Presence of Gas in the Peritoneal Cavity.—Dr. W. J. CHANDLER, of South Orange, N. J., presented a specimen and reported the following case: Mrs. A. L., twenty-eight years of age, married and the mother of one child, eighteen months old, had had an acute endocarditis five years ago. On March 28th she was seized with severe

pain in the right iliac region. A slight menstrual flow
appeared, but soon ceased. She grew steadily worse,
and on March 30th, at 11 P. M., she was admitted to the
Orange Memorial Hospital. The abdomen at this time
was swollen, tympanitic, and tender, and there had been
some vomiting. The bowels had not moved for two
days previously. The urine had a specific gravity of
1.030 and contained a slight trace of albumin. The
pulse was 118, the respiration 24, and the temperature
99° F. During the next day the bowels were moved
with purgatives and high enemata; the vomiting ceased
and the pain lessened. The pulse varied between 100
and 112, the respirations between 20 and 28, and the
temperature between 99° and 100° in the rectum. On
April 1st the respirations were between 30 and 38, with
the pulse and temperature as before. The tympanites
had greatly increased and the patient suffered greatly
The case was supposed to be one of appendicitis complicated with septic peritonitis. Her condition was so
bad that it was decided to perform an exploratory laparotomy. This was done at 4 P. M., the incision being
that usually employed for appendicitis. On opening the
abdominal cavity a *large* quantity of *odorless gas* escaped,
and the abdomen immediately collapsed. This gas had
evidently been *free* in the peritoneal cavity. There was
no fluid visible. The intestines were injected and covered with deposits of lymph. No swelling or accumulation of pus could be felt anywhere. The appendix was
deeply injected, and constricted about an inch from its
free extremity. It was removed and was found to be in
a state of catarrhal inflammation. No other abnormity
being discovered, the wound was closed. The patient
was much relieved by the operation and passed a comfortable night. About 5.30 A. M., April 2d, she was
seized with severe pain; the abdomen again became tympanitic and distended; the pulse and respirations became
very rapid, and she died about 10 A. M. The autopsy
was made at 3 P. M. On opening the abdominal cavity
considerable gas escaped in the same manner as at the
operation on the previous day, and a considerable
amount of dark, thin serum, with flakes of lymph, welled
up. This was removed and amounted to two quarts.
The region about the site of the operation was healthy;
the surfaces of the incised peritonæum were tightly glued
together; the stump of the appendix was intact; there
was no evidence of hæmorrhage. The intestines were
removed entire, and showed no constriction or leak-

age under water pressure. The liver was enlarged and
fatty. The heart, lungs, spleen, and kidneys were normal. The bladder was distended and contained about
half a pint of urine. The uterus was enlarged, measuring about five inches in length. One ovary contained a
corpus luteum of pregnancy; otherwise the ovaries were
healthy. The uterus, on being cut open, showed the
shaggy chorion attached about as it would be near the
end of the second month of gestation. The membranes
had been ruptured and no fœtus was present.

Dr. Chandler said he presented the specimen because
of the presence of free gas in the abdominal cavity without discoverable perforation of the intestine or evidence
of abscess.

Dr. S. ALEXANDER suggested that it would be interesting to have a histological or bacteriological examination made, in order to determine whether the *Bacillus
aerogenes capsulatus* was present in the uterus. In some
of the reported cases the condition had followed attempted abortion.

Paper.

THE TREATMENT OF FRACTURES OF THE PATELLA BY THE PURSE-STRING SUTURE.

By IRVING S. HAYNES, Ph. B., M. D.

IN this paper no attempt will be made to give even
a summary of the many operations and procedures which
at one time or another have been advocated for the
treatment of fractures of the patella.

My purpose is rather to review the principles by
which we should be guided in the selection of the form
of treatment best suited to a given case. Then, if operation be deemed necessary, to place before you the details of the purse-string method, with my reasons for
favoring it, and the results obtained in several cases in
which it has been used.

The treatment of fractures of the patella depends
upon the kind of fracture present, the nature of the
complications, if any, and whether one is satisfied with
ligamentous or strives for bony union. The principles
of treatment are then derived as logical deductions from
the pathology of the fracture. It will be necessary,

therefore, to briefly review the conditions present in such fractures. The pathology is modified according as the fracture is produced by direct or indirect violence.

Fractures by direct violence may or may not be compound. The patella may be broken in any direction and there may be several lines of fracture and fragments. There will be very little separation of these fragments, if any, unless the line of fracture should be directed transversely, as there is very little concurrent laceration of the fibroperiosteal covering and ligamentous structure surrounding the patella.

The effusion into the joint will be small in amount, as a rule, with few blood clots, the condition being more like a synovitis from traumatism without fracture.

The fragments in such a fracture will easily come together, as there is nothing between them to prevent; they can be maintained in close apposition, and bony union is the rule.

Fractures by Indirect Violence or Muscular Action.— The mechanism of the production of this form of fracture is this. In partial flexion of the knee the rounded under surface of the patella is brought against the convex condyles of the femur; its lower end is fixed by the ligamentum patellæ, its upper edge by the quadriceps extensor tendon. This muscle suddenly and violently contracts, usually in some effort to preserve the equilibrium; the patella, being spongy bone and weaker than the ligaments attached to it breaks. Whether the break is the result of this cross strain on the patella pulled against the femur as a fulcrum, or whether it is fractured by the direct pull of the muscles and gives way in its weakest part, are questions not at all vital to the present discussion.

The fact is that the patella breaks. Not only this, but the capsular ligament of the knee with the fibrous expansion of the quadriceps extensor and fascia lata are also torn to a greater or less extent at the sides of the patella in a direction upward and backward, even into the substance of the quadriceps muscle itself. The fibrous covering of the front of the knee may be torn then to a distance of from one to three inches from the patella. The point of fracture of the patella is usually just at or below the middle of the bone; the line of fracture is ordinarily transverse, though it may be slightly oblique. The plane of fracture is directed from above downward and forward. The upper fragment, therefore, presents a sharp, shelving edge. It is by this sharp edge that the fibroperiosteum of the bone is cut or torn through; the level of this tear in the soft parts is lower than the line of fracture in the bone, but continuous with the lacerations in the ligaments at the side of the patella. As the muscle and fibrous tissue contract, this fibroperiosteal flap is firmly drawn over the face of the upper fragment and soon becomes adherent to it.

This fibroperiosteal cap may vary in thickness from less than an eighth to a quarter of an inch, and in width up to half an inch. There are also many shreds of the torn tissue intervening between the fragments. The joint will be filled with blood clots, the synovial membrane injected, and its fringes swollen. The fragments will be separated to all degrees up to two inches, and the degree of separation depends upon four factors: the contraction of the quadriceps extensor muscle, the extent of the laceration of the tissues at the side of the patella, the shortening of the ligamentum patellæ, and the amount of effusion and blood clots in the joint. The fragments are not only displaced longitudinally but also rotated, so that the fractured surface of the lower fragment looks forward and upward, that of the upper fragment downward and backward. This feature of rotation becomes a serious complication in operating upon old fractured patellæ.

The external symptoms and individual circumstances which influence us in determining the kind of treatment are mainly these:

First, all fractures produced by direct violence, not compound, as a rule, do not require operation, because there is not the separation of the fragments nor the in-

terposition of soft tissue between them, neither is there
the quantity of effusion present, nor the difficulty of
bringing the fragments together and maintaining them
in apposition from the very first.

Again, transverse fractures, whether produced by
direct or indirect force, and not compound, in which
there is less than a fourth of an inch separation of the
fragments. Where there is no deep sulcus on either
side of the patella, indicating a minimum amount of
laceration in the lateral ligaments. Where the fragments easily come together, and when together give a
sharp crepitus, showing that there is no tissue between
them, and can easily be retained in close apposition.

With such a case it will be perfectly safe; not only
safe, but also the best plan to treat the fracture by some
form of external dressing combined with the modern
addition of massage.

In such cases you will secure fibrous union, to be
sure, but of a minimum length and with the functional
result almost perfect.

On the other hand, given a compound fracture of the
patella by either direct or indirect force, or given a case
constituting one of the great majority of the ordinary
fractures by muscular action, where the knee is distended
with effused blood and serum, where the fragments are
separated any distance from each other—from half an
inch or more—when they can not be brought together
without great force or not at all, and as soon as the
fragments are released, they retract to their former position. If you find a soft crepitus on rubbing the fragments together, showing the interposition of tissue; if
your fingers sink into a gap on each side of the patella,
indicating that the fibrous structures are badly torn—
then, in such cases, you must perform the open operation if you wish to give your patient the best treatment,
unless there is some contraindication besides the nature
of the injury itself, as Bright's disease, old age, etc.

The treatment of fractures of the patella will then
naturally be divided into the non-operative and the operative.

By non-operative treatment is meant any plan for bringing together the fragments not attended with puncture or incision into the skin. I shall not attempt to mention the many forms of non-operative measures. They all seek to draw together and retain in position the fragments by some forms of splints, strapping, rubber bands or cords with almost innumerable modifications and combinations.

This treatment, before the advent of Listerism the only one seriously considered, is adapted to certain cases at all times, and to all but compound cases at certain times and under certain conditions.

The cases chosen for this plan of treatment would be those already described as fractures by direct and indirect violence, presenting the minimum degree of separation of the fragments with a reasonable certainty that there is no, or at least very little, tissue between the fragments.

Considerations of the position in life held by the patient may also properly enter into the decision, as those in comfortable circumstances who can lead a life of comparatively little physical exertion are also fit subjects for the milder measures and less satisfactory results. The union in these cases will be by fibrous tissue, and if of the minimum amount, the functional result will be very good.

The above class of cases recommended for non-operative treatment are by far in the minority, yet, as they exist, it would be very unwise to insist that they accept the more thorough plan of treatment.

The Principles Underlying the Treatment of Fractures of the Patella by Operation.—The aim of the treatment of a fractured bone is to secure union by bone, not by fibrous tissue.

If the functional disabilities following a fibrous union of the patella were as disastrous as in the long bones of the body, such, for instance, as the femur, we should have our indications more sharply drawn than at present. In the long bones nothing short of bony union is accepted, even if the case demands repeated operation.

11

In the patella the same hard-and-fast rule does not pertain, because a person can get along very well with fibrous union up to a certain degree. Still, the rule holds good that the aim of the surgeon is to secure bony union. How to secure this is the next problem.

Under operative measures I place all forms of treatment attended with puncturing or incising the skin.

The methods for securing union by instruments which puncture the skin, as Malgaigne's hooks, and all the modifications derived from them; by all forms of transverse pins, or sutures, fastened together on the outside of the skin; by sutures placed subcutaneously around the fragments antero-posteriorly, or through several subcutaneous punctures—all these forms and others akin to them are only mentioned to be protested against, because they do not accomplish the object of removing the cause which prevents bony union—that is, the substances between the fragments. Further, they constitute a source of real danger in that about all these punctured holes, where the hooks or pins are left in place, suppuration is sure to follow, and can and has extended to the interior of the joint. There is, then, no logical and practical ground between the old forms of strapping and the open method.

By the open method alone can the joint be freed from blood clot, the fibrous cap covering the upper fragment dissected away, the strands of torn tissue removed, the fragments themselves cleaned and brought into perfect alignment and then fastened together so that this condition will be maintained.

There is another vital reason for the operation besides the immediate conditions in the joint which preclude the possibility of a bony union. It is a condition on which little stress is laid, but one which in itself justifies an operation—namely, to prevent the development of conditions which lead to a weak knee and a refracture of the patella.

Given the last case, as above described, treat it with the best of non-operative measures, and the patient recovers with a fibrous union varying from a half to an inch or more. The lower fragment will be drawn to a considerable distance toward the tubercle of the tibia by the contraction of the ligamentum patellæ. The upper fragment rests upon the front of the condyles of the femur and is nearly immovable vertically and laterally, and is retained in this position by the contraction and consolidation of the lateral expansions of the fibrous hood, together with the cicatricial shortening of the scar tissue which fills in the gap between.

Voluntary and passive flexion of the knee is arrested by the inability of the upper fragment to descend over the rounded condyles of the femur, owing to the contractured tissues at its sides. Forcible flexion carried beyond this limit, either accidental or with intent, will tear through the ligamentous union between the two fragments before the contractured tissues by which the motion is arrested will yield.

If refracture thus does not occur early, the upper fragment seldom descends, but motion is gained by a lengthening of the fibrous union. This elongation may reach the considerable length of four inches. A knee joint, then, with fibrous union sufficiently long between the fragments of the patella to permit of the non-descent of the upper fragment constitutes a constant source of weakness and possesses within itself the predisposing cause for a refracture. To prevent these results would alone justify opening the knee joint.

After this somewhat lengthy review of the principles underlying the treatment of fractures of the patella, and the reasons, pathological and logical, which not only justify, but in the majority of cases demand the open method of treatment for such cases, I will submit to you a brief account of the purse-string suture as used in the patients presented here this evening.

As a rule, patients are not operated upon until about a week has elapsed, during which time the knee is bandaged, lead and opium and an ice bag applied, and the limb fixed to a posterior splint.

The leg is prepared the night preceding the operation. An aseptic operation is performed, no antiseptics

being used except in the preliminary scrubbing of the
patient, operator, and assistants. Sterilized decinormal
salt solution is the only fluid used without and within
the knee during the operation. A vertical incision is
used by preference, as it is not open to the objection
that belongs to the transverse one—viz., that if a refracture occur with a transverse incision the fracture
is apt to be compound. As the scar is adherent to the
deeper tissues, the incision varies in length from three
to five inches, depending upon the conditions present.

The superficial tissues are cut through, the fragments and the quadriceps extensor tendon and the ligamentum patellæ exposed, and dissected up at the sides to
lay bare the entire extent of the tear in the lateral
fibrous tissues. All blood clots are carefully and thoroughly removed by irrigation, all frayed edges and damaged tissue trimmed away, especially along the torn
edges of the capsule.

Attention is now directed to the patella. The fibroperiosteal cap covering the upper fragment is cut away,
the surfaces of the fracture lightly but thoroughly
curetted until they bleed freely. Oozing is checked by
hot irrigating and pressure. The rents in the fibrous
tissues at the side of the patella are sutured with catgut
or silk. The purse-string suture is now inserted. The
suture is of strong braided silk, usually No. 10, capable
of standing a heavy strain, so as not to break in tying.
This silk has been freshly sterilized preceding the operation. Two pieces of silk are used, each about eighteen
inches long, threaded into long half-curved surgical needles. The surgical needle is used in preference to the
Hagedorn, as it passes through the dense fibrous tissues
with greater ease. Before using the sutures the operator should wash his hands and irrigate the joint. The
upper fragment is first semi-encircled. The needle is
entered in the midst of the tissues close to the fractured
edge of the patella, carried upward, with its point closely hugging the bone, and brought out at the lateral and
superior angle; it is reinserted close to the hole of
emergence and carried through the tendon of the quadri-

ceps extensor, always close to the bone, then brought out at the other lateral and superior angle; again it is pushed through the tissues and made to emerge at the side of the fractured edge opposite to that of entrance. The lower fragment is similarly semi-encircled by the other strand of silk which hugs the bone and transfixes transversely the ligamentum patellæ. The joint is washed out for the last time, the two sutures tied with a square knot simultaneously, as much force being used as the silk will stand so as to firmly crowd together the fragments. The knot and cut ends of the silk lie between the torn capsule and are out of the way. The skin is closed with cat or silkworm gut, sealed with an aristo-collodion dressing, and a plaster-of-Paris splint applied over a lint bandage. In seven to ten days the splint should be opened and the sutures, if non-absorbable, removed. A second light splint is applied and worn for two weeks more. This is now taken off daily and passive and voluntary motion instituted, combined with hot- and cold-water douches and massage. Usually there will be ten degrees of motion obtained when the joint is first tested.

The purse-string suture has many points of superiority over the usual method by wiring. The chief one is that the former secures absolute coaptation of the fragments. No matter how carefully one drills the holes for the wire, it is almost an impossibility to get them exactly opposite, and if not opposite, the surfaces of the fragments can not come into direct apposition. For this reason many operators saw off the fractured edges so as to better command a flat surface. With the silk suture this is not necessary, for the encircling suture crowds together the fragments whether there are two or more, and all the little inequalities of surface are brought into accurate apposition and the patella thus united presents a remarkably fine coaptation.

Another objection to wire, as usually applied, is that it is passed through the anterior half of the bone, the posterior surfaces have nothing to hold them together, and there is apt to be a tipping of the fragments and an angular displacement between them. The silk, on the other hand, is applied at the middle of the periphery of the bone and the force holds the fragments evenly balanced.

The amount of bone which can be included within the wire is limited, especially with a small lower fragment, or if there be more than two fragments. If the line of fracture is oblique, then wiring becomes difficult and unsatisfactory. With the purse-string suture it matters not how many fractures there are, or in what direction run the lines of fracture, or whether a fragment is very small, or how irregular the fractured face may be, you will find that as soon as you tie the sutures the fragments accurately come together; there is neither ateral nor antero-posterior displacement, and the patella resumes its normal shape.

In the tissues the silk is better disposed for permanent resistance than is the wire. It is buried deeply within tendinous structures and remains there without causing any secondary symptoms.

On the other hand, a wire in front of the patella often ulcerates through and has to be removed.

There is no operation which gives the appearance of completely fulfilling all the requirements as this one does.

The objections to the operation here described are the objections to all open operations.

These are the opening of the joint and the possibility of infection. I do not wish to belittle the effects of suppuration in the knee joint. It is most serious, resulting eventually in either ankylosis, amputation, or possibly death from septicæmia.

But I think the dangers of infection are too much exaggerated. The fact that in one of our charity hospitals, where there is only one small operating room in which all sorts of cases must be treated, suppuration has not followed in a single case of fractured patella subjected to operation shows that with careful attention to all details of asepsis we can secure union without infection. In a private house the risks are much less.

Therefore, while the danger of septic infection exists, it is no more potent for cases of fracture of the patella than in any case of operation primarily aseptic. An objection which might be urged against this method itself is the dissection of the subcutaneous structures laterally to the full limit of the tears in the capsule of the knee. I do not think this objection can hold. Because if the joint is to be opened at all it is necessary to do the operation thoroughly, and a smaller opening does not admit of this. To me an important part of the operation is the removal of all the torn shreds of tissue, the damaged muscle, and the close suturing of the rents in the soft parts; the conversion, in other words, of a lacerated wound into an incised one.

There is one precaution, however, to be observed— namely, to handle the tissues as little as possible, and then with instruments in preference to the fingers, and most of all to do the handling yourself.

Summary.—Males, three; females, two. Cause, indirect violence in all. Location of fracture: middle, one; middle and lower thirds, three; middle and upper thirds, one. Line of fracture, transverse or slightly oblique. Fibroperiosteal hood present in all. In addition there were fibrous strands between the fragments. Ligamentous structures at the side of the patella torn from one to three inches. Union in skin primary in all; one had a small gap of half an inch, due to infolding of skin, this healed promptly. Union in fragments of patella by bone in four, by fibrous tissue in one. Angle of motion: least, ninety-eight degrees; greatest, a hundred and twenty-five degrees; average in five, a hundred and fourteen degrees and two fifths. Time in hospital, three to four weeks. Average time since operation, a year and seven months.

Case I.—John C., aged fifty-three years; United States, expressman; February 20, 1896.

History.—Fell while loading a wagon and struck his left knee against the tailboard, fracturing the patella transversely at its middle. Brought to Harlem Hospital.

Treatment.—Lead and opium, posterior splint.

February 25th.—Dr. Haubold, then on duty, wired the fragments through a median incision. Periosteal hood found covering face of upper fragment. One silver wire used. No irrigation, the entire operation being conducted after the dry method. Catgut sutures in capsule and skin.

Result: Union primary. Patient discharged at end of three weeks.

May 11th (two months and a half later).—Patient had so far recovered as to have resumed regular work; flexion beyond a right angle; exact amount not known. On this day slipped and fell, refracturing the same patella; lead and opium applied.

18th.—The knee was opened a second time by a vertical incision alongside of the first one. The wire was found broken at the twist; line of fracture at same place as before; fragments covered by thick layer of new connective tissue. On this account the hood hanging over upper fragment was very thick and long. Joint irrigated with saline solution; all blood clots cleaned out; strands of frayed tissue removed; torn capsule sutured up to patella on both sides; surfaces of fragments curetted and encircled by the silk suture close to the bone, but well buried within the tissues. This suture was in a single piece. On tying it it broke from the strain necessary to bring the fragments well together. A second strand had to be passed; this held. In the later operations the suture was used in two pieces and did not break. After tying the knot it was tucked in between the edges of the torn capsule; skin closed with silkworm-gut sutures; aristol-collodion dressing; plaster-of-Paris splint; wound healed by primary union.

June 8th.—Patient discharged wearing a removable splint and using a crutch. Flexion, five degrees.

July.—Twenty degrees of flexion noted.

March 13, 1898.—Patella fragments united by solid union; no motion between them; evidently bone. The patella is freely movable vertically and laterally; angle of voluntary flexion, ninety-eight degrees; has worn a bandage around the knee for fear of another accident, and this has interfered with free motion; told to discard the bandage and work at flexing his leg forcibly every day; has no pain in joint; is working at his business as expressman.

CASE II.—Mary S., married; about thirty-five years of age; September 5, 1897.

History.—Coming down stairs, tripped on next to last step and in the effort to save herself fractured the patella on the left side.

Examination.—Transverse fracture of left patella below middle of bone; joint distended with fluid; fragments separated by wide interval.

Treatment.—Posterior splint and ice bag.

September 6th.—After opening the joint a large amount of clotted blood escaped. The capsule was torn backward and upward on both sides of the patella for between two and three inches into the substance of the vasti muscles. There were many shreds of fibrous tissue presenting between the fragments and a fibroperiosteal hood half an inch wide covering the upper fragment. The usual operation of trimming up the capsule, curetting faces of fractured bone, irrigating joint, introduction of purse-string suture, suturing of torn capsule done. Fragments came evenly together.

, Result: Primary union.

October.—On removal of plaster splint patient at once flexed leg to an angle of about sixty-seven degrees; no pain; patient has done housework for last two weeks without trouble; fragments solid; anterior surface of patella level.

March, 1898.—Angle of motion, a hundred and twenty-five degrees; fragments separated three eighths of an inch; ligamentous union; patella freely movable, however, and flexion normal; has pain in joint preceding bad weather; has had rheumatism in ankle and this knee preceding the injury.

CASE III.—Abram B., aged thirty-one years; May 7, 1896.

History.—While maintaining his equilibrium, as the hospital history reads, he fractured his left patella.

Examination.—Simple transverse fracture of patella below middle; joint swollen; amount of separation of fragments not noted.

Treatment.—Lead and opium and posterior splint for six days.

Operation, May 12th.—Joint opened by vertical incision; large blood clot turned out; the periosteum and fibrous tissue covered over upper fragment, effectually preventing contact of fragments; purse-string double suture used; fragments came together closely; skin incision sutured and sealed without drainage.

23d.—Redressed; wound closed; dermatitis caused by green-soap poultice present; healed under dry dressing.

June 11th.—Discharged.

29th.—Five degrees of motion in joint.

July.—Fifteen degrees of motion present.

March 24, 1898.—Angle of flexion, a hundred and twelve degrees; solid bony union of fracture; patella freely movable.

CASE IV.—Daniel O'K., twenty-eight years old; letter carrier; December 4, 1896.

History.—While making his rounds slipped and fell on stairs. States that the bone broke before he struck the steps. Brought to Harlem Hospital by ambulance.

Examination.—Joint fully distended by effusion; transverse fracture of left patella in middle and lower thirds; fragments separated fully an inch; posterior splint and ice cap. When swelling had somewhat subsided, an attempt was made to bring the fragments together by adhesive strapping, but without success.

December 10th.—Operated on according to the method described. Joint contained a large blood clot; line of fracture was oblique downward and inward. There was an extensive laceration of the lateral ligaments extending into the internal and external vasti muscles; fibroperiosteal hood firmly drawn over edge of upper fragment; shreds trimmed off, rents sutured, surfaces of patella scraped, fragments sutured by two strong braided-silk sutures, and fragments firmly brought into perfect coaptation when tied; dressing and plaster splint.

December 23d.—Wound healed by primary union; silkworm-gut sutures in skin removed; posterior splint applied.

January 3, 1897.—Splint removed; some motion in joint, about five degrees. Discharged from hospital.

July, 1897.—Flexion to forty-five degrees; extension normal; no mobility of fragments.

Angle of voluntary flexion, February 28, 1898, a hundred and twenty degrees; patella freely movable vertically and laterally; union by bone; works full time as letter carrier.

CASE V.—Emma B., aged twenty-six years; housework; September 7, 1897.

History.—Four years ago fractured right patella; to-day slipped down two steps and fractured left one. Brought to hospital.

Examination.—The right patella shows an old fracture at the upper and middle thirds of the bone, with ligamentous union of half an inch; normal range of

motion in joint; left knee swollen and a transverse
fracture of the patella at its upper and middle thirds
found; fragments could be brought together, but crepitus
was too soft to show that the bony surfaces came in contact; ice cap applied and posterior splint.

Operation, September 9th, by the vertical incision.
Joint contained moderate amount of clotted blood in
dark-colored fluid; plane of fracture oblique from behind and above downward and forward; capsule and
deep fascial covering not torn more than an inch laterally; fibroperiosteal hood covering upper fragment; all
blood clots cleaned out by saline irrigation; rent in capsule closed; surfaces of fragments cleaned; fragments
encircled by strong braided-silk ligature in two pieces,
close to the bone and buried within the tissues; ligatures
tied simultaneously; fragments came into perfect apposition; skin closed with silkworm gut and aristol col-
lodion; plaster-of-Paris splint.

September 16th.—Plaster and sutures removed;
union primary, except for a distance of half an inch.

November 8th.—Plaster removed; union throughout;
fragments do not show independent mobility; flexion to
forty-five degrees. Angle of voluntary flexion, February
25, 1898, a hundred and seventeen degrees; patella freely movable laterally and vertically; fragments firmly
united; apparently bony union.

1125 MADISON AVENUE.

Dr. CRARY protested against the name " purse-string
suture," because the latter had become identified in
men's minds with a *subcutaneous* purse-string suture described by Dr. Stimson. The objection given in the
paper to the use of the transverse incision seemed to
him theoretical. The adhesion of the skin to the underlying structures could be readily avoided by making the
transverse incision a little to one side. If a longitudinal
incision was used, and an attempt was then made to
reach the lateral edges of the lacerated aponeurosis, it
would necessitate a considerable undermining of the
skin. It seemed to him that the results obtained by Dr.
Haynes had been largely due to the methods adopted
by him preceding the introduction of the suture—namely, the removal of the clots and of the fibrous portions
between the fragments of bone. Whether the suture
was applied through the bone or around it seemed imma-
terial. The suture material was of importance. As regarded the apposition of the bone, it made no difference

whether an absorbable or a permanent suture was used; if the fragments could be kept in apposition for a few days, or even for a few hours, until a permanent dressing could be applied, the suture would do in that time all that it could accomplish. For this reason he preferred catgut to any so-called permanent suture. In a comminuted fracture undoubtedly the purse-string suture would be better than the direct suture by drilling of the bones, but he could not see that it possessed special advantages in other cases. The objection made that the silver suture usually passed only through the anterior portion, and that consequently there was a tendency to tilting, did not seem well founded. When it was applied by experienced surgeons the entire surfaces were well approximated. Of course, infection of the knee joint must be seriously considered; it was far more dangerous to the life of the individual and to his usefulness than infection of the peritonæum. Infection of the latter, unless of a specially virulent type, was usually shut off and localized by adhesions. Infection of the knee joint on the other hand, always resulted seriously—in ankylosis of the knee joint, amputation, or death. In this connection one should bear in mind the advantages of wearing rubber gloves in operating. These gloves could be absolutely sterilized, as had been proved by Dr. McBurney, and with them any amount of manipulation could be practised without causing infection—in fact, these gloves were practically instruments. With the rubber gloves a simple rinsing of the hands with sterile salt solution rendered the hands absolutely and surgically clean.

Dr. PARKER SYMS said that the practice of treating fractured patellæ by suture had been introduced into this city in 1883. It had given ideal results at that time in many instances, but disastrous results had occurred in a sufficient number of cases to bring most of the operators to a standstill. In considering this question we should do so from the standpoint of the patient. The operation described in the paper seemed to him a most perfect one, and the results, when satisfactory, were certainly ideal; but it must not be forgotten that a review of all the cases of suture of the patella since the introduction of careful antiseptic or aseptic work would show many failures with loss of limb, loss of function, or even loss of life. It seemed to him that this was a matter which should be left for the patient to decide. The reader of the paper had advised waiting about a week to allow of partial recovery from the effects of the traumatism. It was a well-known fact that primary operations on injured joints were very dangerous as compared with operations on joints not thus involved. The indications for operation had been well stated in the paper. It was a mistake to suppose that the silk suture did not give trouble subsequently; it not infrequently required removal even three or four years after operation. As had been said by the last speaker, all that was necessary was to use a suture which would secure apposition for a few days. The invention of the subcutaneous purse-string suture should be credited to one of the house surgeons of the New York Hospital, whose cases had been reported and favorably commented upon by Dr. Stimson.

Dr. HAYNES said that he had been unable to find out to whom credit rightly belonged for the operation. He personally claimed no special originality, but the idea had occurred to him to elaborate the operation recommended by Dr. Stimson. He could not agree with those who thought that the suture material was of little importance. We knew that new bone did not form for three or four weeks; the tissue before that time was a granulation tissue which would yield to strain. He felt very confident that the patient having ligamentous union probably had this form of union because of the giving way of a suture. He heartily agreed to all that had been said about the dangers of infecting the knee joint; nevertheless, it should be remembered that many cases treated by the non-operative method yielded most unsatisfactory results. It seemed to him that a careful comparison of the two methods would show that it was justifiable, and even advisable, to operate, provided always that the proper aseptic precautions were observed.

Meeting of May 4, 1898.

The President, ROBERT J. CARLISLE, M. D., in the Chair.

Cholecystotomy for Occlusion of the Ductus Communis Choledochus; Removal of a Stone.—Dr. JOHN F. ERDMANN reported such a case. The common and cystic ducts had been occluded by a stone, half an inch in diameter, lodging at the junction of the cystic and

hepatic ducts. The patient, Mrs. S., thirty-three years
of age, was of robust physique, and had an excellent
family history. With the exception of a few days in
bed after a birth a few years ago, she had not had a
day's confinement to the house as a result of illness
until the present trouble, which had begun on January
17, 1898, by an attack of rather moderate pain located
in the epigastric region, and accompanied by nausea.
This had disappeared in four days under some mild
treatment. Then she had enjoyed perfect health until
the 1st of March, on which day her family physician,
Dr. V. Piatti, of Greenwich, had been called in, and
had found her suffering with the same symptoms as before, and with pain under the left scapula and in the
region of the spleen. Two days later she had shown
evidences of jaundice, and this had gradually deepened
to a mahogany color. On March 9th, or the ninth day
of the disease, she had a temperature of 103° F., without any previous chill, and a pulse of 132, and had become nervous and restless. When seen by the speaker
on the following day, at 11 A. M., she had a temperature
of 99° F. and a pulse of 108, and, in addition to this
change for the better, her attendant, a woman of considerable intelligence, said that she had observed that
the patient was not so dark as she had been in the
earlier part of the illness. As a result, it had been
thought best to keep her under observation for a few
days before operating, although up to that time there
had been no evidence by the stools of bile entering the
intestine. On the following day the temperature suddenly rose to 105° F. and the pulse to 132, and she had
chills the entire day. When she was seen again, on
March 12th, the temperature was 103° and the pulse
140 to 150, and there was no diminution in the discoloration or evidence of bile in the stools. Immediate
operation was decided upon and, with the patient under
ether, an incision was made in the outer border of the
right rectus muscle. There was no difficulty in finding
the empty and contracted gall bladder, but numerous
bands and a mass of adhesions had to be torn through
before the lesser omentum and the opening of Winslow
were reached. When this had been done, a mass of
about the size of an English walnut could be felt. This
was suspected to be inflammatory rather than malignant.
Careful and prolonged search in this mass failed to detect a stone, and consequently the obstruction was considered to be the result of causes external to the duct—

i. e., the mass of tissue. As it seemed advisable to relieve the pressure as much as possible, and as there was not enough working space, an incision was made at a right angle to the primary one, cutting through the rectus on the right side and partially through that of the left. A careful search then revealed a hard body, at the intestinal end of the mass previously found. This proved to be a stone situated at the beginning of the common duct and at the terminus of the cystic and hepatic ducts. By the use of considerable force the stone was dislodged upward through the cystic duct into the gall bladder. Owing to the patient's condition and the difficulty in bringing the gall bladder to the parietal peritonæum, it was decided to simply incise the gall bladder after first packing the area about it with protective gauze. After this had been done, the stone was easily removed. A forceps was attached to one of the edges of the incision in the gall bladder, and then gauze was packed under the handles of the forceps so as to bring the gall bladder as near as possible to the parietal peritonæum. A small drain was put in the gall bladder and the wounds were sewed up. Within two minutes following the removal of the stone there was quite a flow of bile and mucus from the opening in the gall bladder. The patient was in very poor condition at the close of the operation, having a pulse of 200 and evidences of pulmonary œdema. She responded to strychnine hypodermically, and upon the following day her temperature was normal and her pulse 120. The discharge of bile was so profuse that frequent dressings were necessary throughout the day. On the second day following the operation the stools were found to have bile in them, and on the fourth day the forceps and the drains were removed, but an abdominal drain was introduced. From this time there was no evidence of bile by the stools for three weeks, but an exceptionally large amount came through the opening in the abdomen. This obstruction to the ducts was finally ascribed to the drain, as it was suspected by the family physician that he had been putting the gauze in rather tight. This proved to be the cause, for, after placing a small drain in the opening, bile was again found in the stools. Within a few days the drain had been dispensed with, and this had been followed by a rapid closing of the fistula, so that the entire wound was healed on April 18th. The skin discoloration disappeared in five weeks, and the patient had been allowed to go about since April 20th.

Dr. A. B. Johnson said that the difficulties of these operations were often very great in cases where there were many adhesions and the stone was situated far down in the common duct. The subsequent treatment of the wound in the duct was frequently troublesome on account of the difficulty of applying the sutures, which often tore out repeatedly. The speaker said that he had presented to the society last year a case in which, after the removal of the stone, he had been able to sew up the wound in the duct so as to prevent all leakage, but such cases were the exception rather than the rule.

A method had been devised and used with success in several cases by Dr. Charles McBurney. When the stone was situated far down in the common duct and could not be displaced, the descending portion of the duodenum was incised vertically in front, the papillæ were found, the orifice of the duct was dilated or cut, and the stone was extracted. The opening in the anterior wall of the duodenum was then closed with sutures. The method had given good results.

Dr. J. W. S. Gouley remarked that it was not very many years ago that persons afflicted in this way were simply allowed to die. The celebrated Dr. Granville Sharp Pattison, at one time the professor of anatomy in the New York University, died from the effects of an impacted stone in the ductus communis choledochus. The diagnosis was not made until after death.

Paper.

EXTRA–UTERINE GESTATION OF THE INTERSTITIAL VARIETY TERMINATING BY RUPTURE INTO THE UTERUS. RECOVERY.

By ROBERT MacLEAN TAFT, M. D.

I TAKE pleasure in presenting to you this evening the symptoms observed and the course taken in a case of extra-uterine pregnancy which came under my care some five months ago.

In doing so I will endeavor to be as brief as possible.

Mrs. A., American, aged thirty years, was married at the age of twenty-five. She has had two children—a girl, aged three years and six months, and a boy, aged a year and eight months. Both births were perfectly normal. She has had no miscarriages. She gives no history of previous uterine trouble. The patient began menstruating at the age of fourteen. Her menstrual periods had always been regular, very profuse, and painful until after marriage, when they became regular and profuse, but without pain. On December 16, 1898, I was first called to see this patient in regard to her general ill health and a profuse and troublesome discharge from the vagina.

She gave the following history of her present trouble: She had last menstruated in the latter part of October, 1897. Menstruation ceased about November 4th. There was nothing remarkable about it except that it was very profuse, somewhat painful, and accompanied by the expulsion of a few clots.

About two weeks after this period she began to notice herself becoming nervous, irritable, and morose, with her mind prone to dwell upon morbid subjects.

She suffered from attacks of dizziness and was unable to fix her mind on any one thing.

For the past ten days she had been made miserable by severe pain in the back and dragging down pains in the pelvic region.

Since the latter part of November she had had a profuse leucorrhœal discharge, sometimes rusty in color. Her stomach had been in good condition, with no nausea or vomiting.

Her appetite had been fair and the bowels had been constipated. Since the latter part of November she had experienced severe cramps low down in the pelvis, the pain of which would sometimes make her stoop over and cry out.

At that time she was taking some kind of a " female regulator." At first the pains came at intervals of a day or two, but at this time, December 16th, were more constant. During all this time she had ridden her bicycle constantly, even during her last menstrual period.

She did not menstruate in the latter part of November, but the leucorrhœa was increased in quantity and was rust-colored. When I called to see her, December 18, 1897, her chief complaints were of her miserable nervous condition; cramps low down in the pelvis; dragging pain in the back, made worse by exercise or going up stairs, and the discharge from the vagina. Examination showed the uterus somewhat enlarged, very painful to the touch, and displaced backward, but not markedly so. After the birth of her last child the doctor had told her that her uterus had not properly undergone involu-

12

tion as the result of leaving her bed too soon and too
quickly resuming her household duties. The uterus was
not bound down by adhesions. Examination by speculum showed the cervix large, swollen, red, and œdematous. The results of an old laceration could be seen. The
os was open and from it escaped a thin, rust-colored discharge. On examining the uterus per rectum I found
it tender and displaced backward. She was sensitive on
either side, but not markedly so.

On again examining with the speculum I found that
from the manipulation a considerable amount of bright-
red blood had appeared from the cervix.

I made up my mind that it was either an endometritis which had been associated with amenorrhœa or
else an impending miscarriage.

I advised rest in bed, and decided to wait a few
days for developments.

Temperature at the time, 98°; pulse, 75; respiration,
20. She had a few cramps the next day, and, not knowing what might take place, I introduced a tampon into
the vagina.

On removing the tampon next morning I found it
well saturated with blood, to all appearances that of
menstruation. I introduced another tampon and advised
perfect rest in bed.

She did get up, however, early next morning, and
while at stool was seized with severe pain and the tampon was almost expelled. She removed it, and, after
letting a stream of water flow over the gauze, started
to throw it away, when she thought that it might be
of use to me and saved what was left of it. On examining the gauze I found what appeared to be a small portion of decidual membrane.

She said that the gauze was covered with blood and
that she passed some clots after it. She then flowed
profusely for three days and stopped. I put it down as
a probable miscarriage of three weeks or so, and, as her
general health rapidly improved and the leucorrhœa
diminished under antiseptic and astringent hot vaginal
douches, I discharged her, much improved, with directions for continuing the treatment.

At that time I was in doubt whether or not to use
the curette. The family were much opposed to it and, as
her temperature and pulse remained normal, I believed
it to be unnecessary.

January 29, 1898.—At this time the patient called
at my office and said that the leucorrhœa had again be-

come profuse and that she was feeling ill. At times
there was a dull, grinding, aching pain low down in her
pelvis, and her backache was almost constant. Her abdomen felt enlarged and hard to her. She complained
of a throbbing sensation and of bearing-down pain in
the pelvis, and tenderness on pressure over this region.
Her nervous system was disordered. She was very morbid, with a tendency to weep, and a feeling of isolation
and incapacity for mental work. Nausea and vomiting
were entirely absent, nor was there any enlargement or
sensitiveness of the breasts.

Examination showed the cervix enlarged and swollen, and from the wide-open os exuded a thin muco-
purulent rust-colored discharge, the flow of which would
be increased by manipulation of the uterus. On con-
joined manipulation I found the body of the uterus
much enlarged and very sensitive. I could not make out
any irregularity in the tumor. The cervix pointed a little to the left.

The cervical canal being open and dilated, I cautious-
ly introduced a probe and found the cavity enlarged and
the organ tender and bleeding very readily, and, as I
thought, empty.

A small curette being introduced and withdrawn,
brought away a quantity of gelatinous fungoid tissue.
My mind then dwelt on all the possibilities, and went
through a process of exclusion, the details of which would
take too much time to enumerate. I decided that it
was a case of subinvolution and chronic endometritis,
with a possible retention of secundines. I advised an
anæsthetic for thorough examination of the condition
and the operation of curettage, which was accepted by
the patient.

Operation, February 3d.—Heart and lungs normal;
no abnormal constituents in the urine. Anæsthetic,
chloroform. Under anæsthesia the womb was found
to be much enlarged, slightly retroverted, but I could
not discover any marked irregularity of the tumor. I
proceeded with the operation and removed a great quantity of degenerated and altered mucous membrane and
fungoid vegetations, but nothing which seemed organized tissue.

I concluded the operation by thorough irrigation with
a 1-to-10,000 bichloride solution and packed the cavity of
the uterus with four yards of sterilized iodoform gauze
strips.

After the operation the uterus was within two fingers' breadths of the umbilicus and prominent. The patient recovered rapidly from the effects of the chloroform and I left, trusting that in due course of time the organ would be relieved of its engorgement and overgrowth and return to its normal state.

For the next three days everything went along satisfactorily except for an occasional sharp pain referred to the right side. The temperature remained between 99° and 100° for forty-eight hours and then returned to normal.

The uterine gauze was removed on February 5th. She flowed profusely after removal of packing. On the night of February 6th I was hurriedly called on account of a hæmorrhage. The nurse showed me two large clots, and about twenty small ones, the size of walnuts.

When I arrived the hæmorrhage had ceased. In fact, it had stopped soon after the clots were expelled. With dressing forceps I tamponed the uterus, and left instructions to be followed if there should be signs of more hæmorrhage. The next morning the gauze was removed and no hæmorrhage followed. The discharge continued and was abundant and characteristic of endometritis. Until the 17th of February everything went along uneventfully, except for a feeling of weight and an occasional sharp pain in the suprapubic region.

On the 17th I examined the uterus, and found the organ much reduced in size, being four fingers' breadth below the umbilicus; but with the reduction in the size of the uterus a tumor had developed, or rather was distinguishable, on the right side.

The presentation of the growth might be appreciated if described as an orange placed one half outside and one half inside the uterus at or about the junction of the Falloppian tube, its outer half being palpable from the abdomen above, and giving more resistance to the right than to the left side of the cervix, through the vagina. The cervix was decidedly deflected to the left.

This evidence confirmed my suspicions that other conditions were present besides subinvolution and chronic endometritis.

On the 18th she reported another slight hæmorrhage, a little bright-red blood, but mostly clots.

Heretofore I had entertained the idea of extra-uterine gestation, but not seriously. Now it was uppermost in my mind.

I understood, of course, that other conditions might be present, such as a fibromyoma, a salpingitis, or a pregnancy in a one-horned or double uterus.

Realizing the possibility of an extra-uterine gestation, I brought my battery on the 18th of February with the idea of destroying the life of the fœtus, if there was one, and then proceeding on the advice of consultation. I applied both the faradaic and galvanic currents on the 18th and 19th of February. The patient complained once or twice of a sharp shooting pain, but could not locate it.

On the afternoon of February 19th the patient, being fond of the electrical current, thought she would apply some on her own account. She indulged in a long *séance* of about two hours.

During the night she suffered from sharp shooting pains and bearing-down cramps.

Early on the morning of the 20th I was called in a great hurry and received the following history:

Early in the morning the patient had been seized with a very severe bearing-down pain, and following this felt something coming from her. She supposed it to be a clot of blood, but on examining discovered a fœtus which was held by the cord to the mouth of the vagina.

I found the fœtus small for its presumable age, about two and a half to three months.

It was easily removed to a distance of about two inches from the vagina, but traction on the cord would not budge anything else.

There was some oozing of bright-red blood from the vagina. I introduced my hand into the vagina and passed the index finger through the cervix, following the cord as far as possible, but I was unable to reach the placenta, and did not know where it was situated.

As soon as I could procure a doctor to give chloroform, the patient was anæsthetized and held in the necessary position by a sheet passed under the knees and tied around the neck. Introducing my hand into the vagina, and two fingers through the cervix, by following the cord and bearing down from above I could reach the site of the placenta, high up on the right side and strongly adherent to the upper wall of a dilated pouch with very thin walls. On the left side of the uterus the muscular walls of that body were of natural thickness and contracted. The middle third of the uterus was as would be expected in a womb of that size—that is, the walls were about half an inch in thickness, while on the right side the tissues were dilated into a gourd-shaped pouch, with its walls, as it seemed to me, as thin as parchment. An attempt to loosen the attachment of the placenta brought on a contraction of the uterus, which shut off from access the cavity containing the secundines. Removal of my hand was followed by a gush of blood so serious as to necessitate immediate bimanual compression of the uterus, followed, after the hæmorrhage had been controlled, by the use of a hot douche and subsequent packing with gauze. The blood had simply spurted in all directions in the most alarming manner and, although the pulse stood it well, the general condition of the patient showed the loss of blood.

On removing the gauze the profuse flow of blood was seen to be checked, though there was considerable oozing.

There was no time to be lost, and realizing that the placenta must be removed without delay, and through the vagina if possible, I determined to go ahead and get it out.

The adhesions of the placenta to its unnatural wall were very firm and hard to reach, and any attempt to use instruments, without my fingers in the womb to plug the cervix and control bleeding, resulted in hæmorrhage.

To make a long story short, during the intervals between those measures used to control hæmorrhage, I succeeded in removing the placenta in about twenty small pieces and one large piece containing the membranes. I experienced no little difficulty in doing this, as I was without help except for the double and most valuable assistance rendered by the anæsthetizer.

The uterus was tightly packed with sterilized iodoform gauze and the patient put to bed in a fairly good condition, notwithstanding the serious loss of blood. I presume that during the operation of curettage I opened up a way through which the conception could be expelled into the uterus.

This event was brought about undoubtedly by the death of the fœtus, or the use of the electrical current brought around sufficient contractions to produce this desired result and unexpected termination.

The patient's pulse and temperature, though somewhat elevated, gave no trouble and her recovery was uneventful, save for a few pains in the central pelvic region and right side.

She was very sore and tender on right side and in median line. At the end of three weeks she could walk around with fair comfort, though any exertion, as raising her right arm above her head, would produce a dragging pain in the right side.

On examining her, four weeks after the last operative procedure, the uterus was much decreased in size, and on the right side I could only make out more resistance than on the left, and farther out toward the ovary a cord of about the size of a pencil. The region on right side was sensitive, but not painful.

A little over four weeks from the discharge of the fœtus the patient began to menstruate. The flow was painful, profuse, bloody, and accompanied with clots and membranous material. The flow continued for fourteen days, and then stopped for three days, but reappeared at intervals during the next week, and finally ceased altogether.

I examined her about April 10th and found the uterus small and movable and somewhat displaced backward. There was only a feeling of discomfort on the right side and nothing definite could be made out. On April 15th her menstrual period returned. This time it was almost free from pain, lasted four days, and was perfectly normal, being accompanied with little or no disturbance. Under the use of tonics and restoratives she gained rapidly in strength, and is at the present time in an excellent condition of physical and mental health.

371 WEST END AVENUE.

Dr. JOHNSON expressed his admiration for the way in which this trying case had been treated and brought to a successful issue.

Specimen of Osteosarcoma of the Lung. — Dr. HOTCHKISS presented a specimen of osteosarcoma of the lung which had been taken from a colored boy, aged seven, on whom he had performed an amputation at the hip joint for a large, rapidly growing osteosarcoma of the femur several weeks previously.

When the case was first seen, on January 28th, the child had a large, soft, fluctuating tumor which occupied the anterior and lateral aspects of the lower third of the right femur. The mother said she had noticed a small lump about a month previously in the same situation, which lump was not at first painful, but which had lately become so, and had increased very rapidly in size. She said that the boy had been injured by a blow or fall on the affected side. On admission to Bellevue Hospital, January 28th, the swelling presented so many of the signs of an inflammatory condition that, in spite of a tentative diagnosis of sarcoma, an incision was made, as an acute osteomyelitis could not be excluded on account of the pain, tenderness, fluctuation, and irregular temperature. The incision, however, revealed the presence of a large amount of fluid blood and clot, and a considerable amount of very soft material was scooped out, in which were felt very fine trabeculæ of bone. Some of this soft tissue was sent to a competent pathologist, who reported it to be probably sarcoma, but who later said the growth was probably not sarcomatous and advised delay, asking for further specimens. The growth, however, had rapidly assumed all the clinical features of a rapidly growing sarcoma, and the pain, fever, and emaciation increased markedly. In the mean time the pathologist had examined a second specimen, which had been submitted to him, and reported it to be an osteosarcoma.

On March 7th, at the parents' request, an amputation at the hip joint had been done. Wyeth's pins were used and the hæmorrhage was perfectly controlled. The operation was rapidly done and the patient put to bed in good condition. The child had been free from pain since the amputation and had been able to sit up in the ward. His wound had healed except at the inner end, where infection had occurred from soiling of the dressings with fæces. After about three weeks he had been attacked with bronchitis, at first quite acute, and begun to suffer from dyspnœa. He died about a month after the operation from exhaustion and in a condition of extreme emaciation. The post-mortem revealed osteosarcoma of both lungs. The diaphragm had been converted into a bony arch, which was osteosarcoma. The pleura showed the same changes and was adherent to the ribs, which were in places eroded. There was a distinct bony bar at the transverse arch of the aorta. The heart was uninvolved, as were the other organs. The specimen was presented as showing very beautifully a typical osteosarcoma of the lung which seemed to reproduce perfectly all the gross features of the primary growth on the femur.

Dr. REGINALD H. SAYRE presented in connection with this case a Röntgen picture of an osteosarcoma of the shaft of the tibia. It was a spindle-cell sarcoma of very slow growth. He had not seen the child until it was seven years of age, and the history of the growth apparently dated back about six years.

Paper.

AN OPERATING TABLE AND CHAIR DESIGNED FOR USE IN AN OFFICE OR HOSPITAL.

By ROBERT M. TAFT, M. D.

A YEAR ago I presented before this society an operating chair which I had designed for use in Bellevue Hospital. The chair was introduced at Bellevue in September, 1896, and since that time has seen constant service in the minor surgical room. Many thousands of cases have been dressed upon it. This chair, though well adapted for the uses of a crowded dressing room, was heavy, bulky, elaborate in mechanism, and expensive in construction. I realized that a simpler, less expensive apparatus would better meet the demands of a private office or outside surgical cases, and still be of practically the same value in hospital work. It is such a table as this that I take pleasure in exhibiting to you this evening. The chair, as can be seen by the accompanying illustration, is constructed of a light but strong steel framework, upon which rest thin plates of steel. It is enameled white, with nickel trimmings. A shelf of glass (*E*) is so placed as to add strength to the superstructure, and provide a convenient resting place for instruments, dressings, and solutions. The mechanism is simple in construction and easily cleaned. There is no upholstery upon the table, so a shower of water can be played upon it without injury. Thus it can be kept perfectly clean and aseptic. It is, I think, built on graceful lines, and is both light and strong. Without the glass plate it weighs about twenty-five pounds. If necessary for use in an operation, I have found that it was easily transported to the house of the patient. It can be sent by an express wagon without fear of injury, or can be taken in a cab. According to the manipulations of the head and foot pieces (*B* and *C*), it can be made as required into a chair, a small table, a table for abdominal operations, or a short table for perineal work. If a gynæcological operation is contemplated, the stirrup at-

tachment is easily applied. In this position it can be
used for either examination or operation. If a case is
to be dressed and a hand happens to be the injured
member, it can rest on the central plate (*A*, Fig. 1),

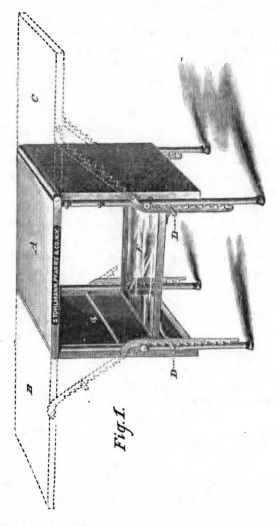

Fig. I.

the patient standing by the table or sitting on a chair.
A Kelly pad may now be placed under the hand, and
by slightly raising the lower section (*C*) you have pro-

vided an inclined plane along which the drainage flows into a receptacle on the floor. This support and drainage leaves both hands of the surgeon free, and enables him to do better and more rapid work, and with far less fatigue to himself. All the necessary instruments and dressings can be placed on the glass shelf out of the sight of the patient. An injury to the arm, head, or face can be conveniently treated in a like manner. A wound of the foot or leg is more handily attended by converting the apparatus into a chair, and the foot piece (*C*) inclined to that degree which best suits the case. A plaster-of-Paris boot is readily applied with the table in this position. The chair is easily converted into a table adapted to almost any surgical procedure. This is done by raising the two outer sections (*B* and *C*). These sections are held in their different positions by a notched steel brace on either side. These braces are connected by a rod (*F*), and consequently work in unison when the power is applied to the knob (*D*). The sides are thus easily lowered or raised. In operations about the perinæum an excellent short table can be formed by lowering the foot piece, as in Fig. 2. It is not then necessary to drag the patient to the foot of the table after ether has produced its effects. The leg holders (*G, G*) can be used instead of a Clover crutch. The table is admirably adapted to gynæcological work, either for examination or operation. Where used in these cases, a Kelly pad is placed under the patient, and several practical demonstrations have proved to me that the drainage is perfect, and not a drop of solution reaches the floor, it all being collected in the pan under the table. In special work about the eye, ear, nose, or throat the chair can be adjusted so that the operator will find it convenient to reach any part of the face or neck. To facilitate this work it would be well to have a simple head piece attached to the back section. At the junction of the central piece (*A*) and the foot piece (*C*) is a nickel-plated roller which allows the patient to get on and off the chair with ease. Leather or rubber cushions could be provided if the operator so wished. The apparatus seems to meet the demands of general surgical work. It is not an expensive chair to make, and the mechanism being simple in construction, needs little or

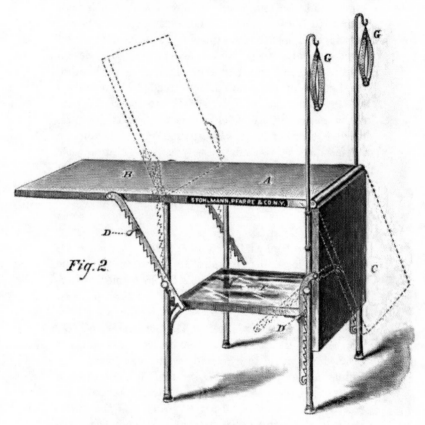

Fig. 2.

no repairing. It is made by George Tiemann & Co., and is sold complete for twenty-five dollars.

May 4, 1898.

A Foreign Body in the Hand.—Dr. FREDERICK HOLME WIGGIN presented two Röntgen pictures of a lady's hand in which a needle had lodged three years previously. One was taken with the palmar surface in position and the other with the dorsal, the result showing plainly that the needle was nearest the palmar surface, where it was afterward found by means of an incision made along the inner side of the dorsal surface of the first metacarpal bone, followed by a separation of the muscular fibres. The wound healed primarily; the mobility of the thumb was in no degree impaired.

A Convenient Retractor for the Abdominal Wall.— Dr. WIGGIN exhibited a pair of large retractors which he had found very useful in retracting the abdominal wall during laparotomy. The instrument, which bore some resemblance to the old duck-bill speculum, was of such a size and shape that the whole thickness of the abdominal parietes was firmly held in its grasp. The instrument was presented because the surgeons in this city did not seem to be acquainted with it.

Paper.

BRAIN ANATOMY AND PSYCHOLOGY.

By STEWART PATON, M. D.

THE study of brain anatomy has been a most important factor in the development of psychology. Weber has said that every science passes through three stages: (1) Theological, (2) metaphysical, and (3) positive or scientific stage. It is proposed to review as briefly as possible some of the influences which have aided psychology in passing from its metaphysical into its scientific period, and to recall the fact that the impetus of the new psychology is largely due to the work of the brain anatomists. Reference will be made chiefly to the influence that the study of the structural conditions of the central nervous system has exerted in determining this development; but, as anatomy and physiology can never be entirely dissociated, attention must necessarily be directed to certain facts in mental physiology. Every student of psychology must be impressed by the force of the affirmation that "the aim of true philosophy should not be so much the discovery of new truths as the prevention of error." Unfortunately, the history of psychology has given little evidence that the workers in this field of science have appreciated this truth. Even to-day there are students of mental phe-

nomena who ignore the source of that vital impulse
which from the time of Thomas Willis has been a factor
of increasing importance in the development of the
" new psychology." Certain ungracious critics often refer to the present very limited knowledge of cerebral
structure and function as bearing testimony to a lamen-
table poverty of facts. These persons forget that it was
the work of years to destroy the old psychological ideals,
the " stuff that dreams are made of," and they ignore
the fact that this process was necessary before the psychological renaissance was possible. The history of the
development of the new conceptions of the structure
and function of the brain is not the story of the evolution of a specialty. Anatomists, physiologists, and
clinicians have all contributed their share to the common store of facts. This is an important lesson. The
investigator who to-day enters upon this field of research must not be blind to the advantages of Plato's
four-sided man as compared with the individual who
looks at psychology only through a high-power lens, or
who, on the other hand and equally as bad, is willing
to call himself one of the purely " introspective school."
It should be very gratifying to the members of the medical profession to recall the fact that psychology developed under the care of the anatomists, physiologists,
and clinicians who founded modern scientific medicine. For centuries the spirit which characterizes the
new psychology gave little evidence of any vitality. Its
reawakening was due to the same causes that resulted
in the birth of the new learning. Descartes, as he conducted his friend to his dissecting room and showed
him the work he was doing there, said " Here is my
library," and thus indicated, as it were, the path along
which psychology must travel to be at last assured a
place among the sciences. It is impossible to fix the
exact date of the psychological renaissance. Thomas
Willis undoubtedly marks a new era in the study of
mental phenomena. He has been called by some the
" father " of the more rational methods of investigating
the structure and function of the brain. It is about

the time of Willis that the psychical functions of the brain were first definitely recognized, although centuries before Alcmæon had stated in a very indefinite way that the brain was the organ of mind. The Platonic trinity of heart, liver, and brain for centuries influenced all the conceptions regarding the structure and function of the central nervous system. This theory received its deathblow from Willis and his followers. The psychical importance of the cerebrum was recognized, and in the reaction of opinion against the Platonic theory the pendulum went too far to the other extreme, and all functions of the nervous system were said to be directly dependent upon cerebral activity. The accumulations of facts from various sources soon rendered this theory untenable. Investigations of the anatomists on anencephalic monsters, the consensus of opinion derived from countless experiments on animals, and the observations of clinicians, all tended to demonstrate the impossibility of adhering to this belief. Willis divided the functions of the soul into " vegetative " and " rational," and in doing this he removed psychology out of the grasp of the scholastics. From the results of imperfectly conducted experiments, Willis located the centre for the vegetative activities in the cerebellum. This error should not make any one forgetful of the real good Willis did by clearly and definitely insisting upon the fact that all functions of the nervous system were not directly dependent upon the cerebrum as a centre. He also demonstrated the possibility of applying the same methods to the investigation of psychical as were used in the study of physical phenomena. The new impetus given by Willis to the study of the brain aroused great interest among the anatomists and physiologists. It is impossible even to mention the names of those who followed in his footsteps. Haller improved the methods of research. He located sensation in the nerves and movement in the muscles, and in doing this Haller opened up a new field in the study of the functions of the nervous system. The domination of every "ism" in psychology, as in other sciences, has been unfortunate, and the rule of materialism established by the Haller school was no exception to the rule. The attempt to explain all forms of psychical activity by recourse to what might be called the coarser forms of materialism was a failure, and this must be kept in mind in considering the influence of Stahl and his pupils. Haller's attempt to account for the functions of the brain by a theory of inherent irritability was unsatisfactory. It was an effort to explain the differences between voluntary and involuntary motions. The Stahlian theory was accepted by many who were unwilling to entirely relinquish the old idea of the soul or *anima* as of great psychical importance. Little by little the anatomists had shown that this "mysterious metaphysical essence" was not to be found in the glandula pinealis or in any other of the various abodes assigned to it by the schoolmen. At last Zinn formulated the belief that the soul was not located in any one part of the brain: "*Anima sedem per omne cerebrum.*" Until this time the brain had been considered the centre of all the functions of the nervous system. Although it is true that from the time of Galen various investigations had been carried on with a view to determining both the structure and function of the cord, these studies had in no way detracted from the supposed despotic sway of the cerebrum. Gradually observers realized that the spinal cord was the seat of independent centres. The medulla was also studied. Fracassati demonstrated that some of the cranial nerves had their origin here. This was the first of a series of investigations which showed the importance of the medulla as a nervous centre, and gave greater emphasis to the fact that the "rational" and "vegetative" functions of the nervous system were dependent upon the activity of different parts of the brain. The structural as well as the functional differences between the higher and lower brain centres were at last recognized.

Although at first glance it appears as if Stahlism or animism was very far from being a scientific interpretation of mental phenomena, it must not be forgotten that the advocates of this belief aided considerably in the promulgation of the new doctrines. Neuberger has called attention to the fact that the Stahlian conceptions were modified by Robert Whytt in England and by Unzer in Germany, and these modified ideas were embodied in the newer and more rational interpretation of the cerebral structure and functions. Whytt said that his investigations led him to believe that the "anima" is nothing more or less than the "indefinite" force which represented the translation of sensation into motion, that this act was at times accompanied by a state of consciousness, while at others there was no conscious cerebration. Unzer recognized certain acts as conscious and others, due only to what he called "nervous forces," as unconscious. This was an important advance; but another step was necessary before the discoveries of Bell and Marshall Hall were possible. In the reaction against the teachings of Haller the idea of cerebral localization had been brought into discredit. For centuries the idea of associating certain functions with certain definite areas of the central nervous system had been looked upon as a favorite theme for the exercise of the speculative and imaginative powers of the schoolmen. In the fifth century Nemesios asserted that memory was located in the posterior, understanding in the middle, and imagination in the anterior ventricle. The work of the anatomists, aided by the observations of practising physicians and surgeons, finally demonstrated the absurdities of these views and the absolute impossibility of establishing any system of psychology which was not founded on a knowledge of the structure of the brain. It was not unnatural that the idea of cerebral localization should have been abandoned for the time by scientific investigators. The dialectic resources of the theologians and scholastics succeeded temporarily in hiding the real element of truth beneath an enormous mass of speculation. "But truth crushed to earth will rise again," and it is to the credit of the anatomists and the surgeons that they were able to give the impulse which was needed. The investigations of François Pourfour du Petit in anatomy and those of

13

Sabourant in surgery were of incalculable value in
stimulating research in this line of study. By their
efforts the theory of cerebral localization was presented
in a newer and more rational form. It was demonstrated that certain functions were localized in certain
definite parts of the nervous system. Gall's well-known
practical application of this idea need not be mentioned.
Science should not forget that Gall was really the first
to direct attention to the importance of the cerebral
cortex in relation to psychical phenomena. The French
surgeons of the eighteenth century made many valuable
contributions which confirmed the work of the anatomists. Investigations in comparative anatomy had already resulted in many valuable contributions which
confirmed the work of the anatomists. Sömmering
concluded that "the soul power" varied in different
animals and was, to a certain extent, dependent on the
size of the brain. He also said (a view in which he was
supported by Ebel) that "the size of the cerebrum in
comparison with the size of the medulla was to a certain extent a measure of the mental capabilities." Investigators soon began to try to determine experimental-
ly the relations of the cerebrum to the psychical process.
Rolando, the Italian anatomist, called attention to the
relation of the cerebrum to the intelligence, will power,
and to the perception of sensation. When at last the
principle contained in the idea of cerebral localization
was firmly reestablished, the way was open for the great
discoveries which marked the first half of the present
century. It is impossible even now to form a correct
judgment regarding the far-reaching consequences of
the discovery of the motor and sensory nerves by Charles
Bell and the theory of reflex action by Marshall Hall.
The discovery of reflex action marks a new era in the
history of psychology. It may be said that although
this discovery threw no light upon the nature of mental
phenomena, it was nevertheless of the greatest importance, as it removed one of the stumbling-blocks which
for centuries had effectively checked the development of
a rational psychology. In other words, this discovery

simplified the problems which remained to be solved. The discovery of the nature of the reflex phenomena was based upon the results of a long series of anatomical investigations. At the same time the more rational methods of investigation were applied to the study of mental phenomena. It is not too much to say that the proper field of investigation for the psychologist was outlined for him by the anatomist. The advances that have been made in the study of the structure and the functions of the brain since the days of Bell and Hall have been due in the main to two factors: First, the introduction of the true scientific spirit into the study of the structure and function of the brain; and second, as a result of this, the improvement of the methods and technique of investigations. In 1833 Ehrenberg called attention to the fact that the organ of mind was composed "of countless small tubes." This was the first definite description of the nerve fibres. In the year 1838 Remak described the ganglion cells, and two years after this Hannover suggested that the cells and fibres were definitely related to each other. This fact was confirmed later by Helmholtz. From this time on the workers in this field have constantly increased in numbers, and in no other science has effort found a better reward. The advances of the last fifty years are, in a general way, known to all. Each new fact regarding the structure and functions of the brain has served to show the marvelous complexity of the central nervous system. This fact has emphasized the truth that the time has not yet come when any definite system of psychology can be deduced from the facts which are now known regarding the structure and function of the brain. Flechsig's investigations on the development of the fibres in the cord and brain mark a new era not only in the study of the brain anatomy, but in psychology as well. He has demonstrated anatomically that the child at birth is, as Virchow said, " a spinal thing," and, as the nerve centres in the cord and medulla at birth are alone capable of functioning, it may be said that the newborn infant is " a vegetative " but not " a rational " being.

As the different nerve fibres in the various tracts receive their myeline sheaths, and connections are established between the higher and lower brain centres, a correlated increase of mental activity is noted as these new tracts develop. The psychologists of the future will undoubtedly make a valuable contribution to science when more systematic studies are made ragarding the correlation which exists between structure and function for all periods in the life of the individual. This structural and functional correlation is emphasized by referring to certain mental diseases which are characterized by definite changes in the brain. For example, the structural conditions which exist in the cortex of the child during the second year of life have many points in common with the lesions of the cortex to be seen in cases of dementia paralytica (Fig. 1).

Fig. 1.—Anterior central convolution. Dementia paralytica. Drawn from a preparation in the writer's possession.

The sparsity of the fibres, the relatively small number of both short and long association fibres, is characteristic of the cortex in both cases. Not only is the structural similarity apparent, but there is a marked functional correspondence. The child's limited power of associating ideas, the inability to fix its attention for any considerable time, are comparable to the chain of symptoms which is often observed in cases of paresis. This structural correspondence between the infantile and pathological conditions of the cortex should be more carefully studied.

" Infant psychology," when studied in connection with the correlated structural changes of the brain, is undoubtedly one of the fundamental necessities upon which the future of psychiatry depends. As the power of associating ideas increases and the ability to concentrate the attention as well as the capacity for prolonged physical effort becomes more apparent, a correlated structural complexity in the higher brain centres is demonstrable. No better idea can be given of the purely theoretical basis upon which the old psychology rested than by recalling Kant's statement in reference to the psychical possibilities of the newborn infant: "The cry uttered by the child just after birth has not the intonation of fear, but that of irritation or anger"; and the philosopher adds, "No doubt, the child would like to move and feel its impotence as it might feel a change restricting its liberty." The anatomist has demonstrated the absurdity of this conception. That the cry has no psychical importance is easily demonstrable, for the structural conditions are such that psychical phenomena at birth are impossible. On the other hand, Preyer's statement that newborn infants during their first days may be pricked with fine needles deeply enough to draw blood, and yet the infant manifests no symptom of consciousness, is in accord with the deductions which can be made from the observations of Flechsig. From birth to the prime of life, as mental activity increases, the connections between the higher and lower brain centres multiply with astonishing rapidity. At the prime of life the cortex has reached its period of greatest complexity. The higher centres are more intimately connected with each other than ever before. When the individual has passed the prime of life and entered upon the period which is marked by the impairment of intellectual power, regressive, correlated structural changes exist. Many arguments may be deduced from the facts discovered by comparative anatomists which emphasize the correlation between structure and function. At birth, so far as functional activity is concerned, the brain of the infant is inferior to that of the trout. In the infant the elements of the cortex are present, but for all practical purposes they resemble the disconnected elements of an electric machine. In

the trout the highest centres are incapable of functional
activity because the trout's cortex consists only of epithelial cells without the presence of any nervous elements. But the fish has a decided advantage. The in-
termediate brain centres are capable of functional
activity, and therefore the structural conditions of the
trout's brain offer a much greater possibility for the
association of the various impulses than is to be found
in the brain of the newborn infant. Gradually the infant rises, as it were, in the animal scale. Its olfactory
tract develops cortical connections. At this stage the
infant's central nervous system is comparable functionally to that of the amphibians. Then the optic tract
develops cortical connections and the infant has developed the structural changes which render a comparison
with the bird possible. The development of the child's
brain shows many correspondences structurally and
functionally to the conditions which are seen in studying
the different brains of the animal series. Comparative
anatomy and comparative psychology have contributed
many valuable facts to the knowledge of the structure
and functions of the human brain, but it is unfortunate
that a more persistent effort has not been made to bring
together and assimilate the results of the investigations
in ontogeny on the one hand with those of phylogeny
on the other. Psychology has made few attempts to
try to solve the simpler problems, and has directed much
attention to the study of the functions of the brain only
at a time when the structural conditions were the most
complex. Much valuable information will undoubtedly
be obtained by the structural and functional comparison of the human brain in the early stages of its development with the brain in the animal series to which, at a
given period, it most nearly corresponds. One example
is sufficient to suggest what is meant. It has been seen
that the infant's brain at a certain period of development is comparable to the bird's brain, for only two of
the sense areas have cortical connections—namely, those
of smell and sight. The structural similarity having
been noted, it would be interesting to see how far func-

tional comparison is possible. The problem might be attacked in another way, and the observer might ask, How is the infant functionally inferior to the bird at the time when the olfactory and visual tracts have no cortical connections? The psychology of the future must be one which is based upon the knowledge of the structure of the organ of mind. It must study more carefully the correlation which exists between structure and function, and to accomplish this it must pay more attention to the solution of the simpler problems in comparative psychology. Brief mention has been made of the fibres which serve as the paths for conduction of impulses. A few words may be said about the elements which are related to the production of these impulses. It is needless to say that the mode of translation of sensory impulses into motor or physical phenomena, or *vice versa,* is not understood. Still, it may be asserted that the truth of Ribot's statement that " psychical phenomena can not be dissociated from their physical conditions " is an excellent " working hypothesis." Although nothing is known regarding the exact method by which the various impulses are produced, it is nevertheless of great importance to study the structural relations which exist between these elements and the various paths of conduction.

In 1854 Remak demonstrated that the ganglion cells of the cord gave rise to two kinds of processes, one of which, the axis-cylinder process, " could be followed into the nerves." Remak had been induced to prosecute the line of research which resulted in this discovery by the suggestions which Rudolph Wagener had made in 1850 regarding the nature of the cells in the electrical apparatus in certain fish. In 1865 Deiters demonstrated that what Remak had shown to exist for the ganglion cells in the cord was likewise true for the nerve cells in all parts of the central nervous system. From Deiters's time until the present day the ganglion cell has been the object of numerous investigations. It is unnecessary for the present purpose to refer to many of the facts that have been brought to light regarding the structure of

the ganglion cell. Golgi's investigations inaugurated a
new era in brain anatomy. His work has been supplemented by the researches of Ramon y Cajál and many
others. It may be said without exaggeration that no
work which has been done since the days of Bell and
Marshall Hall has so revolutionized the ideas and opin-
ions held regarding the structure and function of the
nervous system as has the work of Golgi and his school.
No one can doubt that these conceptions regarding the
structural relations have profoundly modified many
views previously held regarding not only the structure
but the function of the various elements in the nervous system. Since Golgi began his researches in the
early seventies, much light has been thrown upon the
paths of conduction for the impulses after their origin
in the cell. The anatomical relations of the different
nervous centres to each other have also been studied, and
inferences of practical importance have been drawn regarding the governing power of these centres.   The
great number of researches which have been made in
later years, chiefly with the Golgi methods, seem to demonstrate that each nerve cell, with its protoplasmic
branches and its axis cylinder process, was a structural
unit, and that this unit was structurally independent
of any other cell, as no continuity of the elements was
demonstrated. The exact method by which an impulse
is transmitted from one of these structural units to
another is merely a matter of conjecture. No actual
contact of the processes has ever been demonstrated by
the Golgi or other methods.   The investigations of
Wiedersheim several years ago in some of the lower organisms suggested the possibility of the contraction and
expansion of these processes. This idea was accepted
by many as a possible means of explaining certain psychical phenomena, such as sleep and the varying degrees
of consciousness, etc. During periods of " subconscious
activity " it was thought the cell processes were retracted, and during the more active degrees of consciousness they were again extended. Van Gieson has been led
to believe that the fibrillary structure of the cells and

processes suggested contractile powers and had something to do with the supposed movements of the processes. These theories, if true, would doubtless aid in
solving many psychical problems, but unfortunately as
yet the facts do not warrant this deduction. One of the
chief reasons for the writer's skeptical attitude in regard to this theory is that more recent investigations
apparently indicate that the present " neuron conception " of the nervous system is not an established truth.
It is impossible, when referring to the nature of the
single elements which form the various nervous centres,
not to refer to the investigations of Apáthy. If the
results of his researches stand the subsequent tests which
should be applied to them, different conceptions regarding not only the structure but the functions of the
various elements of the nervous system will be essential.
Apáthy's researches have been conducted with great care,
and the results are published in detail.

Although his investigations have been confined mostly to the invertebrates and some few of the lower orders
of the vertebrates, the principle involved is very important. These studies have been so carefully made, the
methods of research so plainly stated, and the results
given with so little reference to purely theoretical conceptions that it is imperative that anatomists as well as
the clinicians should endeavor to test the accuracy of
these results. The main conclusions of Apáthy's investigations are as follows: In the first place he says
there are two chief varieties of cells to be found in the
nervous system. The one which he calls the *nerve cell*
produces the conducting substance; the other cell, or
ganglion cell proper, is the source of the impulse. All
the elements which enter into the structure of the nervous system are said to be connected in unbroken structural continuity. Attention is called to the fact that
at the very beginning, as soon as the cells are differen
tiated in the germ, various branching protoplasmic processes can be distinguished; but at first these processes
consist only of masses of undifferentiated protoplasm.
Later in the development it is evident that small fibrils

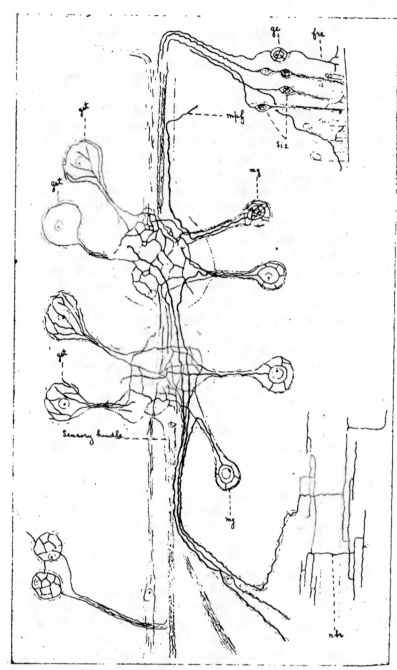

Fig. 2.—Diagrammatic representation of the course and connections of conducting tracts in transverse section of Hirudo somites. *mg*, motor ganglion cell; *gst*, connecting ganglion cell; *mpf*, motor primitive fibril; *fre*, "free end branch" in periphery; *gc*, ganglion cell; *nbr*, connecting bridge between muscle fibres; *siz*, sensory epithelial cell. (S. Apáthy.)

can be seen extending along the processes. These fibrils, which develop from the nerve cells and not from the ganglion cells, serve to connect the various elements. They unite not only groups of nerve cells and ganglion cells, but can often be traced into the peripheral sensory cells, so that, according to Apáthy, the nervous system is not made up of a series of disconnected units, but is structurally as well as functionally one (Fig. 2). A number of the small elementary fibrils unite to form other and larger fibrils, which Apáthy calls the primitive conducting fibrils. A primitive conducting fibril may eventually become split up into a fine network, sometimes inside of the various cells, at other times in the intervals between the cells. It is a curious fact that Apáthy's investigations are in a measure confirmatory of the theory advanced nearly fifty years ago by Gerlach; but, as Apáthy himself says, Gerlach believed in the existence of this " fine network of fibres " only from hypothetical reasons. For nearly half a century the presence of this network has never been actually demonstrated by any observer until the present series of investigations. Apáthy's experience as yet can neither be affirmed nor denied.

The student of brain anatomy should for the present absolutely refuse to construct elaborate theories upon the neurone or any other conceptions of the nervous system. It is far better to assume the spirit indicated in Pasteur's reply to a friend, who asked him what he thought about certain of Liebig's views. " I have no opinion," said the savant; " I will investigate."

One aim of the present paper has been to show the dependence of the new psychology and the new psychiatry upon a knowledge of cerebral structure. The past shows conclusively that no rational study of mind is possible which does not have for its chief end and aim the study of the correlation which exists between cerebral structure and function. Psychology as well as psychiatry should exhibit greater patience in criticising those who claim for the study of brain anatomy a more general recognition than it has yet obtained.

The classification of either normal or abnormal mental processes is as yet impossible. The attempt to study mental diseases only from the clinical side has failed as signally as has the effort of the introspective psychologist to establish his system for the study of mind. The beginnings of a more rational study of both the normal and abnormal workings of the mind have at last been

Fig. 3.—Cortex of the anterior central convolution. Child one year and a quarter. (After Kaes.)

Fig. 4.—Cortex of the anterior central convolution, normal. About the thirty-sixth year. (After Kaes.)

established. But, unfortunately, the old spirit has not been deprived of all its vitality, and is so apparent in the writings and teachings of many psychologists and psychiatrists that the truth in the poet's exclamation—"How," she cried, "you love the metaphysics!"—may be considered as descriptive of the attitude of certain critics of the new psychology.

Literature.

F. Nissl. Psychiatrie u. Hirnanatomie. *Monatsschr. f. Psy. u. Neurol.*, Bd. iii, Heft 2 to 3.

S. Apáthy. *Mittheil. aus der zoolog. Station zu Neapel,* Bd. xii, Heft 4.

Neuburger. *Entwickelung der Gehirn- u. Rücken-marksphysiologie.*

Dr. IRA VAN GIESON said that this most charming discourse gave evidence of most profound reading. It showed among other things that modern scientific research was creating gaps between the different departments, which contained more profound and valuable truths than the individual sciences themselves. Dr. Paton had this evening been bridging over the gap between psychology and cerebral anatomy, and it was precisely in this gap that great generalizations were to be found. There was a class of people who garnered the facts and stopped there; they looked through the microscope and described the swelling of granules and the shrinking of cells, but they gave no answer to the question of the meaning of these things. Another class of people was represented by those who were able to systematize these facts and present them in the form of laws and gneralizations. It was a mistaken notion to believe that science was alone concerned with collecting facts, and not in weaving theories. Medicine, the speaker said, had great need of psychology, for the neurologist had not the means with which to attack his problems without psychology. Psychiatry was hardly a science; it was simply an art. The psychiatrist was like a squirrel traveling around in a cage, and not making any headway, and the reason was to be found in the absence of all methods of investigation—it was a pretense. The term " psychiatry " should be replaced by the words " pathological psychology." Possibly the psychiatrist had been held apart from the brain anatomist by the fear of falling into the pitfall of materialism, because, after all, it must be remembered that if we possessed the ultimate knowledge of molecules of the ganglion cells, and the most perfect knowledge of all their connections, it would not help us to postulate the phenomena of consciousness, because thought could not be weighed or measured. Thought was not the equivalent of ganglion-cell activity; the brain did not secrete ideas, as the kidney secreted urine. It was Huxley, he thought, who had brought out the idea that the phenomena of consciousness lay parallel with these activities of the ganglion cells; but we could not say that one was the equivalent of the other. Psychology was the

science of consciousness, but we could not define consciousness. Although the science of the geometer
dealt with the relations of space, he was unable to define
space; but that did not prevent him from ascertaining
the properties of spatial relations. So it was with the
psychologist; he could not define consciousness, but he
could study its phenomena. The crowning glory of the
psychology of the present day was its entire emancipa-
tion from metaphysics. It had been shown that the
human mind could be studied by the same methods
as those employed in studying the distant stars, or a
tiny organism, or any other phenomena in the physical world. Dr. Paton had shown how the brain consisted of a relatively small part communicating with
the outer world, and a very large part, which did not
come in contact with the outside world, but which took
the impressions coming from the smaller part and
correlated them. This was the last attainment in man's
evolution—these supreme centres which had to do with
self-control and self-consciousness. Perhaps the two
greatest factors in dissipating the mysteries of the abnormal phenomena of consciousness were this conception
of Flechsig's plan and the retraction of the ganglion cell.
Dr. Van Gieson said that, to his mind, this subject could
be very graphically presented by a comparison with an
octopus. Like that animal, the ganglion cell had a number of tentacles on one side, and on the other side exceedingly long arms which conveyed an impression from one
distant part to another. Like the octopus, it assimilated
food from the vessels, and was able to retract and expand
its tentacles. The education of some of our lower centres had been going on through such long periods of time
—for instance, the centre of respiration and circulation
—that the channel had become ingrown; the nerve cells
had positively grown together. There was no thought of
retraction in such of the elementary portions of the nervous system as those of circulation and respiration, and it
would be a very dangerous thing if the nerve-cell octopus
were to withdraw its arms from the systems concerned
in the control of respiration and circulation; it would
be a constant menace to life. Those centres which were
developed first in the nervous system, and which had
been working for millions of years, had been educated
through these ages until they had made connections so
stable that they had actually grown together. But in
the higher centres the ganglion cells were not grown together; with these cells, which were the basis of human

intelligence, the condition was different. The neurones were constantly shifting, and it seemed absolutely impossible to explain in any rational way all the mysterious phenomena of loss of consciousness, the curious phenomena of hysteria, and such things as double consciousness. For instance, we knew that in hysteria the anæsthesia or hemiplegia might be absolute while it lasted, and yet the hemianæsthesia might disappear very rapidly. That could only be explained, he thought, by retraction or expansion of the nerve-cell octopus. What happened when the arms of the nerve-cell octopus were withdrawn? The entire current was broken, and, moreover, it was a signal of fatigue in the higher centres. The lower centres never rested, except in a rhythmical way. It was a pity that some Darwin did not come into medicine and weave the scattered facts of pathology into a theory like his grand one of selection and the survival of the fittest. Whatever in Darwinism applied to the body at large must apply to the cells themselves. Apáthy's studies were in the leech, which had no nervous system beyond that attending to the vegetative functions, and hence it was quite natural that such a chain of these nerve-cell octopuses should be absolutely stable—so stable as to be ingrown; but in the higher or association spheres of the brain it seemed to him entirely incompatible with the doctrine of concrescences. The associations would become ingrown and grooved, and would always travel in one channel.

In conclusion, Dr. Van Gieson said that to attempt to add to the charming discourse of the evening seemed very much like bringing " coals to Newcastle."

Dr. EDWARD D. FISHER said that he could only echo what had been said by the last speaker regarding the immense grasp of the subject that had been displayed by the author of the paper. In the investigation of psychology and anatomy there were unfortunately three sets of investigators, all working with only a partial knowledge—*i. e.*, the pathologist, who frequently had no clinical knowledge, the psychologist, who certainly had none, and the clinician, who usually had very little advanced knowledge and very little opportunity to make the necessary investigations in the laboratory. He was glad to say that Dr. Paton apparently represented a happy combination of the pathologist and the clinician. He did not believe we should ever find the cells which represented thought, although we might find cells which probably had little or nothing to do with thought. He

could not believe that we could go at it in the easy way
described by Dr. Van Gieson, as in the study of the stars
—indeed, such a method would hardly give us much
help.

As to the comparison of the brain of a child to the
brain of a paretic, it must be admitted that there were
certain striking resemblances. For instance, in both
there was the absence of association; in paretics the
association fibres were destroyed; in infants they were
not developed. This was a fortunate provision, because
ideas were simply impressions from external sensation,
which were repeated until they became fixed in the brain,
and if the association fibres were developed at birth, the
child would act with great muscular violence, because
it would not have the experience of a lifetime to
guide it.

Regarding the matter of consciousness, he said that
a distinction should be made between consciousness and
self-consciousness. The first was a mere function of the
cell itself, and was represented by the simple activity
of the cells. It was entirely different from self-consciousness, which represented the experience of a lifetime. He did not believe it possible to think of an hysterical babe—in other words, self-consciousness had not
yet been established.

On motion of Dr. S. Alexander, the society unani-
mously tendered a vote of thanks to Dr. Paton for the
trouble he had taken in coming to New York, and for
the very interesting discourse he had given the society
on the occasion of its one hundredth meeting.

Meeting of June 1, 1898.

The President, ROBERT J. CARLISLE, M. D., in the Chair.

**Penetrating Wound of the Abdomen; Peritonitis
from Infection through the External Wound.**—Dr.
ALEXANDER B. JOHNSON reported such a case. He said
that in times past wounds of the peritonæum were regarded as particularly dangerous; now we considered
this membrane as one possessing peculiar powers which
enabled it to limit and to eliminate infections.

The following case would serve to illustrate the fact

that in apparently slight injuries of the peritonæum
grave dangers might exist, and serious complications
arise, unless promptly met by operative interference:
A. M., forty years of age, an Irish laborer, had been admitted to the Roosevelt Hospital April 1, 1898. A few
hours previously he had been stabbed in the abdomen
and leg while quarreling. The patient was a large, robust man. There was a wound a quarter of an inch in
length, and apparently an inch and a half deep, at the
outer border of the right rectus muscle, about midway
between the ensiform cartilage and the umbilicus. There
were no signs of injury to the abdominal viscera. The
wound was disinfected and dressed, drainage being
with a shred of iodoform gauze. On the day following
the patient had no pain or tenderness in the neighborhood of the wound, which was again packed. The
next day the patient's temperature rose to 101° F. and
the pulse to 120. He complained of abdominal pains
and the abdomen was moderately distended, rigid upon
the right side, and very tender upon percussion and
pressure. During the afternoon of this day the patient
looked severely ill, and exploration of the wound was
made under nitrous oxide and ether anæsthesia, a vertical incision being made through the skin, with its centre at the site of the original wound. A considerable
quantity of thin pus escaped from a pocket which led
through the muscular layers of the abdomen. The
wound in the skin was enlarged to a length of six
inches, the fat layer being very thick. Further exploration showed that the suppurating tract led to a hole in
the peritonæum, through which a small portion of inflamed omentum protruded. The external wound was
thoroughly flushed with salt and water, and wiped dry,
when a small amount of pus could be seen escaping
through the hole in the peritonæum. On enlarging the
peritoneal wound, an area six inches in diameter, including the transverse colon and the omentum, was
found to be intensely red and coated with fibrin and a
little pus. There were no limiting adhesions, and no
perforation of intestine was found. The inflamed intestine and omentum were drawn out of the belly and
thoroughly washed with hot salt and water, and replaced.
The wound was then partly closed by suture of the several layers of the belly, except at the middle, where a
strand of gauze was left in the peritoneal cavity for
drainage. The patient required considerable stimulation after the operation, and his pulse became rapid and
feeble on the following day, but with no rise of tem-

14

perature above 100°. Signs referable to disturbance within the belly did not occur, but the external wound suppurated, so that the stitches were removed and the wound was not in a healthy granulated condition for two weeks. On May 1st there was only a superficial granulating wound, and the patient was allowed to walk out. He left the hospital on May 11th, with a fairly strong abdominal wall.

Thoracic Aneurysm with Unusual Symptoms.—Dr. ALEXANDER LAMBERT presented a specimen from a case of thoracic aneurysm, together with the following history: E. W., a moderate drinker, who had had no venereal disease other than gonorrhœa, had enjoyed excellent health with the exception of an attack of typhoid fever when fourteen years old. For the past six months he had been losing flesh. On May 6th, after having been out in the wet and cold, he had begun to have some pain in the chest, with slight cough and expectoration. There had been no chill or rise of temperature. On May 10th he had begun to have trouble in swallowing, and pain at the upper and lower ends of the sternum on trying to swallow solid food. On May 13th he had experienced a sudden attack of dyspnœa, and had had more or less dyspnœa ever since, especially at night. Since May 14th his deglutition had improved, and on coming under observation he was able to take solid food without any difficulty. Examination showed the patient to be well nourished and well developed. His face was anxious; he sat up in bed, and his breathing was of a peculiar stenotic character. Phonation was not impaired. The extremities were cold and cyanotic. The apex beat was in the fifth intercostal space at the nipple line; the heart action was extremely rapid but regular; there were no murmurs. The pulse was rapid, regular, and of slight tension. Over the entire right side of the thorax, both anteriorly and posteriorly, the percussion sound was normal, but the breathing and voice were rather high-pitched. Over the left side, in front, there was an area in which the percussion sound was nearly flat, and the breathing and voice were diminished. Over the upper part of the scapula there was a peculiar whistling character to the breathing, and over the rest of this side behind, while the percussion note was normal, the breathing and voice were diminished. On May 17th the patient's condition was generally improved; the breathing was less stenotic, and the area of flatness over the left lung was smaller. The patient's temperature ranged from 101° to 103° F. Death occurred on May 20th. On opening the thorax, at autopsy, the left pleural cavity was found to have been obliterated by recent thin adhesions. About one hundred cubic centimetres of cloudy yellow fluid were present. The upper lobe of the left lung was pale and slightly œdematous. The lower lobe was solid. The bronchi contained yellowish pus. There was slight peribronchial infiltration. The vessels were apparently normal. The upper lobe of the right lung was markedly congested and œdematous; the lower lobe was the seat of a hypostatic pneumonia. The pericardial cavity contained twenty cubic centimetres of clear fluid. The heart was of average size, and its muscle light reddish in color. The left ventricle was free from clot. There was marked atheromatous degeneration throughout the entire thoracic aorta. About eight cubic centimetres above the aortic valve, on the concave surface of the arch, was a large, recently organized clot, extending through the aorta into the middle mediastinum. This clot measured about ten cubic centimetres in diameter and was almost circular. Extending toward the concave surface of the arch, at the beginning of the transverse portion, was a rupture of the sac, measuring about three centimetres in diameter, and filled with partially organized clot. The right heart was dilated. The spleen was slightly enlarged and its capsule thickened. The stomach showed no lesion of its mucous membrane. The pancreas measured sixteen centimetres in length, and its tail was adherent to the spleen and vessels, and was markedly congested. The left kidney was decidedly enlarged, and its pelvis distended with clear yellow fluid, apparently due to obstruction at the beginning of the ureter. There was slight thickening at the proximal end of the ureter. Both kidneys presented evidence of passive congestion. A superficial examination showed no pathological change in the intestine. Examination of the abdominal vessels showed general arterial sclerosis.

Dr. JOHNSON said that a man had been brought to Roosevelt Hospital with a history of six weeks' illness, indefinite in character. There had seemed to be some obstruction of the left ureter; he had had severe pains in the loins, had passed but little urine, and had suffered from pains shooting into the testicle. When admitted he had presented the appearance of one suffering from severe sepsis. Dr. Delafield diagnosticated the case as peritonitis, and the man was transferred to the surgical ward. A large tumor was found on the left side, occupying the region of the loin, and seemingly larger than the head of an infant at term. The inference was drawn that it was a case of sarcoma. An incision was made, and what appeared to be a tumor was found in the bowel. At this juncture a severe hæmorrhage took place, necessitating the prompt packing of the opening. The patient died twenty-four hours later, and the autopsy revealed an aneurysm of the aorta and a large rupture at the transverse portion of the aorta. Neither of these had been suspected during life.

Intestinal Obstruction from an Enterolith; Operation; Recovery.—Dr. GEORGE D. STEWART reported the following case of enterolithiasis which had been transferred to him for operation by Dr. Phelps, in whose service at St. Vincent's Hospital it had occurred: A. C., thirty-five years of age, an Italian laborer was admitted to the hospital on May 16th. On Friday, the thirteenth day of May, the patient had eaten for his midday meal a great quantity of baked beans, and at supper he had eaten heartily of meat. Early in the evening he had been seized with severe, colicky abdominal pains, and a little later had begun to vomit undigested food. The vomiting and general abdominal pains had continued during Friday night and all of Saturday. On Saturday the vomited matter was greenish (evidently from bile), and the patient noticed that the tenderness was greater in the left iliac region. The bowels did not move on either Friday or Saturday. On Sunday a physician, who had been called, gave an enema with but very little result. The vomiting became stercoraceous, probably, and the pain was distinctly localized in the left iliac region. On Monday, the 16th, the patient was brought to the hospital by ambulance. He was then suffering from severe shock; the extremities were cold and the face was pinched. His temperature was 98° F., pulse 96 and very feeble, and respiration 26. The vomiting on Monday was certainly stercoraceous, but not very persistent. The abdominal wall was flat and slightly rigid, and the hepatic dullness normal. There was but little abdominal tenderness except in the left iliac region, where a tumor, apparently of about the size of a small apple, could be felt beneath the abdominal wall. This tumor was freely movable and disappeared occasionally from beneath the examining fingers. Quick, interrupted pressure made with the other hand in the opposite iliac fossa caused the tumor to strike against the palpating fingers with a sudden impact. It was irregular in outline, and this, with its size and mobility, led to the opinion that it consisted of hardened fæces.

Operation was decided upon, but delayed for a time to permit the patient to react from the shock. Accordingly, stimulants were administered and artificial warmth was applied, to which measures the patient responded quickly and well, the skin becoming warm and the pulse of better tension. An enema was given, but with no result. The operation was performed on the afternoon of the day of admission. The portion of intestine containing the tumor, which was afterward found to be the ileum, was easily located and brought out through a median incision of the abdominal wall below the umbilicus. The tumor was quite hard, irregularly cuboid in outline, and presented several projecting prominences, over which the walls of the ileum were much thinned by stretching. Except at these points the gut looked normal. As the tumor could not be moved in either direction without using undue force, it was removed through a longitudinal incision in the intestinal wall.

This incision was closed by two series of sutures, the first a continuous, the second an interrupted, Lembert. The gut was then put back and the abdominal wound closed in the usual way. The after-history was uneventful. The bowels were moved on the third day by enema, and on the fourth by calomel. A slight amount of suppuration occurred in the abdominal wound, due, probably, to the hurried preparation and to the previous unsanitary condition of the patient's abdominal wall.

After removal it was found that the tumor cut easily, and showed a fibrous surface resembling somewhat the cut surface of a meat ball. This mass certainly contained some of the meat eaten on Friday, but one could not speak so positively about the beans. The speaker raised the question as to whether any cathartic could have broken up or caused the expulsion of this mass.

So-called Aneurysm of the Heart.—Dr. N. E. BRILL presented a case of what he stated was at times incorrectly called aneurysm of the heart. It was that of a patient who was admitted into one of his wards at Mount Sinai Hospital about a month before. The patient stated that thirty-five years before that time a diagnosis had been made of his disease by Traube, of Germany, who said he had phthisis, that it would be a disease of long standing, and would not be fatal. In the light of the subsequent history of the patient this was a diagnosis and prognosis which a progress of thirty-five years could not make any of us devoted to clinical work improve upon; perhaps we could not do so well.

On admission the patient gave the following history:

He was seventy-two years of age, and, with the exception of his illness in his thirty-seventh year, had not been suffering with any serious illness. During the preceding seven months he had begun to feel weak, and lost flesh and strength. He had occasionally severe pain in the epigastrium and would vomit but seldom. A marked pallor, prominent signs of cachexia, and extreme anæmia were the indications, by merely glancing at the patient, for a diagnosis of carcinoma. The patient was a large man, whose mucous membranes were very pale, who was much emaciated, and who had very feeble heart sounds, accompanied by a slight systolic murmur over the mitral and aortic areas, without a history of rheumatism. An examination of his lungs confirmed the diagnosis of a consolidation at both apices.

His stomach contents showed an absence of free HCl. This fact, together with the pain of which he complained, which was very severe when present, the age of the patient, and the previously mentioned data, suggested the diagnosis of carcinoma of the stomach, notwithstanding no tumor could be felt. The cardiac murmur suggested atheroma of the aorta and of the mitral valves.

In four weeks the patient died. The autopsy revealed cheesy nodules in the apices of both lungs surrounded by dense lung substance. The heart showed some thickening of the mitral valve and a very well organized thrombus in the lower aspect of the left ventricle.

The heart muscle was atrophied and brown in color, showing retrogressive degenerative changes. Where the thrombus was attached the heart wall was very thin and transparent, bulging outward somewhat. This represented the condition which was sometimes erroneously called chronic aneurysm of the heart. The condition was due to deficient nutrition of the heart wall by reason of a diminished blood supply. On opening the left coronary artery, the atheroma of the vessel was found well marked and the presence of an old thrombus in that vessel explained the entire condition of the organ.

This pathological condition was not often found in the post-mortem rooms in this country, probably because it was not looked for; but the speaker had no doubt that it must be almost as common here as it was abroad, where it was not infrequently demonstrated.

The aorta was the seat of atheromatous degeneration. The stomach showed the presence of a carcinoma limited to the pyloric end, where it had produced a well-marked stricture. Notwithstanding this stricture, there was but little gastric dilatation. Both kidneys revealed the presence of an atrophic cirrhosis. The liver was the seat of two large carcinomatous metastases. There was some perisplenitis.

The speaker apologized for making an extemporaneous presentation of this interesting pathological condition of the heart, but, owing to the death of the patient on the eve of presentation, he had not had time to commit the report to writing or to look up the details of the case more closely.

A New Electric Urethral Sound.—Dr. WINFIELD AYRES presented a new electric urethral sound. Dr. Ayres said this was an improvement on the Newman sound. The instrument was intended for the treatment of resilient strictures and strictures of large calibre. The objection to the Fort instrument was that the stricture was absorbed only on one side; also, if the stricture was cut widely enough to relieve the symptoms, a deformed penis might result. The objection to the Newman sound was that it could not be absolutely controlled and healthy tissue might be injured.

For these reasons he had devised a sound with an insulated point which would guide the instrument in the canal and at the same time bring the entire circumference in contact with the circumference of the stricture. The insulated point was conical, running through three sizes. The electrode projected as a shoulder from and was three sizes larger than the base of the cone. The shaft was of the same size as the base of the cone. The sounds ran from No. 17 to 30 F. Every second size was required.

In using the instrument, a sound of the same size as the stricture was selected and passed to the face of the stricture. The current was then turned on. In from thirty seconds to ten minutes the sound would be felt to pass through, when the current must be turned off and the sound withdrawn. The amount of electricity that might be used with this instrument was considerable. Dr. Ayres had used as high as fifty milliampères, though he had found that ten to fifteen were usually all that were required. He thought that this instrument would obviate the necessity of cutting a great many strictures.

Paper.

THE HISTORY OF A CASE OF CEREBRAL ABSCESS OF UNUSUAL ORIGIN.

By CHARLES PHELPS, M. D.

ABSCESS of the brain disconnected with disease of the internal ear is still sufficiently infrequent to justify the record of individual cases, and the history of the one which follows is so far unique as to be specially worthy of detailed description:

The subject was a young man, twenty-five years of age, who had never suffered disease of any part of the auditory passages, who had never received an injury of the head, and who had never been contaminated by the poison of syphilis. He was evidently of a strumous diathesis. His right lower extremity was shortened from the effects of an arthritis of the hip which had existed in childhood, and he bore many deep cicatrices occasioned by abscess in various parts of the body, including the neck and extremities. These abscesses and the arthritis were in progress from his fifth to his thirteenth year. During the later years of this period abscess so repeatedly formed in the left posterior parietal region as to make it probable that a persistent sinus existed, which was closed from time to time, with consequent purulent accumulations. No history could be obtained of pulmonary or glandular lesion. For an interval of ten years there were no suppurations, and his health remained good. In February, 1896, an abscess not preceded by cephalic injury was again formed in the left posterior parietal region, and was attended by intense pain in the head until relief was afforded by incision. In August, 1897, another abscess formed in the same region, and intense pain in the head was again at once relieved by incision made after the lapse of many days. The pain, which was at first dull and general, gradually increased in severity and became localized in the parietal region as the swelling became evident. The wound healed by granulation. The remembrance of the intensity of the pain he had suffered was afterward always in his mind and the source of constant apprehension. He felt no doubt of its recurrence, and at length sought other medical advice in the hope of earlier relief by operation when the paroxysm should come. During this period, as before, his mental faculties and muscular functions were unimpaired and his special senses undisturbed. His health was good and he was engaged in his usual occupations. On February 1, 1898, he consulted Dr. D. J. Donovan, who suspected intracranial disease. He was then suffering from a dull headache during the day which became sharp and piercing at night and prevented sleep. The pain was sometimes frontal or temporal and sometimes occipital. He was anæmic, though his pulse was slow (65), and his stomach was disturbed. His heart and lungs were in normal condition. A little later he was sent to me by Dr. Donovan, for examination. From this time the pain became more severe, and the constitutional condition more deranged; loss of sleep, anorexia, nausea, and constipation continued, with increasing prostration; food and medicine were vomited; no mitigation of pain was obtained by medication; temperature ranged from 99.6° to 100°. During the night of March 7th to 8th there were two left unilateral convulsions, and on March 9th two more. After the first convulsion the left upper extremity was paretic, with muscular twitching, and the mental condition became dull.

He was sent to St. Vincent's Hospital, March 10th, and was then stupid, though conscious and rational. His nutrition was good and vision normal; temperature, 98.7°; pulse, 76; respiration, 24. Pain in the right side of the head was especially severe; the pupils were slightly dilated but responsive to light; the mouth was slightly drawn to the right side; there was incomplete paralysis of the left upper extremity with contraction of the fingers. There was no other loss or impairment of muscular function. In the evening, during a paroxysm of pain, he threw himself upon the bed and contused the left eye; this was followed by a tetanic convulsion of the left face and left upper extremity lasting four minutes. The temperature rose to 99.2°; pulse, 72; respiration, 24.

On the following day, March 11th, he was subjected to operation. The site of cicatricial depression upon the left side had been originally selected for trephination, but the later development of focal symptoms of abscess led to the making of the cranial opening over the motor centre for the left arm. It was ascertained by a preliminary curved incision that no obvious disease of the bone existed in the situation first mentioned. The trephine used was an inch and a quarter in diameter;

the bone and pericranium at the site of operation were found to be of normal thickness and unaltered in character. Pus at once flowed freely from a wound made in the dura mater posteriorly by the trephine, and afterward from an incision made in the central part of its exposure. This discharge, which was thick, yellow, and inodorous, and from three to four ounces in amount, afforded upon subsequent examination pure cultures of the *Staphylococcus pyogenes aureus.* A small quantity of darker and less laudable pus was also seen to flow from the upper surface of the dura mater, though the inferior surface of bone, so far as it could be reached, was smooth and apparently free from disease.

After irrigation with a solution of mercury bichloride, 1 to 10,000, a drainage tube was placed between the dura mater and the bone, and some strands of silkworm gut in the cerebral cavity, and the wound in the scalp was closed by sutures, except in its posterior portion, in order to restrain the exuberance of the inevitable fungus cerebri. During the operation, which required little time, the pulse became exceedingly weak, rapid, and irregular, and much stimulation was required, but reaction from the anæsthetic was rapid. The mental condition of the patient was at once notably improved and his headache relieved. Temperature rose to 102°; ten hours later the temperature was 99°, pulse, 72, and respiration, 24.

From ten o'clock in the morning till nine in the evening of the following day he had nineteen convulsions, of which seventeen were left unilateral; one also involved the right leg, and one was general; each began in the left upper angle of the mouth. Five occurred in the last two hours. As their frequency was increased and it was thought possible that they might be occasioned by dural irritation, the epidural drainage tube was removed; two slight paroxysms occurred during the night, and none at any time thereafter.

The wound was dressed daily; the silkworm drainage strands were removed on the third and fourth days and their track irrigated; from this time intracranial discharge definitely ceased.

On the day following operation ophthalmoscopic examination, which had been hitherto neglected, was made by Dr. P. A. Callan, and was repeated by him at intervals of one to two weeks during the progress of the case. At the first examination choking of and œdema of both of the discs was noted, with hæmorrhages into the left;

at the second examination hæmorrhages had also occurred into the right. The œdema and choking of the discs was found to increase at successive examinations and became intense. There was moderate photophobia during the first month and slight dilatation of the left pupil late in the second. Vision, in the opinion of the patient, was unaffected, and the movements of the eyes were unimpaired. He was able to read the daily journals till within a few days of his death.

On the second day urinary control was regained, headache further relieved, paralysis diminished, and mental condition improved. On the fifth day after operation paralysis of the left upper extremity began to again increase and was soon complete. On the eighth day pulsation was felt through the scalp, and on the fourteenth day the incision was reopened and a fungus cerebri exposed. Until the twenty-first day the fungus, which was about the size of a mandarin orange and was covered by simple granulation tissue, did not increase. There was pulsation at only a single point, and moderate purulent discharge from the granulating surface. The left upper extremity could be moved only at the shoulder joint and by the action of the extensor muscles alone. The mental condition was normal, the appetite was good, and the special senses were all unimpaired. Pain in the right side of the neck was each morning of sufficient severity to cause complaint. The temperature became normal on the fourth day, and afterward during this period ranged from normal to 99° +, and but once reached 100°. The pulse was usually below 90, with a maximum of 96, and the respiration varied from 22 to 26.

On the twenty-first day a mass of softened and necrotic material, apparently disintegrated brain tissue, was forced upward through a small opening in the centre of the fungus and through a larger opening in its anterior portion. The extrusion and detachment of this necrotic tissue continued afterward in greater or less degree.

From the twenty-first to the thirty-first days the patient's general health improved, his appetite was still good, and with the use of tincture of chloride of iron his color became better. His mental condition was normal, he was cheerful, and he slept well. Considerable masses of brain tissue continued to be extruded and were detached, and the fungous mass was rather larger and more compressible. Pain occurred at intervals in the left foot and leg. The temperature, pulse, and respiration had essentially the same range as in the former period.

At the beginning of the second month paralysis of
the left upper extremity was complete, and the left
lower extremity was paretic. Tactile sensibility was
diminished in both left extremities and in the whole left
side of the body. The fungus increased in size. A little
later the patient became stupid and apathetic, his sleep
was disturbed, and his appetite failed. The fungus was
then removed by a catgut ligature, and as it reformed,
superficial portions were afterward detached and removed from day to day. His mental condition became
brighter and his general health again improved. Pain
occurred at frequent intervals throughout the month,
almost daily, always on the left side of the body, and
usually in the leg or shoulder. Left hemiplegia became
complete; but facial paralysis was still noticeable only
in a slight retraction of the angle of the mouth upon the
right side when he smiled. An intercurrent bronchitis
of some severity somewhat later was followed by renewed constitutional disturbances: mental dullness, loss
of appetite, and increasing anæmia. The temperature,
pulse, and respiration were not markedly higher than
in the first month, though the temperature occasionally
rose to 100° or 100° +, and the pulse rather more frequently reached 100.

On the fiftieth day the fungus had decreased in size,
was no longer sloughy, and its margin was well covered
by healthy simple granulations. His general mental
and physical condition was in every way satisfactory and
hopeful. His temperature was normal.

On the fifty-first day he rather suddenly began to
suffer pain in the back of his head and right side of his
neck; he vomited a considerable amount of undigested
food, and his temperature rose from 98° in three hours
to 103°. On the fifty-second day he was stupid, and at
night slightly delirious. His temperature throughout the
day was 104.4° The fungus was sloughy, and was again
ligated and cut away.

On the fifty-third day he was mentally dull, slightly
delirious, restless, and suffering pain in the head, right
side of the neck, and left lower extremity. There was
dilatation of the left pupil, with muscular twitching of
the left side of the face and lower extremity, and for the
first time since the day following operation loss of
fæcal and urinary control. Temperature rose to 105.4°,
and receded to 104°. The cervical glands on the right
side, beneath the sterno-mastoid muscle, which were already enlarged, became swollen and painful.

On the fifty-fourth and fifty-fifth days he was less

stupid and more rational, his temperature was lower, 104.6° to 102.4°, and, as he said, he felt better.

On the fifty-sixth day semiconsciousness lapsed into coma, with Cheyne-Stokes respiration, and temperature rose to 107.4°.

On the fifty-seventh day after operation he died, the temperature having risen to 107.8° F. Thirty minutes post mortem the temperature had fallen to 106.6°. During the last fifteen minutes of life respiration was reduced to three in the minute.

Portions of tissue removed from the fungous mass were submitted to Dr. D. H. McAlpin, pathologist of the hospital, and examined at the Carnegie Laboratory during the life of the patient. I insert the report which I have received from Dr. Carlin Phillips detailing its microscopic characters:

" Many of the sections show areas of necrosis with colonies of bacteria, evidently staphylococci. About these areas are evidences of newly formed granulation tissue with branching capillaries, fibroblasts, leucocytes, hæmorrhages, etc. In all the sections purulent foci are seen in abundance. In the midst of the granulation tissue, which is extremely œdematous, are seen evidences of cortical substance infiltrated with inflammatory products. The various layers of ganglion cells with neurogliar network are in places easily made out. There are no nuclear changes in the neuroglia cells that present evidences of a proliferation. Hence we must explain the presence of cerebral tissue by assuming that it is an extrusion produced, first, by the marked œdematous condition of the cortical tissue, and second, by the accumulation beneath these areas of the purulent material which tends to force outward the cortical tissue in front of it. The exact origin of the granulation tissue can not be made out microscopically."

Dr. Alexander Lambert, to whom the same fungous material was sent for microscopical examination, found it to contain " irregular masses of brain tissue markedly infiltrated in places with leucocytes, and with hæmorrhages scattered through the brain substance, also areas of granulation tissue and of necrosis, and in some places cells which resemble the spider cells of glioma."

Necropsy made five hours post mortem: Body still warm, and fungus still protruding from the anterior and external borders of the semicircular flap raised from the scalp during life in the right posterior parietal region. Semicircular incision in left posterior parietal region, including in its extent two small depressed cicatrices entirely healed. Periosteum much thickened in parietal and occipital regions on the left of the median line; on the right side, of normal thickness and appearance.

Calvaria: External surface normal in appearance, except for trephine and rongeur opening on the right side, of which the margin was still sharp and unaltered; small opening existed through the median line in the mid-vertex, barely admitting a large probe, and having its margin of external table eroded and exposing the diploe. Internal surface: A depression in bone on the left side, an inch and a half antero-posteriorly by an inch laterally in diameter, underneath old cicatrices in the scalp, the site of former caries of bone now cicatrized; caries of internal table, extending four inches anteriorly from the occipital tuber in the line of the sagittal suture, and at two points each of one inch in length broadening to three fourths of an inch; edge of trephine opening, anteriorly and externally, necrotic, with small loosened fragments; calvarium in its left half of nearly twice the thicknes sof the right, measuring three eighths of an inch in parietal and three sixteenths of an inch in squamous portion.

Dura mater: Normal on the right side of the brain, but much thickened on the left, an eighth of an inch diminishing to a sixteenth of an inch in thickness from median line to temporal region; falx cerebri and walls of longitudinal sinus also much thickened; pachymeningitis externa, with grumous pultaceous exudation, confined to site of old carious process on the left side and to that of the present active process in the median line; internal surface of the membrane normal.

Arachnoid membrane: Small quantity of thin, semiopaque, yellowish fluid covering surface of brain, mainly upon the left side, and occurring in larger amount in posterior basic fossa; under surface of cerebellum, pons, and left temporal lobe, and anterior surface of medulla covered with a thick, yellowish, pasty exudation.

Brain: Calvaria removed without disturbing fun-

gus cerebri, and the adjacent dura covering vertex of
both hemispheres left *in situ;* whole viscus softened, but
much more markedly upon the right side; dura mater
adherent to the cerebral surface about the margin of the
fungus. Sections made by Dr. McAlpin.

I am again indebted to Dr. Carlin Phillips, who has
studied the topography of the diseased area.

Longitudinal section: The right hemisphere just
anterior to the Rolandic fissure is a dark, fungous mass
projecting through and involving the dura mater. This
mass measures about six centimetres in diameter and
extends to within two centimetres of the longitudinal
fissure. Owing to the disintegration of the brain substance, its exact relationship can not be made out. A
longitudinal section of the hemisphere, taken four centi-

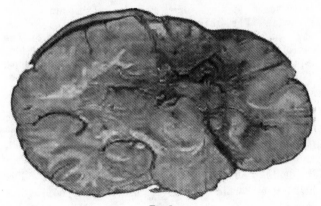

FIG. 2.

metres from the longitudinal fissure, presents the following picture: From the surface of the dura in the pre-
Rolandic region a dark mass extends downward, involving everything, even into the floor of the lateral ventricle. Passing backward, the involved areas seem to
follow the lines of the ventricle even into the posterior
horn. In this region the hæmorrhagic area extends from
one centimetre to two centimetres on either side of the
ventricle; anteriorly the mass involves the upper posterior portion of the corpus striatum, extending forward and involving the upper posterior third of the
white matter of the frontal lobe. The cortex of the
frontal lobe appears in the gross to be uninvolved.

Transverse section, looking forward: The dura mater over the left ventricle and the falx cerebri are seen to be markedly thickened, and on the right side all the membranes are included in the morbid process. The

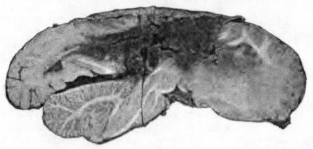

FIG. 3.

third ventricle is distended and filled with hæmorrhagic material. The outline of the right ventricle is obliterated, and apparently all its walls are included in the morbid process. In the right temporo-sphenoidal lobe especially are small groups of punctate hæmorrhages. The entire right centrum ovale is softened and œdematous, and also the left, but in a much less marked degree.

Had the consistence of the tissues permitted section without resort to a hardening process, the exact limits of the diseased part might have been better observed, and the extent of the abscess cavity which has been incidentally obliterated might have been displayed. The brain itself, which I present, has suffered no further change; and the photographs made by Mr. Mason, of Bellevue Hospital, the eminent photographer of pathological subjects, exactly reproduce its minutest lines. I regret my inability to show the calvarium or its photographic reproduction, of which I am deprived owing to the circumstances under which necropsy was made.

The post-mortem revelations make clear not only the recent, but the earlier procession of related pathic processes in the formation of this rather unusual instance of cerebral abscess. In the absence of a detailed history of the early epicranial suppurations it is not certain whether they were the result of antecedent caries of the

inner table of the calvaria, or whether they constituted the primary lesion from which the bone became
infected; there can be no doubt as to the relation of
the more recent and still active caries to the later abscesses. In the long interval of health which followed
the epicranial suppurations of childhood the osseous
lesion healed. At a later period a renewed carious process, involving the mid-parietal region, was followed by
an epidural accumulation of pus upon the left side,
which in time (February, 1896) came to exert such pressure as to at length force itself through the biparietal
suture and to form an epicranial abscess which was
tardily relieved by incision and subsequently healed. A
similar epidural pyogenic process with a similar history
of secondary superficial abscess, relieved by long-de-
ferred incision, occurred in August, 1897, and was followed by another prolonged interval of apparent recovery. It is conceivable that sufficiently careful examination at either of these crises might have discovered the
intracranial source of suppuration, and suggested such
radical methods of treatment as would have arrested
the subsequent progress of the disease to a fatal termination. In February, 1898, or at some time during the
period which had elapsed since the outbreak in August
preceding, the continuance of the epidural suppurative
process resulted in an infection of the opposite (right)
parietal lobe and the formation of this cerebral abscess
which in March reached the surface.

On each of the two occasions upon which epidural
pus, by increasing pressure, was forced through the
minute opening in the biparietal suture to form an
epicranial abscess, the crisis was marked by pain in the
head, at first dull and diffuse, but gradually increasing
in severity and diminishing in area, until it became at
length almost intolerable, and strictly limited to an evident external tumor. The patient and his family expected with absolute conviction a repetition of this se-
quence of pain, external abscess, and relief by incision;
and when in February last dull pain began and gradually increased in severity, it is not strange that their

15

anticipations should have been shared by his physician and myself. I had correctly interpreted the nature of the previous attacks, culminating in epicranial abscess, and had therefore advised operation, but was quite unprepared for the development of a cerebral abscess which became manifest during the short interval of delay which circumstances compelled.

Certain points in symptomatology invite special remark.

The choking and œdema of the optic discs and the retinal hæmorrhage, which were observed by ophthalmoscopic examination immediately after the operation, when intracranial pressure had been measurably relieved, and which progressively increased throughout the progress of the case, afforded an almost conclusive prognostic indication. The extensive nutritive changes which were thus known to have existed at the time the abscess was evacuated, and the advance of which, as it was thus seen, the removal of their cause was powerless to check, could only result in the continued disintegration and extrusion of the cerebral tissue until terminated by the exhaustion of the patient or by the intercurrence of some new infective process. Even the hope engendered by a long continuance of a satisfactory general condition—an almost normal pulse and temperature, unimpaired mental faculties, and improving nutrition—could only prove to be illusive in view of this obvious persistence of pathic structural changes.

The sudden occurrence of the unilateral convulsions and limited paralysis, which immediately preceded the evacuation of the abscess, indicate its central origin and the final invasion of the cortex; and the instant free discharge of pus upon incision of the dura mater makes it no less evident that the cerebral surface had already been ruptured. The patient certainly should have suffered at the time of superficial rupture a consequent acute arachnitis of intensity, but his whole history shows remarkable powers of resistance, not less to pathogenetic influences than to the ravages of acquired disease.

The great number of convulsions, commencing on the morning after operation and continuing with increasing frequency through the day, it was thought might have its source in a dural irritation caused by the drainage tube which had been left in the existent epidural space. The extreme sensitiveness of the external surface of the dura mater to irritation has been exemplified in the history of certain pistol-shot wounds in which excessive pains or violent convulsions were induced by a small fragment of bullet resting upon that membrane. The fact that in this case convulsions at once ceased upon the removal of the tube, without subsequent recurrence, seemed to confirm the correctness of the view which had been taken of their immediate cause.

The focal or localizing symptoms presented were unusually distinct, and of the highest importance in the clinical study of the case. Cerebral abscess is so generally central, or if it approach the surface so preferably tends toward the basal cortex, that the motor zone is rarely implicated. The primary paralysis of an upper extremity, with digital contraction, pointed unmistakably to its centre of control as the seat of a pathic process. The progressive and eventually complete hemiplegia, and the later hemianæsthesia, with trivial and stationary facial paralysis, supplemented ophthalmoscopic examination and the direct visual observation of the disintegration and extrusion of cerebral tissue, by determining the limit as well as the direction of the extension of disease.

The absolute integrity of all the mental faculties, without either aberration or decadence, may perhaps be regarded as having a negative value in localization. The observation of this case is at least in line with that of others made and published by the writer, which tend to show a special control, resident in the left frontal lobe, over the intellectual manifestations. In those cases, which were those of traumatisms, the same amount of structural alteration of the right frontal lobe which this case presented was unattended by deviations from the normal mental condition aside from delirium or unconsciousness, while lesions of the left lobe were marked by perverted or deficient mental activity.[*]

The enlargement of the cervical glands, which was noted in connection with a previous case reported by me,[†] and was again observed in the present instance, may or may not prove to have a diagnostic significance. Two cases are insufficient for generalization, but they are two out of five, which has been the limit of my experience, and as an attendant condition seem to me deserving of further attention in order to determine whether it is an accidental complication or a resulting symptomatic indication of the cerebral lesion.

The normal or but slightly elevated temperature and the unaccelerated pulse and respiration which attended the formation of this abscess, continuing even at the time of its evacuation, were rather characteristic than exceptional conditions of its progress. The persistence of a scarcely higher temperature and pulse rate during the many weeks of subsequent illness up to the time of access of the final complication was consistent with the nature of the altered pathogenic process, which, no longer to any great extent pyogenic, had become a simple disintegration of tissue from passive serous infiltration.

The termination of the case by a late meningeal infection was marked by an abrupt change of symptoms which in traumatic cases of arachnitis, ingrafted upon cerebral lesions, I have found to be characteristic. The sudden rise in temperature from 98.8° to 103°, which occurred between nine o'clock in the evening and midnight of the fifty-first day after operation, and was succeeded by stupor and delirium, undoubtedly indicated not only the day but almost the hour of the new septic invasion. An abrupt exaltation of temperature, with a coincident access or increase of mental disturbance, I believe to be diagnostic of the supervention of arachnitis, if of pyogenic grade, in the class of cases mentioned. In

[*] Phelps. *New York Medical Journal*, vol. II, No. 3, 1890.
[†] Phelps. *Injuries of the Brain*, etc.

this case of similar cerebral lesion of different origin it was inferred, correctly as the event proved, that a similar development of symptoms should have the same interpretation.

Dr. LAMBERT said that a microscopical examination of the section of the brain from the case presented by Dr. Phelps had shown areas of necrosis, with irregular areas of brain tissue, a few areas of normal neuroglia, and small areas of hæmorrhage and of tissues infiltrated with leucocytes. There were also some cells resembling the spider cells seen in glaucoma, and areas of granulated tissue extending into the cerebral tissue, and sometimes abruptly separated from it.

Dr. JOSEPH COLLINS said that the case which had been so admirably presented by Dr. Phelps was very interesting from both a pathological and a diagnostic standpoint. As Dr. Phelps truly said, cases having a preceding and clinical history similar to this one were very rare, and the individual did not encounter many of them. A number of cases had been reported in which the pathogenesis had been similar to this case, but in the majority of them trauma, with an open wound communicating with the air, was an ætiological factor. He ventured the belief that in Dr. Phelps's patient the abscess formation had been of long duration, and had perhaps causal connection with the caries of the cranial bone. He believed that the pyogenic process had existed for a year or longer before it had manifested itself significantly. A case had been reported from Glasgow of a man who had been struck on the head with a musket, resulting in an abscess, though there was no connection with the open air. The pathogenesis was not difficult to interpret if one kept in mind the anatomical relations. One remark had been made that some might take exception to—viz., that abscesses in the central portion of the brain were extremely rare. They were relatively rare, but when they did occur, they were usually from trauma. Those located in other parts of the brain came more often under medical than surgical supervision in the beginning. He wished to ask if Dr. Phelps had made the diagnosis of abscess positively before operation.

In regard to treatment, it seemed to him that the present mortality justified laying bare the abscess, scraping out the cavity, and thoroughly cleaning the affected area. The occurrence of the epileptic condition was remarkable. It was important to see if some measure could not be devised which would prevent the hernia cerebri and subsequent vegetations, and thus the facility with which the secondary infection took place and destroyed the brain. He was not inclined to attach any importance to the spider cells found in this case, or the glioma cells found in the pieces of vegetation removed, even if they were present. This case showed the importance of the pathology of infections of all kinds. It might have been possible to utilize lumbar puncture in the early weeks of the disease, and thus had the attention drawn earlier to intracranial suppuration.

Dr. C. L. DANA said that the history was a very typical one of cerebral abscess. These abscesses could generally be recognized and their origin traced, but the difficulty was to remove them without killing the patients, as the brain was an organ very peculiar in its susceptibility to injury and its power of absorption. No other organ had such extended lymphatics, and no other organ had such an absorbent area. For this reason the brain, when affected, became œdematous, and the pressure prevented resorption and carrying off of the œdema. He thought the patients might be benefited by extensive bleeding, counter-irritation, etc., and that it was possible, by relieving the blood pressure, to secure the resorption of the congestion, and the carrying off of this matter. It was important that the medical side of the question should be studied as well as the surgical.

Dr. EDWARD D. FISHER said he had been interested in the cases reported before by Dr. Phelps. It was very probable that in case of trauma the point of infection was overlooked, and in many cases there was a small nidus for infection. The rise of temperature in these cases was important from a diagnostic standpoint. The question as to which side of the brain was affected, for instance, in an injury, reminded him of a case which came under his observation some years ago. An Italian had a portion of the frontal lobe shot away, yet he made a good recovery, with no special mental disturbance.

Dr. PHELPS said that the origin of the trouble in the case under consideration was not known to be trauma. He could not say that the man had never received an injury in the head, but he could find no history of one. He thought there was nothing strange in a case of infection through the lymphatics. During the time from August till February he was not able to find any symptoms that pointed to cerebral abscess, and the man considered himself in good health, interrupted only on the two occasions on which superficial abscess formed. In reference to the localization in the frontal lobe, he did not consider this case conclusive; only one in line with others.

At the time of the operation the abscess was not more thoroughly opened and curetted on account of the patient's condition, for it was difficult to keep him alive. The patient's strength often failed during the operation, and he was glad to get through with the case as well as he had. Cases of this form of infection were rare. He had records of five hundred and seventy-three cases of injuries of the head, and out of these, four were cases of cerebral abscess. One patient was operated on just before death. In the past, when it was considered wrong to remove bullets, spicula of bone, etc., cerebral abscesses were more common than at the present time. He did not see anything in the case to lead to the conclusion that the abscess had existed for a long time, even a year before. He had not mentioned in the history that the diagnosis had been correctly made, as it seemed sufficiently indicated.

INDEX.

LaVergne, TN USA
03 February 2010
171938LV00007B/78/A